The BIG BOOK of DESIGN IDEAS

editor
DAVID E. CARTER

art director
SUZANNA M.W.

designers
CYNTHIA B. COMBS
ANTHONY B. STEPHENS

The Big Book of Design Ideas

First published in 2000 by HBI,
an imprint of HarperCollins Publishers
10 East 53rd Street
New York, NY 10022-5299

ISBN: 0688-17896-X

Distributed in the U.S. and Canada by
Watson-Guptill Publications
1515 Broadway
New York, NY 10036
Tel: (800) 451-1741
            (732) 363-4511 in NJ, AK, HI
Fax: (732) 363-0338

Distributed throughout the rest of the world by
HarperCollins International
10 East 53rd Street
New York, NY 10022-5299
Fax: (212) 207-7654

First published in Germany by Nippan
Nippon Shuppan Hanbai
Deutschland GmbH
Krefelder Strasse 85
D-40549 Dusseldorf
Tel: (0211) 5048089
Fax: (0211) 5049326
nippan@t-online.de

ISBN: 3-931884-77-5

Printed in Hong Kong by Everbest Printing Company through Four
Colour Imports, Louisville, Kentucky.

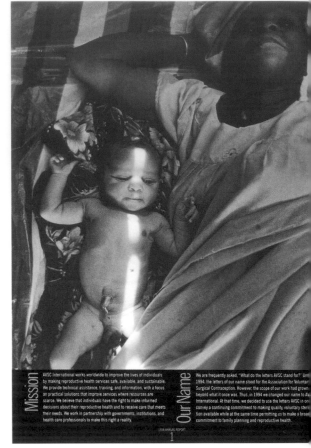

creative firm
EMERSON,
WAJDOWICZ
STUDIOS
New York, New York
creative director
JUREK WAJDOWICZ
senior art director
LISA LaROCHELLE
client
AVSC INTERNATIONAL

creative firm
LOUEY/RUBINO DESIGN GROUP, INC.
Santa Monica, California
creative director
ROBERT LOUEY
client
KAUFMAN AND BROAD HOME CORPORATION

creative firm
SIBLEY PETEET DESIGN
Dallas, Texas
designer
DAVID BECK
photographers
JOHN PARRISH, GREG BOOTH
client
ZALE CORPORATION

It is likely that Kim's material condition will improve as she finds higher-paid employment. But like most people in the United States, finding work provides more than merely a source of income: it is an organizing principle of her daily life and social interaction. Without a job, Kim is not only cut off from earning a good living but also shut out of much of the city's social order – perhaps even more than other jobless people in Seattle, since as a new immigrant she speaks hesitant English and often feels culturally isolated.

creative firm
EMERSON, WAJDOWICZ STUDIOS
New York, New York
creative director
JUREK WAJDOWICZ
senior art director
LISA LaROCHELLE
client
THE ROCKEFELLER FOUNDATION

creative firm
ARNOLD SAKS
ASSOCIATES
New York, New York
creative director
ARNOLD SAKS
designer
MICHELLE NOVAK
client
GENERAL CHEMICAL

The General Chemical Group   *1997 Annual Report*

Global Growth

Development

Innovation

The EMI Group   Annual Report 1999

creative firm
TOR PETTERSEN
& PARTNERS
London, England
designers
JEFF DAVIS, JIM ALLSOPP
client
THE EMI GROUP

5

creative firm
  HEINEY & CRAIG, INC.
  San Francisco, California
creative director
  TIM CRAIG
senior designer
  SHARON BACKURZ
client
  PUMA TECHNOLOGIES

creative firm
  BBK STUDIO INC.
  Grand Rapids, Michigan
creative director
  STEVE FRYKHOLM
designer
  YANG KIM
copywriter
  CLARK MALCOLM
typesetter
  KIM LAPP
client
  HERMAN MILLER INC.

The Hybrid Strategy: Superior Technology/Customer Focus

True broadband solutions for any environment or user need

The superior broadband Internet access of wireless and cable represents an important new value-added revenue opportunity for wireless and cable companies, network systems integrators, resellers, and even traditional telephone-access

Hybrid Networks, Inc. Annual Report 1997

Work
that
ing stro
as RCN
tomorro

download in seconds rather than minutes

Hybrid *we make the internet fly*

creative firm
 HEINEY & CRAIG, INC.
 San Francisco, California
creative director
 TIM CRAIG
senior designer
 JANET CARPINELLI
client
 HYBRID NETWORKS, INC.

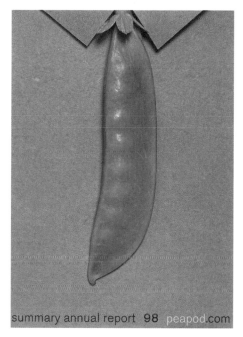

summary annual report **98** peapod.com

creative firm
 PARAGRAPHS DESIGN
 Chicago, Illinois
designer
 SCOTT HICKMAN
client
 PEAPOD

CTIONS NOW

WORKPLACE RESEARCH

Because business is changing, the way people work is changing too.

At Herman Miller, our researchers spend time looking ahead, anticipating our customers' needs. As work processes evolve, workplaces evolve. Our researchers are staying ahead of the game by focusing on the future and the impact of change on worker effectiveness.

SERVICE CENTER

Herman Miller offers more than office furniture

At our service center, we can offer you the full spectrum of services, from customization of products to leasing options. And our Customer Service representatives are also ready to assist you with your questions and requests. Here are some of the services we provide.

PEOPLE / TECHNOLOGY

A Report on the Environmental Stewardship of Herman Miller and its Subsidiary Companies

"On spaceship Earth there are no passengers—only crew."
—Buckminster Fuller

SELLING >>

Connecting seeing and believing, perception and reality. 1:1 keeps us connected to our dealers and salespeople, a vital part of selling and servicing our products. Z-Axis shows people the office they are ordering from Herman Miller before it arrives. Then prices it. Perfectly. Every time. OnSite is redefining how our larger customers get their furniture—with speed, convenience, and reliability. Customers connected directly to manufacturing. A complete process. A working connection.

creative firm
DEVER DESIGNS
Laurel, Maryland
art director
JEFFREY L. DEVER
designer
AMY WHITE SUCHERMAN
client
U.S. DEPT OF LABOR

creative firm
HEINEY & CRAIG, INC.
San Francisco, California
creative director
TIM CRAIG
senior designer
SHARON BACKURZ
client
UNION BANK

creative firm
HEINEY & CRAIG, INC.
San Francisco, California
creative director
TIM CRAIG
designer
KRIS MATSUYAMA
client
APEX PC SOLUTIONS

The Company continues to increase its presence as one of North America's premier specialty retailers of men's tailored apparel by offering customers a shopping experience that combines quality merchandise, value pricing and a high level of customer service. At the end of 1998, the Company operated 431 stores in 40 states. Through a merger completed in early 1999, the Company also operates Moores Retail Group Inc. under the name Moores the Suit People, which has 107 stores throughout Canada.

Even with the changing look of business, taste still remains **in style.**

* Before extraordinary item.

creative firm
HEINEY & CRAIG, INC.
San Francisco, California
creative director
TIM CRAIG
senior designer
SHARON BACKURZ
client
THE MEN'S WEARHOUSE

creative firm
CASPER DESIGN GROUP
Berkeley, California
creative director, designer
BILL RIBAR
photographer
DAVID POWERS
client
PROBUSINESS SYSTEMS

Jenny Craig

Personal support **makes** the difference.

Jenny Craig, Inc. is one of the most successful weight management service companies in the world. What truly sets it apart is an emphasis on personal support. Consultants help clients one-on-one to develop a healthy relationship with food, build an active lifestyle, and create a more balanced approach to living.

In turn, Jenny Craig, Inc. relies on expert personal support from ProBusiness to automate its payroll processing and payroll tax filings for more than 2,900 employees at 524 company-owned Centres in the United States.

"We've been extremely pleased with the level of service provided by ProBusiness," says Jim Kelly, vice president and CFO for Jenny Craig, Inc. "ProBusiness has enabled us to save time and focus our resources on more strategic initiatives."

ProBusiness Account Team for Jenny Craig
Dan Keeber, Tom Lamb,
and Kimberly Haring

Jamie Filippone, director of finance, has found several tangible benefits to working with ProBusiness. "One of the challenges that we had in the past was a lack of direct access to our own information," she says. "We were with another payroll provider, and we always had to go through them to get any type of detailed report. With ProBusiness, we're able to generate detailed reports at the push of a button. Before, it took days to generate these reports—now it takes minutes."

"Working with ProBusiness has been a very positive experience—from the people to the product to the training," says Filippone. "If I call them with questions, they get back to me right away. They do quality work. It's always 'How can we do that better?' It's been great."

Powering businesses by empowering people.

Personal motivation is key to the success of Jenny Craig, both with its clients and with its employees. The company reengineered the commission process to reward performance on an individual basis — and to teams of employees — who meet their goals. Monthly team commissions apply to everyone in a Centre, from consultants to program directors to the Centre director, even to support staff. ProBusiness has allowed Jenny Craig to reduce processing time for the entire payroll process — including commissions, vacation accruals, benefits administration, and tax deposits — by a day and a half each pay period.

CALAVO
98 Annual Report

creative firm
McNULTY & CO.
Thousand Oaks, California
creative director
DAN McNULTY
designer
EUGENE BUSTILLOS
illustrator
LIZ WHEATON
copywriter
GERRY FREISLEBEN
client
CALAVO GROWERS OF CALIFORNIA

creative firm
ARNOLD SAKS ASSOCIATES
New York, New York
creative director
ARNOLD SAKS
designer
MICHELLE NOVAK
client
VF CORPORATION

Our brands buck all the trends. Because we know our success doesn't depend on being first in fashion. It's about satisfying consumers with innovative products that set the standard for value. Using technology to break new ground in flexible manufacturing and retail service. And speaking directly to consumers who know that things like quality, comfort, function and fit never go out of style.

Always in Style

vf We Fit Your Life www.vfc.com

a strong diversified customer base.

creative firm
LOUEY/RUBINO DESIGN GROUP, INC.
Santa Monica, California
creative director
ROBERT LOUEY
client
RELIANCE STEEL & ALUMINUM COMPANY

1998 Annual Report

Harvest

Prune

Fertilize

Protect

TREE TOP

creative firm
HORNALL ANDERSON DESIGN WORKS
Seattle, Washington
art director
KATHA DALTON
designers
KATHA DALTON, JANA NISHI
client
TREE TOP

creative firm
MULLER + CO.
Kansas City, Missouri
creative executive officer
JOHN MULLER
creative director, copywriter
DAVID MARKS
designer
MARK VOSS
client
BOY SCOUTS OF AMERICA

creative firm
  MINALE TATTERSFIELD + PARTNERS
  Richmond, England
creative director
  PAUL ASTBURY
senior designers
  GRANT RUSSELL, ROBIN CHAPMAN
client
  EXPRESS DAIRIES

creative firm
  HEINEY & CRAIG, INC.
  San Francisco, California
creative director
  TIM CRAIG
senior designer
  JANET CARPINELLI
client
  UNION BANK OF CALIFORNIA

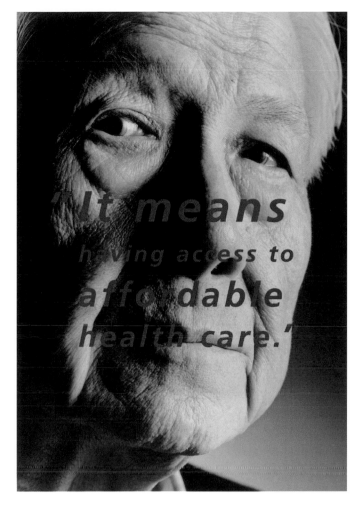

"It means having access to affordable health care."

creative firm
CASPER DESIGN GROUP
Berkeley, California
creative director
BILL RIBAR
designer
CHRISTOPHER BUEHLER
photographer
DAVID POWERS
client
THE CALIFORNIA ENDOWMENT

ESTERLINE TECHNOLOGIES
1998
N Y S E
ESL
ANNUAL REPORT

creative firm
LEIMER CROSS DESIGN
Seattle, Washington
creative director, art director
KERRY LEIMER
designers
KERRY LEIMER, MARIANNE LI
photographers
JEFF CORWIN, TYLER BOLEY
copywriters
KERRY LEIMER, BRIAN KEOGH
client
ESTERLINE TECHNOLOGIES, INC.

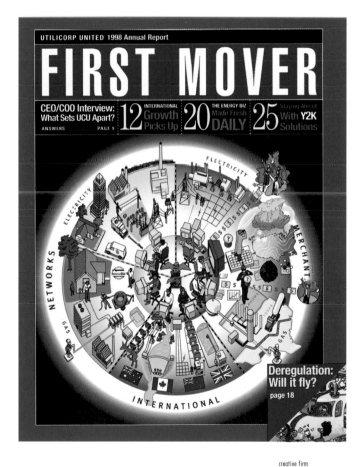

UTILICORP UNITED 1998 Annual Report

FIRST MOVER

CEO/COO Interview:
What Sets UCU Apart?
ANSWERS   PAGE 9

12 INTERNATIONAL Growth Picks Up

20 THE ENERGY BIZ Made Fresh DAILY

25 Staying Ahead With Y2K Solutions

Deregulation:
Will it fly?
page 18

creative firm
MULLER + CO.
Kansas City, Missouri
creative directors
JOHN MULLER, MARK EINER
art director
MARK EINER
designer
JENNIFER JAHDE
client
UTILICORP UNITED

13

creative firm
  SQUIRES & COMPANY
  Dallas, Texas
designer
  BRANDON MURPHY
photographer
  JAY ROUSQUICH
client
  BELLWETHER

creative firm
  BONNIE MATHER DESIGN
  Edmunds, Washington
graphic designer
  BONNIE MATHER
client
  EVERETT PARKS FOUNDATION

 knowledge keeps like fish

creative firm
  PARAGRAPHS DESIGN
  Chicago, Illinois
designer
  SCOTT HICKMAN
client
  DIAMOND TECHNOLOGY—JULIA POTTER

creative firm
  LOUEY/
  RUBINO
  DESIGN
  GROUP,
  INC.
  Santa Monica,
  California
creative director
  ROBERT LOUEY
client
  FREMONT
  GENERAL

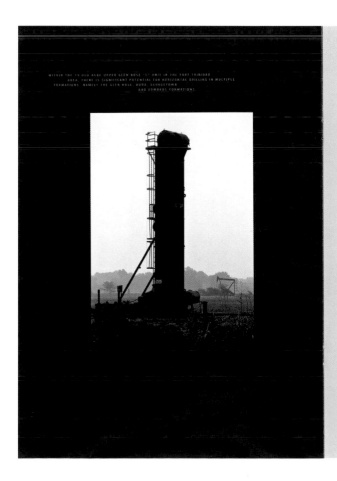

the productivity of the new structure is expected to exceed that of the Point Pedernales Field, where the wells initially averaged production rates of 2,300 barrels of oil per day.

SHIP SHOAL AREA *Offshore Louisiana*   In the April 1997 acquisition, Bellwether acquired working interests ranging from 10–29% in eight producing blocks in the Ship Shoal Area, covering three fields in 125 feet of water. In the fourth quarter 1997, production from these fields accounted for 8% of total Company production.

In April 1997, Bellwether also acquired 65 square miles of a 3-D seismic survey covering the area and participated in the drilling of two successful development wells which had initial production rates net to the Company's interest of 1.7 MMcf of gas per day and 309 barrels of oil per day.

In September 1997, the operator commenced a two well workover program to be followed by a two well development drilling program on a block in which Bellwether has a 29% working interest. Initial production rates from these four wells, if successful, could reach 50 MMcf of gas per day.

In August 1997, pursuant to a contractual right, Bellwether acquired a 19% working interest in an adjacent undeveloped block with attractive exploration potential from the operator of the area.

Bellwether anticipates that an annual eight to ten well program of workovers, development drilling and exploratory drilling can be sustained on these nine blocks for the next three to four years.

FORT TRINIDAD AREA *Houston and Madison Counties, Texas*   Bellwether acquired its interests in the Fort Trinidad Area through the Hampton Resources acquisition that was completed in February 1995.

The Dexter Waterflood Unit, in which Bellwether has a 48% working interest, has

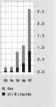

PRODUCTION
OIL EQUIVALENT

creative firm
  SQUIRES & COMPANY
  Dallas, Texas
designer
  PAUL BLACK
photographers
  GARY McCOY, KIETH WOOD
client
  BELLWETHER

McWhorter Technologies, Inc.
Annual Report 1998

Growth through Technology

creative firm
  PARAGRAPHS DESIGN
  Chicago, Illinois
designer
  SCOTT HICKMAN
client
  McWHORTER

creative firm
  CASPER DESIGN GROUP
  Berkeley, California
creative director
  BILL RIBAR
designer
  CHRISTOPHER BUEHLER
illustrator
  WARD SCHUMAKER
photographers
  LONNIE DUKA, SLAN MUSILEK,
  KINGMOND YOUNG
client
  PEOPLESOFT

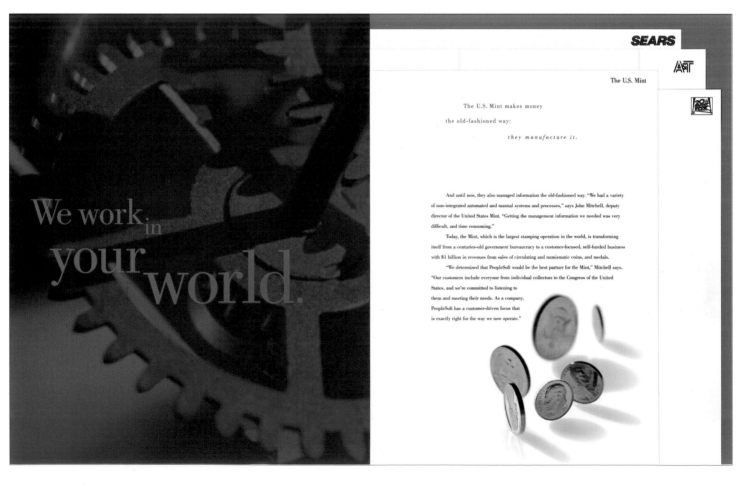

We work in your world.

SEARS

AT&T

The U.S. Mint

The U.S. Mint makes money

the old-fashioned way:

they manufacture it.

And until now, they also managed information the old-fashioned way. "We had a variety of non-integrated automated and manual systems and processes," says John Mitchell, deputy director of the United States Mint. "Getting the management information we needed was very difficult, and time consuming."

Today, the Mint, which is the largest stamping operation in the world, is transforming itself from a centuries-old government bureaucracy to a customer-focused, self-funded business with $1 billion in revenues from sales of circulating and numismatic coins, and medals.

"We determined that PeopleSoft would be the best partner for the Mint," Mitchell says. "Our customers include everyone from individual collectors to the Congress of the United States, and we're committed to listening to them and meeting their needs. As a company, PeopleSoft has a customer-driven focus that is exactly right for the way we now operate."

Community Involvement

"Logan Airport is as much at the center of local and regional economic development as were the shipyards of Donald McKay in the late 1800s."

DAVID MIGLIACCIO

PRESIDENT,

EAST BOSTON CHAMBER OF COMMERCE

The continued strength of New England's economy in the 21st century is the reason Massport is investing so heavily to improve its facilities. But the burden of those improvements is borne most directly by those living and working near these vital transportation facilities. As it pursues business opportunities around the globe, Massport also works hard in its own backyard to ensure Massport's neighbors benefit directly from the economic growth its facilities generate.

In Chelsea, Massport forged a far-ranging economic development compact this year that guarantees $2.5 million over five years for the city. The agreement also creates joint economic ventures that combine Chelsea's economic goals with Logan's need for additional parking, maintenance and freight forwarding space as the airport gets ready for the crush of as many as 10 to 15 million new passengers a year by 2010.

In East Boston, Massport is collaborating with the community on a waterfront development agenda that keeps maritime uses alive, and opens the waterfront to the public while providing economically feasible development opportunities needed to drive new building.

For many local businesses, Massport can be their best customer. Massport's on-going "Logan and Beyond" contract forums give local businesses the information they need to begin a profitable relationship supplying Massport's many needs.

With *South Boston A to Z*, and *The Local Advantage* Massport helps open doors for East Boston and South Boston vendors who want to do business with companies located at Logan Airport and the Port of Boston. The second edition of Massport's popular *Taste of Eastie* East Boston restaurant guide doubled the number of listings. And with its support for the new "Eastie Express" shuttle service, Massport is making it even easier for Logan's 17,000 workers to patronize East Boston businesses.

While it continues to support local businesses, Massport hasn't forgotten the important investment in young people. Each summer, Massport sponsors Student Internship and Community Summer Jobs programs that help get young people off to a good start. Students are put to work in every department at Massport and throughout their local communities as maintenance workers, camp counselors, peer leaders, and lifeguards. Massport-sponsored students work with at-risk youngsters, in day care centers, senior centers and in Head Start programs. Through these programs, young people get the chance to build a brighter future for themselves and their community.

14

15

creative firm
KOR GROUP
Boston, Massachusetts
art director
ANNE CALLAHAN
designer
JIM GIBSON
photographer
BETSY CULLEN
client
MASSPORT

creative firm
EDWARD WALTER DESIGN
New York, New York
designer
MARTIN BAYNELL
client
MERCURY COMPUTER SYSTEMS

1999 ANNUAL REPORT

17

"Did you get Tony's message?"

PORTICO. NEW PRODUCTIVITY FROM AN OLD CONNECTION.
As the pace of business quickens, so does the opportunity to fall behind. Staying in touch, staying in the loop, becomes ever harder. Particularly when you're on the road. So you juggle phones and pagers, PDAs and computers, unsure whether to check voice mail or email when time is tight, worrying that you might not get the message. Why can't a device you already own connect you to both? Now it can, with Portico.

We've developed an integrated voice and data communication service that acts as a second-generation virtual assistant for mobile professionals. Our service, Portico, offers subscribers access to all of their important information at any time, from any location, using just a phone or a favorite Web browser. But that's only the beginning. The real productivity of Portico comes from its ability to link the world of voice and data. Subscribers accessing Portico will use natural language – just as they would talk to another person – to direct a virtual assistant to read emails and voice mails, forward phone calls and look up contacts. No awkward menus. No irritating prompts. Because voice and data are integrated, the subscriber is in the driver's seat. And that's not all. Portico will offer a rich array of access services. It will answer subscribers' inbound calls, try to find them, have them paged, or simply take a message. Follow-me routing will maximize a subscriber's availability to callers. Intelligent filtering will screen calls and emails per the subscriber's directions, and will forward only priority messages to the subscriber's cell phone. Accessing Portico through a Web browser will be just as convenient.

creative firm
HORNALL ANDERSON DESIGN WORKS
Seattle, Washington
art directors
JACK ANDERSON, JANA NISHI
designers
JACK ANDERSON, JANA NISHI, MARY CHIN HUTCHISON, MICHAEL BRUGMAN
client
GENERAL MAGIC

TECHNOLOGY

that connects.

creative firm
HEINEY & CRAIG, INC.
San Francisco, California
creative director
TIM CRAIG
senior designer
JANET CARPINELLI
client
SILICON VALLEY GROUP

BIOGEN

DELIVERING ON THE PROMISE OF BIOTECHNOLOGY

1998 Annual Report

creative firm
GILL FISHMAN ASSOCIATES, INC.
Cambridge, Massachusetts
creative director
GILL FISHMAN
designer
MICHAEL PERSONS
photographer
JOHN EARLE
client
BIOGEN, INC.

creative firm
HORNALL ANDERSON DESIGN WORKS
Seattle, Washington
art directors
JOHN HORNALL, LISA CERVENY
designers
JOHN HORNALL, LISA CERVENY, HEIDI FAVOUR, BRUCE BRANSON-MEYER
client
AIRBORNE EXPRESS

creative firm
SIBLEY PETEET DESIGN
Dallas, Texas
designer
DON SIBLEY
photographer
PETER KRAEMER
client
TEXAS UTILITIES

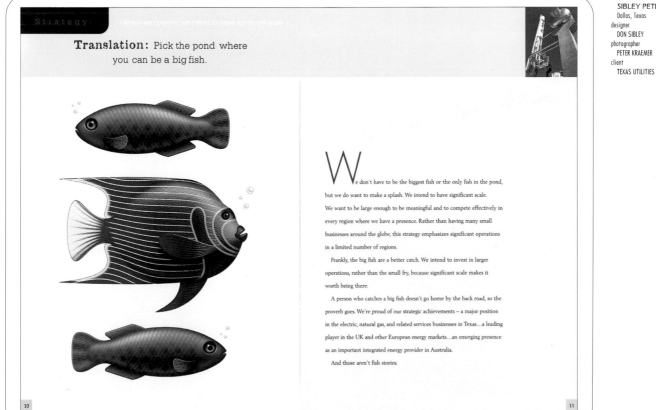

Strategy: (Where we operate, we intend to have significant scale.)

Translation: Pick the pond where you can be a big fish.

We don't have to be the biggest fish or the only fish in the pond, but we do want to make a splash. We intend to have significant scale. We want to be large enough to be meaningful and to compete effectively in every region where we have a presence. Rather than having many small businesses around the globe, this strategy emphasizes significant operations in a limited number of regions.

Frankly, the big fish are a better catch. We intend to invest in larger operations, rather than the small fry, because significant scale makes it worth being there.

A person who catches a big fish doesn't go home by the back road, so the proverb goes. We're proud of our strategic achievements – a major position in the electric, natural gas, and related services businesses in Texas…a leading player in the UK and other European energy markets…an emerging presence as an important integrated energy provider in Australia.

And those aren't fish stories.

10

11

19

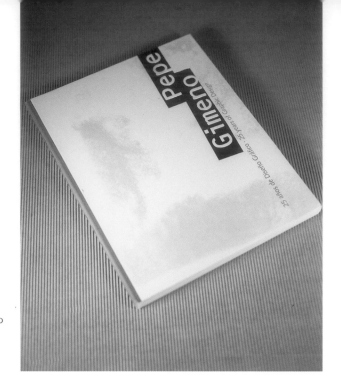

creative firm
PEPE GIMENO—PROYECTO GRÁFICO
Valencia, Spain
designer
SUSO PÉREZ
client
EXPERIMENTA EDICIONES DE DISENO

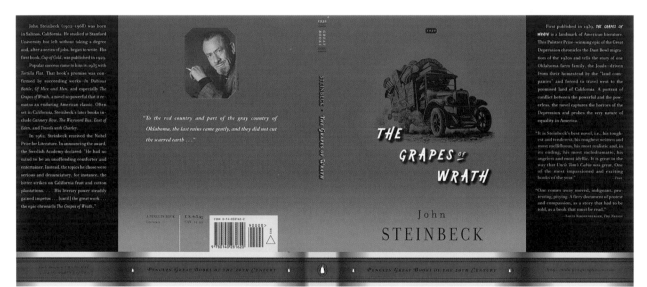

creative firm
PENGUIN PUTNAM INC.
New York, New York

creative firm
PENGUIN
PUTNAM INC.
New York, New York

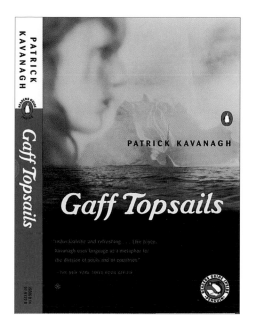

creative firm
PENGUIN PUTNAM INC.
New York, New York

creative firm
FROST DESIGN LTD
London, England
creative director
VINCE FROST
client
D&AD

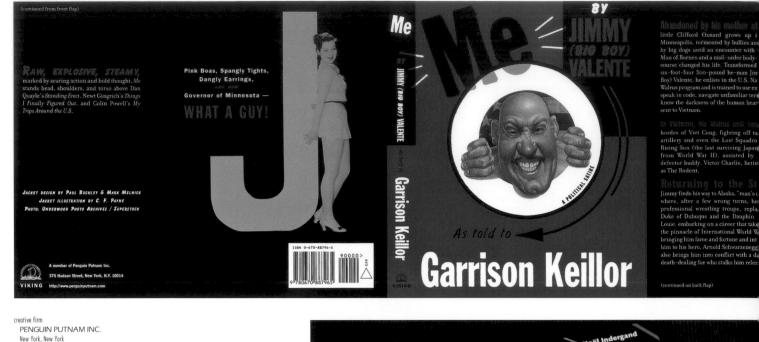

(continued from front flap)

RAW, EXPLOSIVE, STEAMY,
marked by searing action and bold thought. *Me*
stands head, shoulders, and torso above Dan
Quayle's *Standing Erect,* Newt Gingrich's *Things
I Finally Figured Out,* and Colin Powell's *My
Trips Around the U.S.*

Jacket design by PAUL BUCKLEY & MARK MELNICK
Jacket illustration by C. F. PAYNE
Photo: UNDERWOOD PHOTO ARCHIVES / SUPERSTOCK

A member of Penguin Putnam Inc.
375 Hudson Street, New York, N.Y. 10014
VIKING   http://www.penguinputnam.com

ISBN 0-670-88796-X

90000>

9 780670 887965

Pink Boas, Spangly Tights,
Dangly Earrings,
AND NOW
Governor of Minnesota —
WHAT A GUY!

Me
BY
JIMMY
(BIG BOY) VALENTE

Me
BY
JIMMY
(BIG BOY) VALENTE

As told to

Garrison Keillor

A POLITICAL SATIRE

Abandoned by his mother at
little Clifford Oxnard grows up i
Minneapolis, tormented by bullies an
by big dogs until an encounter with
Man of Borneo and a mail-order body-
course changed his life. Transformed
six-foot-four 3oo-pound he-man Jim
Boy) Valente, he enlists in the U.S. Na
Walrus program and is trained to use ex
speak in code, navigate unfamiliar terr
know the darkness of the human hear
sent to Vietnam.

In Vietnam, his Walrus unit rans
hordes of Viet Cong, fighting off ta
artillery and even the Lost Squadro
Rising Sun (the last surviving Japan
from World War II), assisted by
defector buddy. Victor Charlie, bette
as The Rodent.

Returning to the St
Jimmy finds his way to Alaska, "man's o
where, after a few wrong turns, he
professional wrestling troupe, repla
Duke of Dubuque and the Dauphin
Louie, embarking on a career that take
the pinnacle of International World W
bringing him fame and fortune and int
him to his hero. Arnold Schwarzenegg
also brings him into conflict with a d
death-dealing foe who stalks him relen

(continued on back flap)

creative firm
PENGUIN PUTNAM INC.
New York, New York

Jean-Noël Indergand
Suzanne Vitacco
Jürgen Sell

Holzhausbau
Qualität+Detail

EMPA
Lignum
Baufachverlag

creative firm
MIRIELLO GRAFICO INC.
San Diego, California
designers
MICHELLE ARANDA, MAXIMO ESCOBEDO, DAN RENNER
client
HARCOURT BRACE

creative firm
ALBERT GOMM SGD
Basel, Switzerland
graphic designer
ALBERT GOMM
architect
CHARLES VON BUEREN
client
BAUFACHVERLAG

creative firm
  JILL TANENBAUM GRAPHIC DESIGN & ADVERTISING
    Bethesda, Maryland
creative director
  JILL TANENBAUM
art director
  SUE SPRINKLE
designers
  LEAH GERMAN, HANNA CHANG
client
  U.S. POSTAL SERVICE

creative firm
  PEPE GIMENO—PROYECTO GRÁFICO
    Valencia, Spain
designer
  JOSE P. GIL
client
  FERIA INTERNACIONAL DEL MUEBLE DE VALENCIA

THROWING THINGS
DAVID KASPAREK

REVIVAL
ROBERT DRY

creative firm
KINETIK COMMUNICATION GRAPHICS, INC.
Washington, D.C.
designer
BETH CLAWSON
client
NORTH CAROLINA STATE UNIVERSITY

Wallowa Llamas

Raz and Louise Rasmussen • Steve Backstrom
Rt. 1 Box 84 • Halfway, OR 97834
phone: (541) 742-2961 • email: wallama@pdx.oneworld.com

Since 1985, Wallowa Llamas has conducted guided tours of small groups into the state's largest wilderness area, the Eagle Cap. Here, at the southern edge of Eastern Oregon's spectacular Wallowa Mountains, amid towering peaks, glacier-sculpted valleys and sparkling mountain streams, our llamas carry the amenities, unburdening hikers to experience ease and luxury normally unavailable to backcountry travelers in such rugged environs.

Packing with even-tempered llamas, we can enjoy delightful meals prepared without freeze-dried ingredients. Wallowa Llamas provides tents, eating utensils, and all meals, beginning with lunch the first day and ending with lunch the last day.

The llamas will carry up to 20 pounds of each guest's personal gear. Anything above that must be carried by the guest. A daypack is highly recommended for carrying cameras, binoculars or rain gear.

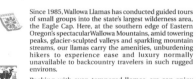

"One of the highlights of my life" Deanna Watkins

creative firm
FIFTH STREET DESIGN
Berkeley, California
production
ALLISON VALERIO
copywriter
MAURIZIO VALERIO
client
PICKED-BY-YOU

NIKKI GEMMELL

Alice Springs

A NOVEL

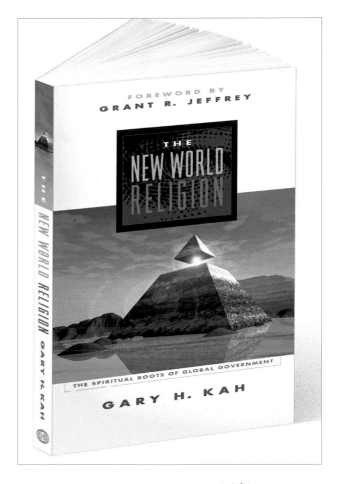

FOREWORD BY
GRANT R. JEFFREY

THE
NEW WORLD
RELIGION

THE SPIRITUAL ROOTS OF GLOBAL GOVERNMENT

GARY H. KAH

creative firm
  THE RIORDON
  DESIGN GROUP INC.
  Oakville, Canada
designer, illustrator
  DAN WHEATON
client
  FRONTIER RESEARCH
  PUBLICATIONS

creative firm
  PENGUIN PUTNAM BOOKS
  New York, New York
designer
  JENNIFER HEISEY
client
  VIKING

Glarner und St. Galler Alpen, Alpstein

Tödi, Glärnisch, Walensee, Churfirsten

creative firm
  ALBERT GOMM SGD
  Basel, Switzerland
designer
  ALBERT GOMM
typesetter
  MARCO VOLKEN
illustrator
  GUIDO KOEHLER
photographer
  REMOKUNDERT
client
  SWISS ALPINE CLUB

25

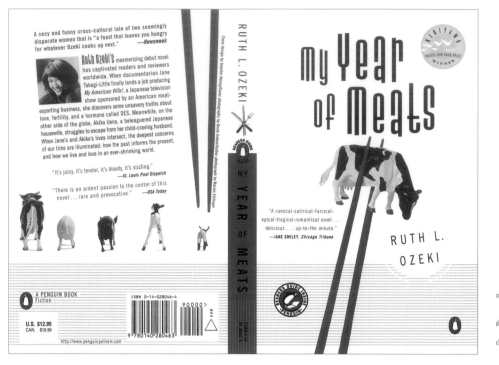

creative firm
PENGUIN PUTNAM BOOKS
New York, New York
designer
JENNIFER HEISEY
client
PENGUIN

creative firm
PENGUIN PUTNAM BOOKS
New York, New York

27

creative firm
 ST. MARY'S PRESS
 Winona, Minnesota
art director
 MAURINE R. TWAIT
typesetter
 HOLLACE STORKEL
copy editor
 LAURIE A. BERG
client
 ST. MARY'S PRESS

creative firm
 ST. MARY'S PRESS
 Winona, Minnesota
cover designer
 STEPHAN NAGEL
cover painting
 CHARLES PERKALIS
manuscript editor
 REBECCA FAIRBANK
client
 ST. MARY'S PRESS

creative firm
 ST. MARY'S PRESS
 Winona, Minnesota
cover designer
 CINDI RAMM
cover illustrator
 ROSEAN TISHMAN
copy editor
 LAURIE A. BERG
client
 ST. MARY'S PRESS

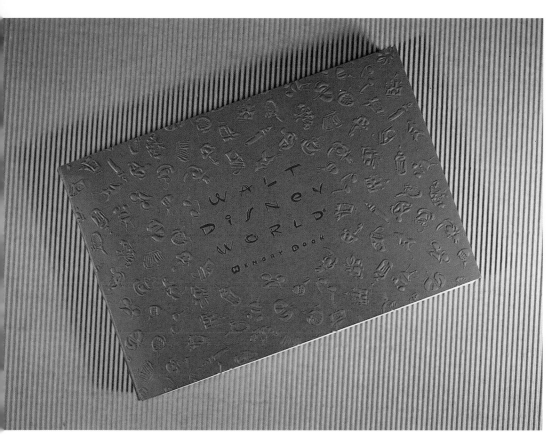

creative firm
DISNEY DESIGN GROUP
Lake Buena Vista, Florida
creative director
MICHELE KEATING
art director
MARK SEPPALA
designer
THOMAS SCOTT
illustrators
LARRY MOORE, CHRISTIAN MILDH
client
WALT DISNEY WORLD SALES & MARKETING

creative firm
SAYLES GRAPHIC DESIGN
Des Moines, Iowa
art director, illustrator
JOHN SAYLES
client
HOTEL PATTEE

29

BOOKS

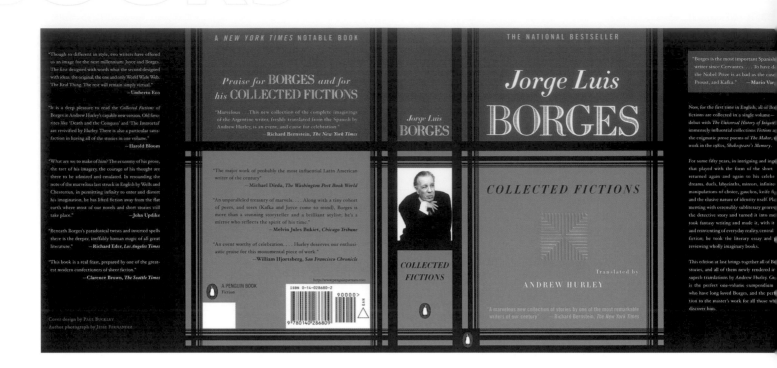

creative firm
PENGUIN PUTNAM BOOKS INC.
New York, New York

creative firm
PENGUIN PUTNAM BOOKS INC.
New York, New York

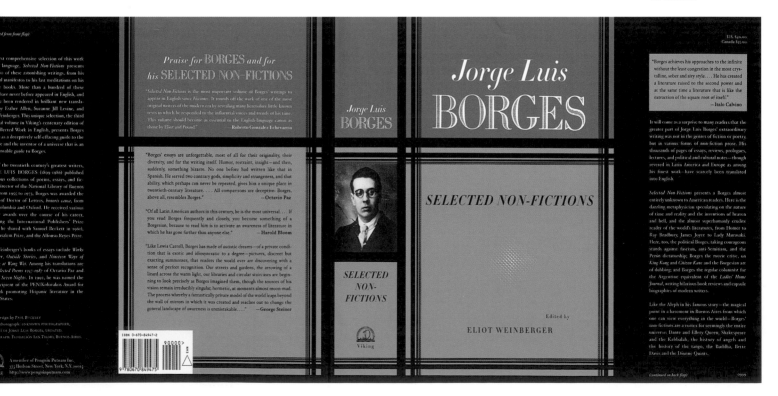

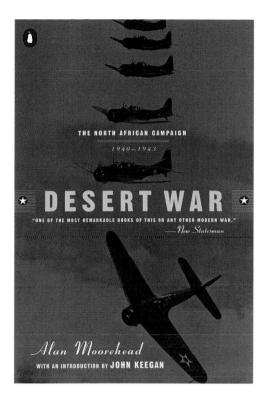

THE NORTH AFRICAN CAMPAIGN
1940–1943

★ DESERT WAR ★

"ONE OF THE MOST REMARKABLE BOOKS OF THIS OR ANY OTHER MODERN WAR."
—*New Statesman*

Alan Moorehead

WITH AN INTRODUCTION BY **JOHN KEEGAN**

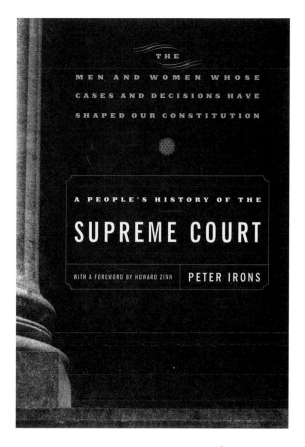

THE
MEN AND WOMEN WHOSE
CASES AND DECISIONS HAVE
SHAPED OUR CONSTITUTION

A PEOPLE'S HISTORY OF THE
SUPREME COURT

WITH A FOREWORD BY HOWARD ZINN | PETER IRONS

creative firm
PUTNAM PENGUIN INC.
New York, New York
designer
JENNIFER HEISEY
client
PENGUIN

creative firm
PUTNAM PENGUIN INC.
New York, New York
designer
JENNIFER HEISEY
client
VIKING BOOKS

"*Billy Dead* is a brave, heartwrenching debut. I couldn't look away."
—ALICE MUNRO

"This is a compelling work, reminiscent of both Dorothy Allison and Caroline Chute, that evokes empathy for those who lead bleak, savage lives and even finds a measure of dignity and love in people raised in a world where all the rules and taboos are broken on a daily basis."
—PUBLISHERS WEEKLY

LISA REARDON

BILLY DEAD

BILLY DEAD

a novel by
LISA REARDON

VIKING

ISBN 0-670-88224-0
90000>
9 780670 882243

creative firm
PUTNAM PENGUIN INC.
New York, New York
designer
MAGGIE PAYETTE
client
VIKING BOOKS

creative firm
NIKLAUS TROXLER DESIGN
Willisau, Switzerland
designer, typographer, illustrator
NIKLAUS TROXLER
client
LARS MÜLLER PUBLISHERS

creative firm
DESIGN GUYS
Minneapolis, Minnesota
art director
STEVEN SIKORA
illustrator
JAY THEIGE
copywriter
AMIE VALENTINE
client
TARGET STORES

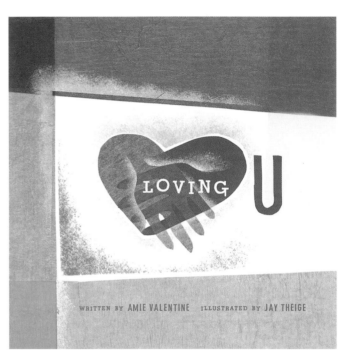

creative firm
JACK SCHECTERSON ASSOCIATES
Little Neck, New York
concept
BARBARA HARRIS
design director
JACK SCHECTERSON
illustrator
THERESA DELLA CERRA
copywriter
LIANE ONISH
client
EURPSVILLE, USA, INC.

creative firm
  SIBLEY PETEET DESIGN
  Dallas, Texas
designer
  BRENT McMAHAN
photographer
  MICHAEL ROYTEK
client
  BOY SCOUTS OF AMERICA

creative firm
  PLATINUM DESIGN, INC.
  New York, New York
art director, designer
  VICTORIA STAMM
client
  CLARKSON POTTER/PUBLISHERS
  (BEAUTIFUL AMERICAN ROSE GARDENS)

creative firm
DISNEY DESIGN GROUP
Lake Buena Vista, Florida
creative director
MICHELE KEATING
designer
MIKE WOOD
photographers
JOE BROOKS, WALT DISNEY WORLD PHOTOGRAPHY
client
WALT DISNEY ATTRACTIONS MERCHANDISE

creative firm
UKULELE DESIGN
CONSULTANTS PTE LTD
Singapore
design director
KIM CHUN-WEI
designer
LYNN LIM
client
THE ASIA INSURANCE CO. LTD

creative firm
WARNER BOOKS
New York, New York
designer, artist
DANIEL PELAVIN
client
WARNER BOOKS

A PARKER NOVEL

RICHARD STARK

The Outfit

Count on This

The castle was in Buffalo and the king was in the castle. The car was in the pine woods of Georgia and Parker was on the move: slowly plotting his attack on the head of the powerful criminal outfit that had put a contract on his life. Armed with a new face and the old iron will, Parker is declaring coast-to-coast war. And after Parker's associates pull off twelve robberies in five days against Outfit targets, the man in the castle starts to get the picture. All except one part: with a hot car and a cold tenacity, Parker is coming after him…

"AS DONALD E. WESTLAKE OR RICHARD STARK, THIS CRIME NOVELIST GIVES THE BEST LINES TO THE BAD GUYS."—*TIME*

"WESTLAKE KNOWS PRECISELY HOW TO GRAB A READER, DRAW HIM OR HER INTO THE STORY, AND THEN SLOWLY TIGHTEN HIS GRIP UNTIL ESCAPE IS IMPOSSIBLE."—*Washington Post Book World*

Visit our Web site at http://warnerbooks.com

$12.00 US / $14.99 CAN.
ISBN 0-446-67467-2

9 780446 674676   51200

RICHARD STARK   *The Outfit*

"PARKER IS A TRUE TREASURE….THE MASTER THIEF IS BACK, ALONG WITH RICHARD STARK (AKA DONALD WESTLAKE)."
—MARILYN STASIO, *NEW YORK TIMES BOOK REVIEW*

MYSTERIOUS PRESS

GRANT SPEAKS
A Novel

GRANT SPEAKS

by EV EHRLICH

author of BIG GOVERNMENT

A NOVEL

creative firm
WARNER BOOKS
New York, New York
designers
JACKIE MEYER, JON VALK
client
WARNER BOOKS

the neighbors

a novel by carol smith author of *Charmed Circle*

creative firm
WARNER BOOKS
New York, New York
designer
JACKIE MERRI MEYER
photographer
ALEXA GABANINO
client
WARNER BOOKS

35

The new Pelican Shakespeare series incorporates the more than thirty years of Shakespeare scholarship undertaken since the acclaimed original series, edited by Alfred Harbage, appeared between 1956 and 1967.

The general editors of the new series of forty volumes—the renowned Shakespeareans Stephen Orgel of Stanford University and A. R. Braunmuller of UCLA—have assembled a team of six eminent scholars who have, along with the general editors themselves, prepared new introductions and notes to all of Shakespeare's plays and poems. Redesigned in an easy-to-read format that preserves the favorite features of the original, including an essay on the theatrical world of Shakespeare, an introduction to the individual play, and a note on the text used.

The new Pelican Shakespeare will be an excellent resource for students, teachers, and theater professionals well into the twenty-first century.

Cover design: Gail Belenson
Cover illustration: Riccardo Vecchio
http://www.penguinputnam.com

A PENGUIN BOOK
DRAMA

U.S. $3.95
CAN. $5.99

ISBN 0-14-071480-4

90000>

9 780140 714807

THE PELICAN SHAKESPEARE

MUCH ADO ABOUT NOTHING

MUCH ADO ABOUT NOTHING

Edited by
Peter Holland

THE PELICAN
SHAKESPEARE

creative firm
PENGUIN PUTNAM INC.
New York, New York

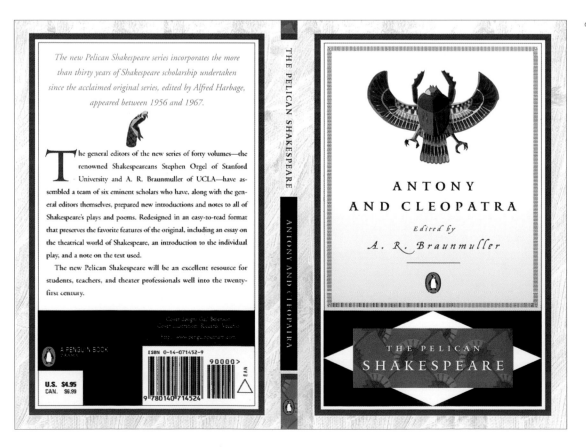

The new Pelican Shakespeare series incorporates the more than thirty years of Shakespeare scholarship undertaken since the acclaimed original series, edited by Alfred Harbage, appeared between 1956 and 1967.

The general editors of the new series of forty volumes—the renowned Shakespeareans Stephen Orgel of Stanford University and A. R. Braunmuller of UCLA—have assembled a team of six eminent scholars who have, along with the general editors themselves, prepared new introductions and notes to all of Shakespeare's plays and poems. Redesigned in an easy-to-read format that preserves the favorite features of the original, including an essay on the theatrical world of Shakespeare, an introduction to the individual play, and a note on the text used.

The new Pelican Shakespeare will be an excellent resource for students, teachers, and theater professionals well into the twenty-first century.

Cover design: Gail Belenson
Cover illustration: Riccardo Vecchio
http://www.penguinputnam.com

A PENGUIN BOOK
DRAMA

U.S. $4.95
CAN. $6.99

ISBN 0-14-071452-9

90000>

9 780140 714524

THE PELICAN SHAKESPEARE

ANTONY AND CLEOPATRA

ANTONY AND CLEOPATRA

Edited by
A. R. Braunmuller

THE PELICAN
SHAKESPEARE

creative firm
PENGUIN PUTNAM INC.
New York, New York

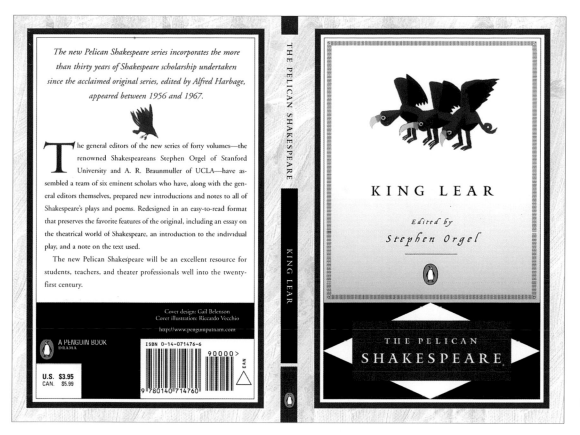

The new Pelican Shakespeare series incorporates the more than thirty years of Shakespeare scholarship undertaken since the acclaimed original series, edited by Alfred Harbage, appeared between 1956 and 1967.

The general editors of the new series of forty volumes—the renowned Shakespeareans Stephen Orgel of Stanford University and A. R. Braunmuller of UCLA—have assembled a team of six eminent scholars who have, along with the general editors themselves, prepared new introductions and notes to all of Shakespeare's plays and poems. Redesigned in an easy-to-read format that preserves the favorite features of the original, including an essay on the theatrical world of Shakespeare, an introduction to the individual play, and a note on the text used.

The new Pelican Shakespeare will be an excellent resource for students, teachers, and theater professionals well into the twenty-first century.

Cover design: Gail Belenson
Cover illustration: Riccardo Vecchio
http://www.penguinputnam.com

A PENGUIN BOOK
DRAMA

ISBN 0-14-071476-6

90000>

U.S. $3.95
CAN. $5.99

9 780140 714760

THE PELICAN SHAKESPEARE

KING LEAR

KING LEAR

Edited by
Stephen Orgel

THE PELICAN
SHAKESPEARE

creative firm
PENGUIN PUTNAM INC.
New York, New York

creative firm
PENGUIN PUTNAM INC.
New York, New York

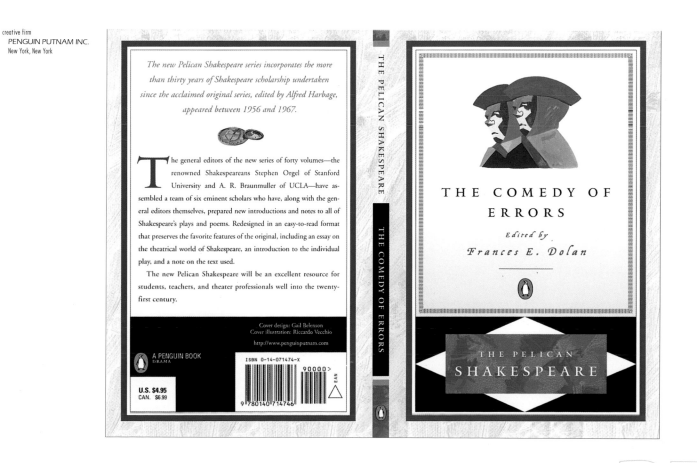

The new Pelican Shakespeare series incorporates the more than thirty years of Shakespeare scholarship undertaken since the acclaimed original series, edited by Alfred Harbage, appeared between 1956 and 1967.

The general editors of the new series of forty volumes—the renowned Shakespeareans Stephen Orgel of Stanford University and A. R. Braunmuller of UCLA—have assembled a team of six eminent scholars who have, along with the general editors themselves, prepared new introductions and notes to all of Shakespeare's plays and poems. Redesigned in an easy-to-read format that preserves the favorite features of the original, including an essay on the theatrical world of Shakespeare, an introduction to the individual play, and a note on the text used.

The new Pelican Shakespeare will be an excellent resource for students, teachers, and theater professionals well into the twenty-first century.

Cover design: Gail Belenson
Cover illustration: Riccardo Vecchio
http://www.penguinputnam.com

A PENGUIN BOOK
DRAMA

ISBN 0-14-071474-X

90000>

U.S. $4.95
CAN. $6.99

9 780140 714746

THE PELICAN SHAKESPEARE

THE COMEDY OF ERRORS

THE COMEDY OF
ERRORS

Edited by
Frances E. Dolan

THE PELICAN
SHAKESPEARE

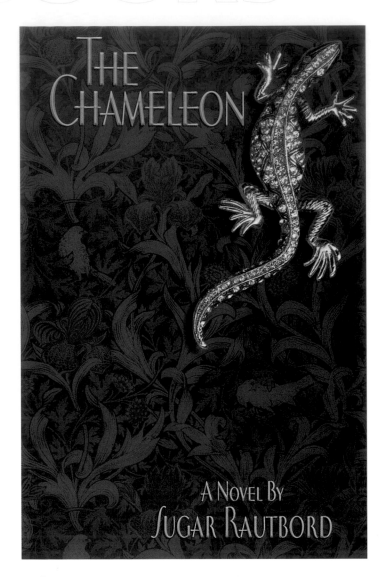

creative firm
   WARNER BOOKS
   New York, New York
designer
   JACKIE MERRI MEYER
illustrator
   FRANCO ACCORNERO
client
   WARNER BOOKS

creative firm
   WARNER BOOKS
   New York, New York
designer
   FLAG
client
   WARNER BOOKS

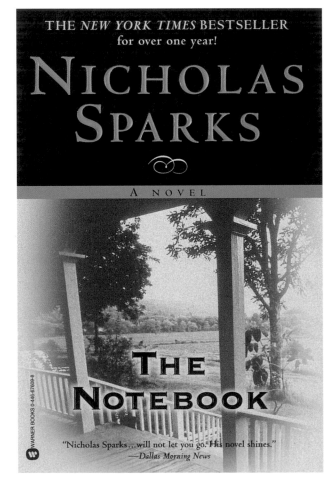

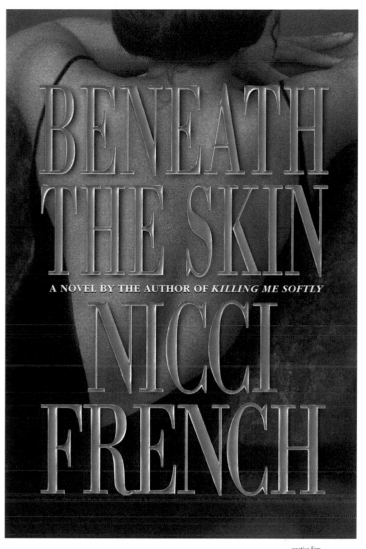

BENEATH THE SKIN

A NOVEL BY THE AUTHOR OF *KILLING ME SOFTLY*

NICCI FRENCH

creative firm
  WARNER BOOKS
  New York, New York
designer
  LOUISE FILI
photographer
  ALICE GANIK
client
  WARNER BOOKS

Traveling Light

A NOVEL

KATRINA KITTLE

creative firm
  WARNER BOOKS
  New York, New York
designer
  DIANE LUGER
photographer
  FRANCO ACCORNERO
client
  WARNER BOOKS

creative firm
  WATERSDESIGN.COM
  New York, New York
creative director
  JOHN WATERS
designer
  DIRK ROWNTREE
client
  LAZARD FRERES

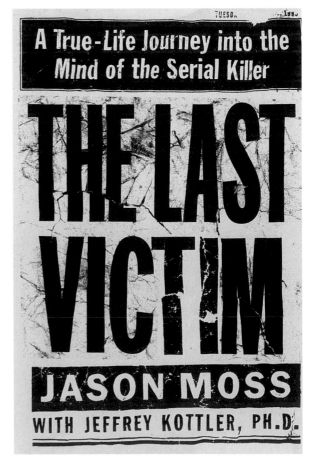

A True-Life Journey into the
Mind of the Serial Killer

THE LAST
VICTIM

JASON MOSS

WITH JEFFREY KOTTLER, PH.D.

creative firm
  WARNER BOOKS
  New York, New York
designer
  FLAG
client
  WARNER BOOKS

AMPERSAND ISSUE 3 JANUARY/FEBRUARY 1999 BRITISH DESIGN & ART DIRECTION

creative firm
FROST DESIGN LTD.
London, England
creative director
VINCE FROST
client
D&AD

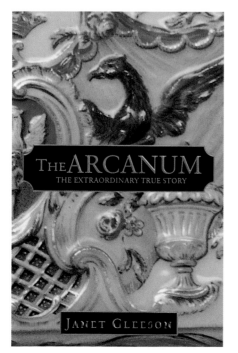

THE ARCANUM
THE EXTRAORDINARY TRUE STORY

JANET GLEESON

creative firm
WARNER BOOKS
New York, New York
designer
JACKIE MERRI MEYER
image courtesy of
ALEXANDER'S ANTIQUES OF NEW YORK CITY
client
WARNER BOOKS

41

creative firm
  WARNER BOOKS
  New York, New York
designer
  RACHEL McCLAIN
illustrator
  JOHN MARTINEZ
client
  WARNER BOOKS

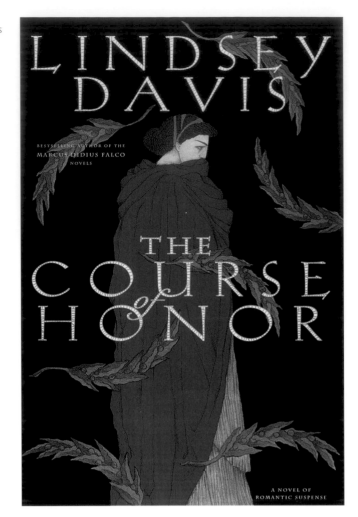

creative firm
  WARNER BOOKS
  New York, New York
designer
  RICHARD FAHEY
client
  WARNER BOOKS

creative firm
  WARNER BOOKS
  New York, New York
designer
  RACHEL McLAIN
illustrator
  JOHN MARTINEZ
client
  WARNER BOOKS

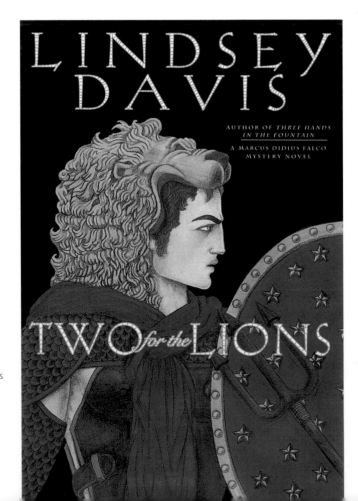

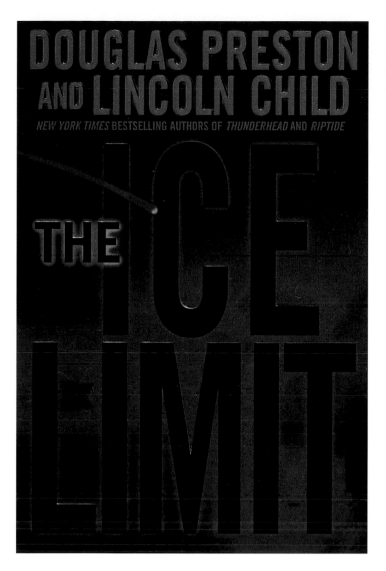

creative firm
WARNER BOOKS
New York, New York
designer
FLAG
illustrator
FRANCO ACCORNERO
client
WARNER BOOKS

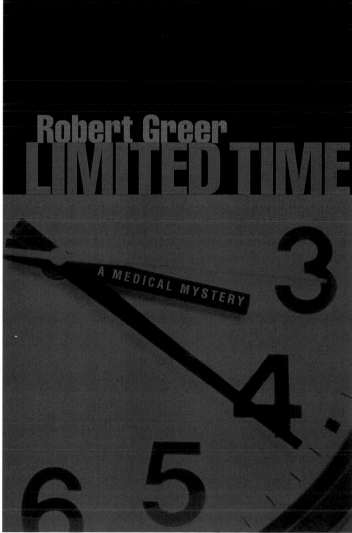

creative firm
WARNER BOOKS
New York, New York
designer
DIANE LUGER
client
WARNER BOOKS

43

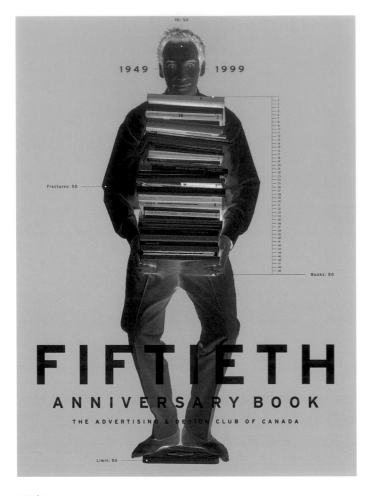

creative firm
VIVA DOLAN COMMUNICATIONS AND DESIGN INC.
Toronto, Canada
designers
FRANK VIVA, DOMINIC AYRE, JOHN GUDELJ
photographers
RON BAXTER SMITH (cover),
BRIAN BOYEL (interior)
copywriters
PETER GIFFEN, ROBERT STACEY
client
THE ADVERTISING AND DESIGN CLUB OF CANADA

creative firm
SIBLEY PETEET DESIGN
Dallas, Texas
designer
DON SIBLEY
client
BELLAGIO RESORT & CASINO

creative firm
BRUNAZZI & ASSOCIATI/
IMAGE + COMMUNICATION
Turin, Italy
art director
GIOVANNI BRUNAZZI
client
MALGRÉ TOUT...LA PITTURE

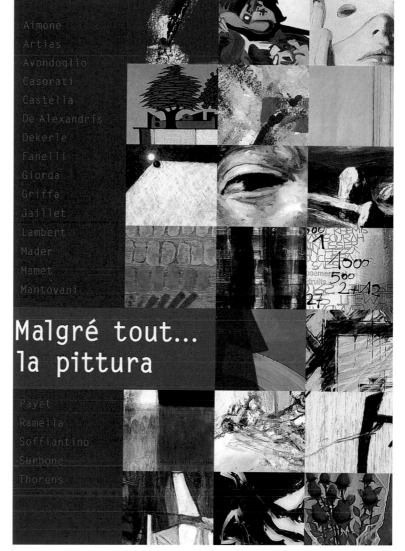

Aimone
Artias
Avondoglio
Casorati
Castella
De Alexandris
Dekerle
Fanelli
Giorda
Griffa
Jaillet
Lambert
Mader
Mamet
Mantovani

Malgré tout...
la pittura

Payet
Ramella
Soffiantino
Surbone
Thorens

james harte

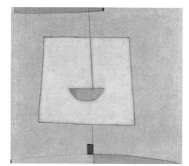

new paintings

creative firm
ALBERT GOMM
Basel, Switzerland
graphic designer
ALBERT GOMM
painter
JAMES HARTE
client
JAMES HARTE

PETER GAY

Edna O'Brien on James Joyce
Jonathan Spence on Mao Zedong
Jane Smiley on Charles Dickens
Carol Shields on Jane Austen
Mary Gordon on Joan of Arc
Karen Armstrong on the Buddha
Patricia Bosworth on Marlon Brando
R. W. B. Lewis on Dante
Janet Malcolm on Anton Chekhov
Marshall Frady on Martin Luther King, Jr.
Elizabeth Hardwick on Herman Melville
John Keegan on Winston Churchill
Wayne Koestenbaum on Andy Warhol
Roy Blount, Jr., on Robert E. Lee
David Quammen on Charles Darwin
Sherwin Nuland on Leonardo da Vinci
Nigel Nicolson on Virginia Woolf
Bobbie Ann Mason on Elvis Presley
Louis Auchincloss on Woodrow Wilson
Douglas Brinkley on Rosa Parks
Francine du Plessix Gray on Simone Weil

PETER GAY

Mozart

Mozart

ISBN 0-670-88238-0
9 780670 882380
90000>

Viking

Penguin LIVES

creative firm
PENGUIN PUTNAM INC.
New York, New York

LOUIS AUCHINCLOSS

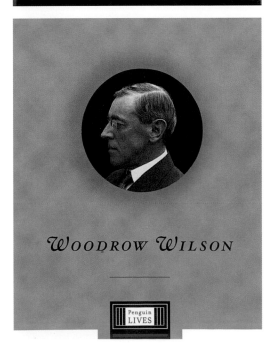

Woodrow Wilson

Penguin LIVES

creative firm
PENGUIN PUTNAM INC.
New York, New York

creative firm
ST. MARY'S PRESS
Winona, Minnesota
cover designer
CINDI RAMM
copy editor
REBECCA FAIRBANK

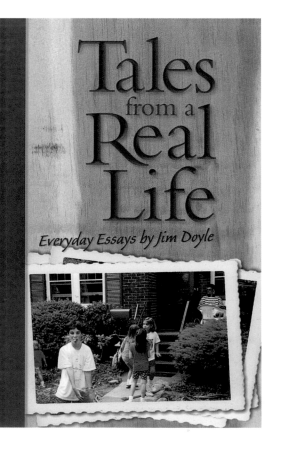

Tales from a Real Life

Everyday Essays by Jim Doyle

UNIVERSAL

"Psycho" 1960

UNIVERSAL

"The Birds" 1963

8	9	10	11	12	13	14	15	16	17	18	19	20	21	22	23	24	25	26	27	28	29	30	31
mon	tue	wed	thu	fri	sat	sun	mon	tue	wed	thu	fri	sat	sun	mon	tue	wed	thu	fri	sat	sun	mon	tue	wed

8	9	10	11	12	13	14	15	16	17	18	19	20	21	22	23	24	25	26	27	28	29	30
thu	fri	sat	sun	mon	tue	wed	thu	fri	sat	sun	mon	tue	wed	thu	fri	sat	sun	mon	tue	wed	thu	fri

IVERSAL

"Vertigo" 1958

PTEMBER

2	3	4	5	6	7	8	9	10	11	12	13	14	15	16	17	18	19	20	21	22	23	24	25	26	27	28	29	30
thu	fri	sat	sun	mon	tue	wed	thu	fri	sat	sun	mon	tue	wed	thu	fri	sat	sun	mon	tue	wed	thu	fri	sat	sun	mon	tue	wed	thu

TOBER

2	3	4	5	6	7	8	9	10	11	12	13	14	15	16	17	18	19	20	21	22	23	24	25	26	27	28	29	30	31
sat	sun	mon	tue	wed	thu	fri	sat	sun	mon	tue	wed	thu	fri	sat	sun	mon	tue	wed	thu	fri	sat	sun	mon	tue	wed	thu	fri	sat	sun

creative firm
  AREA STRATEGIC DESIGN/ROME
  Rome, Italy
creative director
  ANTONIO ROMANO
art director
  KEVIN MOULT
photographer
  MASSIMO PIERSANTI
client
  UNIVERSAL STUDIO/ROME LOS ANGELES

creative firm
  TOM FOWLER, INC.
  Stamford, Connecticut
art director, designer, illustrator
  ELIZABETH P. BALL
client
  GRAPHICS THREE, INC.

47

THEY GROW AND SURVIVE
WITH LITTLE HELP FROM MANKIND
FINDING THEIR OWN WAY

grow and survive

Coho, 27" x 31", 1991

SUN	MON	TUE	WED	THU	FRI	SAT
			1	2	3	4
5	6	7	8	9	10	11
12	13	14	15	16	17	18
19	20	21	22	23	24	25
26	27	28	29	30		

SKAGIT
WATERSHED
COUNCIL
A Community
Partnership for Salmon

november

creative firm
BONNIE MATHER DESIGN
Edmunds, Washington
graphic designer
BONNIE MATHER
client
SKAGIT WATERSHED COUNCIL
(a community partnership for salmon)

creative firm
AERIAL
San Francisco, California
designer, copywriter
TRACY MOON
client
AERIAL

creative firm
ARєA STRATEGIC
DESIGN/ROME
Rome, Italy
creative director
ANTONIO ROMANO
art director
STEFANO AURELI
illustrator
FRANCESCA MONTOSI
photographers
MARCO TEMPERA, GIUSEPPE FADDA
client
ARєA STRATEGIC DESIGN/ROME

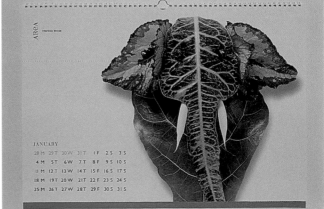

creative firm
  JULIA TAM DESIGN
  Palos Verdes, California
client
  JULIA TAM DESIGN

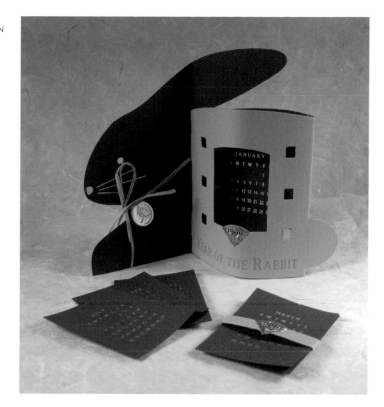

a. Heteropteryx dilatata

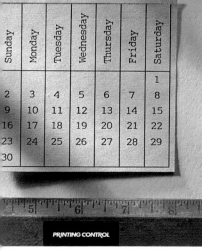

Sunday	Monday	Tuesday	Wednesday	Thursday	Friday	Saturday
						1
2	3	4	5	6	7	8
9	10	11	12	13	14	15
16	17	18	19	20	21	22
23	24	25	26	27	28	29
30						

PRINTING CONTROL

creative firm
  GREG WALTERS DESIGN
  Seattle, Washington
designer
  GREG WALTERS
photographer
  TOM COLLICOTT
client
  PRINTING CONTROL

creative firm
  BELYEA
  Seattle, Washington
art director
  PATRICIA BELYEA
designer
  RON LARS HANSEN
letterer
  JOCELYN CURNY
photographer
  ROSANNE OLSEN
client
  BELYEA

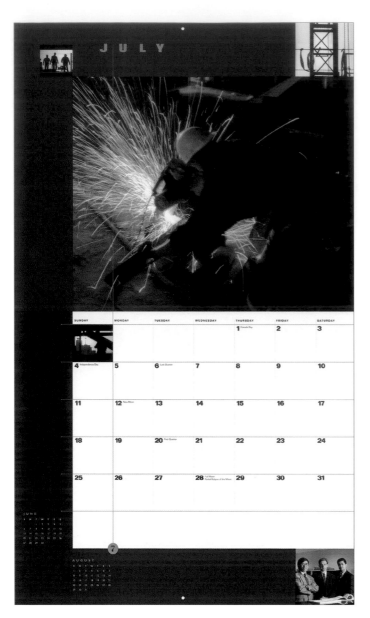

creative firm
  BIG CAT
  MARKETING
  COMM.
    Colorado Springs, Colorado
designer
  ANNA BARNES
client
  COLORADO SPRINGS
  UTILITIES

creative firm
  SACKETT DESIGN ASSOCIATES
    San Francisco, California
creative director
  MARK SACKETT
designers
  JAMES SAKAMOTO, ERIC SIEMENS
photographers
  HOLLY STEWART PHOTOGRAPHY, MENUEZ PICTURES
client
  SAN FRANCISCO INTERNATIONAL AIRPORT

creative firm
  TRICKETT & WEBB LTD
    London, England
designers
  LYNN TRICKETT, BRIAN WEBB, MARCUS TAYLOR
client
  FOREIGN & COMMONWEALTH OFFICE

creative firm
30SIXTY DESIGN, INC.
Los Angeles, California
creative director
HENRY VIZCARRA
art director
JAIME FLORES
designers
ANNA KALINKA, RICKARD OLSSON,
THOMAS GUNDRED
client
MUSEUM OF FLYING

creative firm
BRUNAZZI & ASSOCIATI/
IMAGE + COMMUNICATION
Turin, Italy
photo editor
ADA BRUNAZZI
client
CARTIERE BURGO

51

A DISCOUNT STORE WITH STYLE

"TARGET IS THE DISCOUNT ANSWER TO THE DEPARTMENT STORE EXPERIENCE."
—New York Times Reporter

THE SECOND YOU WALK INTO A TARGET STORE, YOU'LL KNOW YOU'VE DISCOVERED SOMETHING UNIQUE "IS THIS A DISCOUNT STORE?" YOU'LL FIND THE DISCOUNT STORE BASICS, SODA POP TO TOOTHPASTE, TOILET PAPER TO UNDERWEAR. (And yes, we have very competitive prices.) "OR A DEPARTMENT STORE?" YOU'LL ALSO FIND FASHION-FORWARD APPAREL JUST LIKE YOU'VE SEEN IN THOSE DEPARTMENT STORE WINDOWS, AND TREND-RIGHT HOME FASHIONS LIKE THOSE FOUND IN MAGAZINES. (But take a look at the price tag. Lower than you expected, huh?) DO SOME RESEARCH AND YOU'LL DISCOVER THAT TARGET IS THE LARGEST CHARITABLE CONTRIBUTOR IN THE RETAIL INDUSTRY. (All this and nice too.) I GUESS YOU COULD SAY, WE'VE FOUND OUR NICHE RIGHT SMACK DAB IN THE MIDDLE OF IT ALL, AND WE KIND OF LIKE IT HERE. FOR NOW, WE'LL SAY WE'RE A MULTI-DEPARTMENTAL/UPSCALE DISCOUNT STORE. BUT YOU CAN JUST CALL US BY OUR FIRST NAME...TARGET. (Or "Tar-zhay" as our loyal guests have nicknamed us.)

creative firm
  GRAPHICULTURE
    Minneapolis, Minnesota
designer
  CHERYL WATSON
illustrator
  ROBIN ZINGONE
client
  TARGET

creative firm
  DOTZLER CREATIVE ARTS
    Omaha, Nebraska
client
  JOHN DAY COMPANY

DEDICATED TO

BUILDING RELATIONSHIPS

BY PRODUCING

COMPLETE SOLUTIONS

WITH INNOVATIVE

PRODUCTS, TECHNICAL

EXPERTISE, AND

PERSONALIZED SERVICE

creative firm
  SIGN
  Frankfurt, Germany
creative director
  KARL W. HENSCHEL
client
  SIGN I TOKYO

creative firm
  DEVER DESIGNS
  Laurel, Maryland
creative director
  JEFFERY L. DEVER
art director
  EMILY MARTIN KENDALL
designer
  EMILY MARTIN KENDALL,
  CHRISTINE DRAUGHN
client
  INSTITUTE OF MUSEUM AND LIBRARY SERVICES

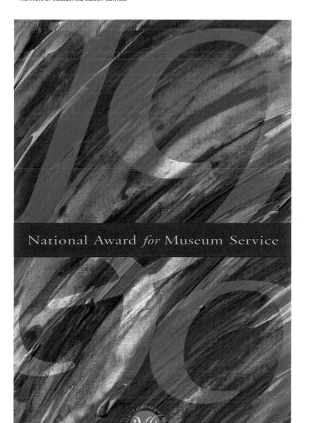

National Award *for* Museum Service

creative firm
  McNULTY & CO.
  Thousand Oaks, California
creative director
  DAN McNULTY
designer
  BRIAN JACOBSON
client
  MOTOROLA

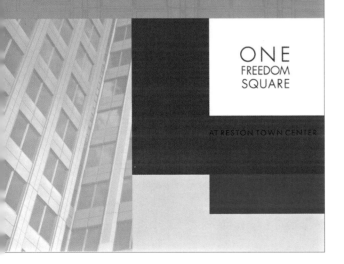

DEFINING THE **FUTURE** OF NORTHERN VIRGINIA

ONE FREEDOM SQUARE

AT RESTON TOWN CENTER

creative firm
KINETIK COMMUNICATION GRAPHICS, INC.
Washington D.C.
designers
JEFFREY FABIAN,
SCOTT RIER,
SAM SHELTON
client
BOSTON PROPERTIES

TECHNOGYM SYSTEM®

SOFTWARE

WELLNESS

W

IN MOTION

creative firm
HORNALL ANDERSON DESIGN WORKS
Seattle, Washington
art director
JACK ANDERSON
designers
LARRY ANDERSON, MARY HERMES, MARY CHIN HUTCHISON
client
TECHNOGYM (WELLNESS)

creative firm
AMY NEIMAN DESIGN
Berkley, California
designer
AMY NEIMAN
photographer
WES WALKER
client
INCA (INTERNATIONAL NATURE &
CULTURAL ADVENTURES)

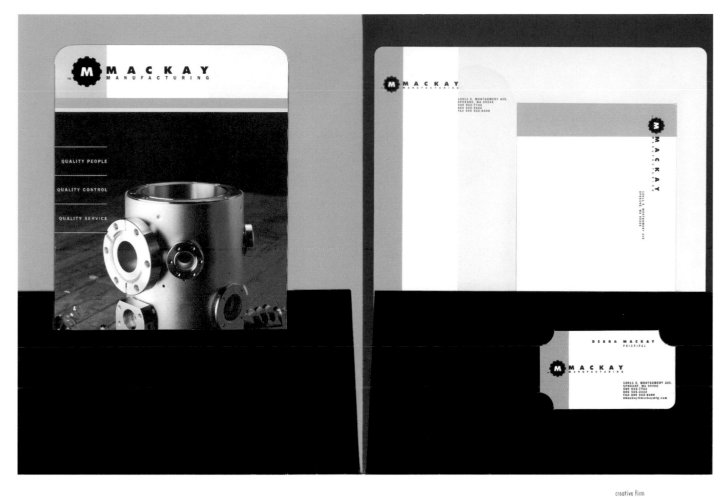

creative firm
KLUNDT HOSMER DESIGN
Spokane, Washington
designers
BRIAN GAGE,
DARIN KLUNDT
client
MacKAY

creative firm
MIRIELLO GRAFICO INC.
San Diego, California
designers
MAXIMO ESCOBEDO,
DENNIS GARCIA
client
OMEGA MARINE

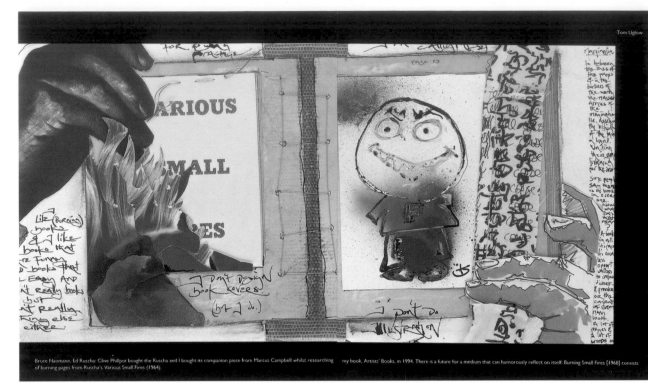

Tom Uglow

Bruce Naumann, Ed Ruscha: Clive Phillpot bought the Ruscha and I bought its companion piece from Marcus Campbell whilst researching my book, Artists' Books, in 1994. There is a future for a medium that can humorously reflect on itself: Burning Small Fires [1968] consists of burning pages from Ruscha's Various Small Fires (1964).

creative firm
 TRICKETT & WEBB LTD
 London, England
designers
 LYNN TRICKETT,
 BRIAN WEBB,
 KATJA THIELEN
client
 THE LONDON INSTITUTE

creative firm
 GARDNER DESIGN
 Wichita, Kansas
art directors
 BILL GARDNER,
 BRIAN MILLER
designer
 BRIAN MILLER
client
 EXCEL

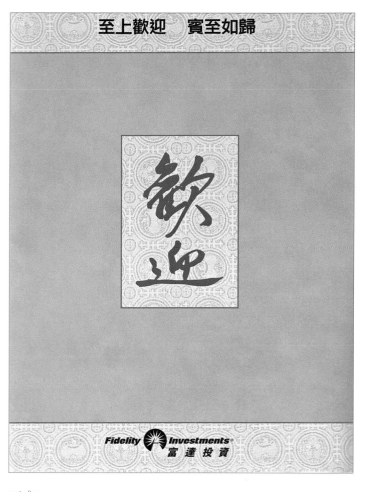

creative firm
  GARDNER DESIGN
  Wichita, Kansas
art directors
  BILL GARDNER, TRAVIS BROWN, BRIAN MILLER
designer
  TRAVIS BROWN
client
  EXCEL

creative firm
  WONG WONG BOYACK, INC.
  San Francisco, California
art director
  BEN WONG
calligrapher
  H.W. WONG
copywriters
  BEN WONG, SHINY HUANG
client
  FIDELITY INVESTMENTS

creative firm
  HORNALL ANDERSON
  DESIGN WORKS
  Seattle, Washingtona
art directors
  JACK ANDERSON, LARRY ANDERSON
designers
  JACK ANDERSON, LARRY ANDERSON,
  MARY HERMES, MIKE CALKINS,
  MICHAEL BRUGMAN
client
  U.S. CIGAR

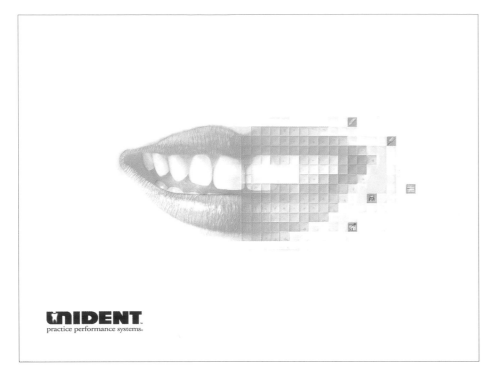

UNIDENT
practice performance systems.

creative firm
  DOTZLER CREATIVE ARTS
  Omaha, Nebraska
client
  UNIDENT

creative firm
  NAKATSUKA DAISUKE, INC.
  Tokyo, Japan
designers
  DAISUKE NAKATSUKA, TOM NAKATSUKA,
  KENJI INOUE, JUNKO NAKATSUKA,
  YOSHIFUMI NAKASHIMA, FUMIYO KITAZUME,
  HIROMI YAMADA, TOMOKO KANOU
photographers
  FRANCOIS GILLET, GORO ARIZONA,
  SHOZO NAKAMURA, ERNST HAAS
client
  H+B LIFESCIENCE CO., LTD.

creative firm
  WAGES DESIGN
  Atlanta, Georgia
designer
  RANDY ALLISON
photographer
  JERRY BURNS
client
  CADMUS

HAYASHIBARA
GROUP

creative firm
WDA PINFOLD
Leeds, England
art directors
**MYLES PINFOLD,
RICHARD HUNT**
design manager
ANDY PROBERT
designer
PHIL MOMSON
client
WATERFORD-WEDGEWOOD

GET ME TO THE CHURCH ON TIME

Floral Tapestry is a fruitful marriage of the traditions of fine needlework and great ceramic design.
The pattern is inspired by the richly detailed embroidery of Tudor and Stuart times.
Here it is worked with Sage Green Jasper: an original Wedgwood colour now enjoying a splendid renaissance in this varied range of giftware.

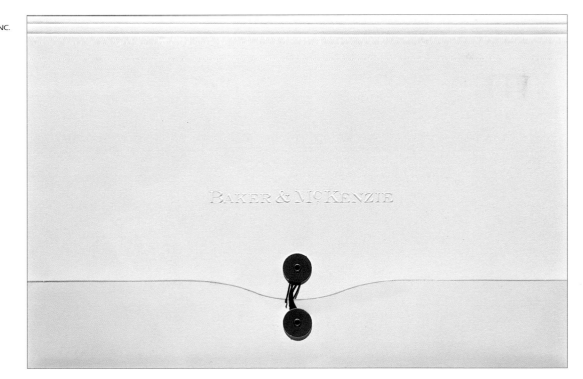

creative firm
PIVOT DESIGN, INC.
Chicago, Illinois
creative director
BROCK HALDEMAN
designer
HOLLE ANDERSON
client
BAKER & McKENZIE

k Commerce™

inference

creative firm
HORNALL ANDERSON DESIGN WORKS
Seattle, Washington
art directors
JACK ANDERSON,
JANA NISHI
designers
JACK ANDERSON,
JANA NISHI,
MARY CHIN HUTCHINSON
client
INFERENCE

creative firm
SHEILA HART DESIGN, INC.
Strongsville, Ohio
art director
SHEILA HART
client
MIDWEST CURTAINWALLS

QUALITY

creative firm
ARNOLD SAKS ASSOCIATES
New York, New York
creative director
ARNOLD SAKS
designer
ROBERT YASHARIAN
client
CONSOLIDATED PAPERS

creative firm
5D STUDIO
Malibu, California
art director, designer
JANE KOBAYASHI
client
BROWN JORDAN

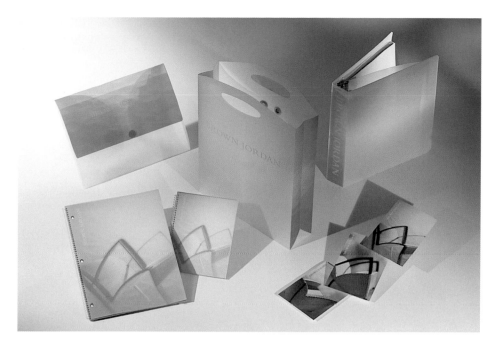

creative firm
MacVICOR DESIGN + COMMUNICATION
Arlington, Virginia
art director, designer
CATHY BROADWELL
illustrator
CHRIS O'CONNOR
photographer
CHRIS USHER
client
EU SERVICES
(COLLATERAL)

creative firm
DOUGLAS JOSEPH PARTNERS
Los Angelos, California
art director
DOUG JOSEPH
designer
JULIE SLOTO-MELLEN
illustrators
JULIE SLOTO-MELLEN, JOHN HERSEY
photographers
RICK BRIAN, JERRY GARNES
copywriter
MARK SCAPICCHIO
client
3D SYSTEMS CORPORATION

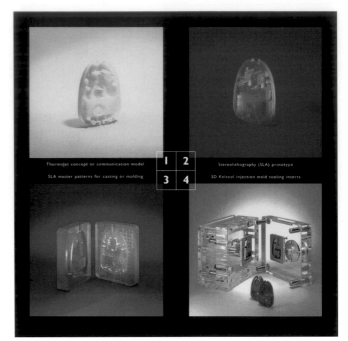

creative firm
JAMES ROBIE DESIGN ASSOCIATES
Los Angelos, California
creative director
JAMES ROBIE
design director
WAYNE FUJITA
designer
WAYNE FUJITA
photographer
HENRY BLACKHAM
client
JAMES ROBIE DESIGN ASSOCIATES

creative firm
HORNALL ANDERSON DESIGN WORKS
Seattle, Washington
art director
JACK ANDERSON
designers
JACK ANDERSON, LISA CERVENY,
HEIDI FAVOUR, JANA WILSON ESSER
client
NOVELL, INC.

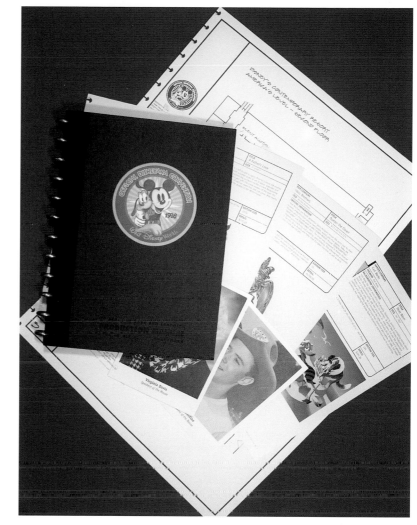

creative firm
DISNEY DESIGN GROUP
Lake Buena Vista, Florida
creative director
MICHELE KEATING
art director
MARK SEPPALA
designers
THOMAS SCOTT, DARREN WILSON
illustrators
THOMAS SCOTT, DARREN WILSON, MARK SEPPALA,
COSTA ALAVEZOS, JON BISHOP, DAVID WHITAKER,
ALEX MAHER, MONTY MALDOVAN, CODY REYNOLDS,
JOHN TRENT, ROBERT VANN, BRIAN BLACKMORE,
DOUG STRAYER, KERI MURPHY, RICHARD SZNERCH,
MICHAEL MOJHER
production coordinator
CHRISTINE MacFARLANE
client
WALT DISNEY WORLD SPECIAL EVENTS DEVELOPMENT

creative firm
ROSS ADVERTISING
creative director
SKIP DAMPIER
art director
MICK JIBBEN
copywriter
JOHN RUEBUSH
client
CATERPILLAR

65

creative firm
DOUGLAS JOSEPH PARTNERS
Los Angeles, California
art directors
DOUG JOSEPH, SCOTT LAMBERT
designer
SCOTT LAMBERT
illustrators
DAVID PLUNKERT, AUGUST STEIN
photographer
ERIC TUCKER
copywriter
SCOTT LAMBERT
client
SPICERS PAPER

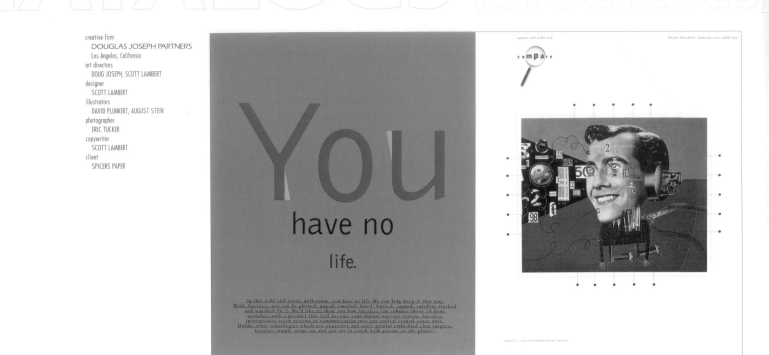

creative firm
GRETEMAN GROUP
Wichita, Kansas
creative director
SONIA GRETEMAN
art director
SONIA GRETEMAN, JAMES STRANGE
designer
CRAIG TOMSON
client
LEARJET

creative firm
DISNEY DESIGN GROUP
Lake Buena Vista, Florida
creative director
MICHAEL KEATING
designers
MIKE WOOD, DARREN WILSON
illustrators
BRIAN BLACKMORE, ALEX MAHER
client
WALT DISNEY WORLD SPECIAL EVENTS DEVELOPMENT

Learjet 31A

creative firm
  HORNALL ANDERSON DESIGN WORKS
  Seattle, Washington
art directors
  JACK ANDERSON, KATHA DALTON
designers
  JACK ANDERSON, KATIIA DALTON,
  RYAN WILKERSON, BELINDA BOWLING
client
  BOUILLION AVIATION SERVICES

creative firm
  HORNALL ANDERSON DESIGN WORKS
  Seattle, Washington
art director
  JACK ANDERSON
designers
  JACK ANDERSON, BRUCE BRANSON-MEYER,
  HEIDI FAVOUR, MARGARET LONG
client
  DDB SEATTLE

The Sony of Canada story, like so many great stories, begins with a stroke of luck. It is October 1955. Albert Cohen, a 41-year-old entrepreneur from Winnipeg, is in his room at Tokyo's Imperial Hotel. It is his second trip to Japan at a time when few Westerners come here. He is shopping for products to expand his distributing business: watches, lighters, any kind of reasonably priced gadget that will appeal to Canadian consumers.

Browsing through the English-language *Nippon Times*, Cohen notices an item on Japan's first transistor radio. He has been following the new transistor technology with interest, looking for an alternative to battery-powered tube radios (whose short life span cost him profits on an earlier import deal). Of course, it isn't likely that a small, unknown company, Tokyo Tsushin Kogyo (TTK) Ltd., will have the solution. But it's worth a shot. He calls and sets up a meeting for the following afternoon.

Arriving by taxi, Cohen feels his hopes sink still lower when he sees TTK's office, a ramshackle wooden house in the Shinagawa district. He is greeted by a Mr. Naruse, who informs him cautiously that the news story was a bit premature: the new radio is not quite ready for market. Without fanfare, he presents this historic Japanese first: the TR-55.

Cohen is intrigued. The five-transistor set measures 5″ by 3″ by 1.25″ and is powered by four inexpensive penlight batteries with a fairly long life span. Canadian consumers will buy this, provided the price is right. Mr. Naruse allows that TTK has not considered exporting the new radio. After some calculations, he arrives at a wholesale price of $27. Cohen is taken aback: that becomes $79.95 retail, far more than the $25 people typically pay for a tube radio. Still, the distributor is impressed by the TR-55's compactness and long battery life – and even more so by a brief meeting with one of TTK's founders, a gentleman named Akio Morita.

4 · 5

creative firm
   VIVA DOLAN COMMUNICATIONS ANDDESIGN, INC.
   Toronto, Canada
designer
   FRANK VIVA
illustrator
   MICHAEL BARTALOS
photographer
   HILL PEPPARD
copywriter
   DOUG DOLAN
client
   SONY CANADA

creative firm
   VIVA DOLAN COMMUNICATIONS AND DESIGN, INC.
   Toronto, Canada
art director
   FRANK VIVA
designers
   FRANK VIVA, JIM RYCE
client
   GOLDEN BOOKS FAMILY ENTERTAINMENT

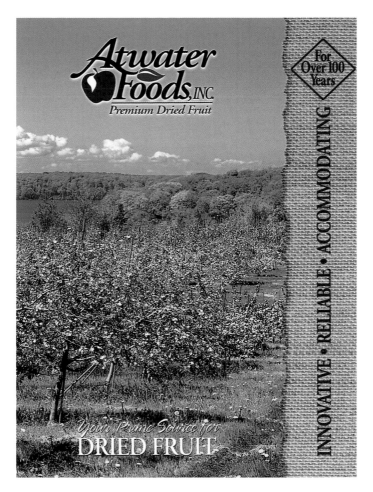

creative firm
  McELVENEY + PALOZZI DESIGN GROUP, INC.
    Rochester, New York
creative director
  WILLIAM McELVENEY
art director
  LISA WILLIAMSON
client
  ATWATER FOODS, INC.

creative firm
  SIGN KOMMUNIKATION GMBH
    Frankfurt, Germany
creative director
  KARL W. HENSCHEL
client
  SIGN KOMMUNIKATION GMBH

creative firm
  BBK STUDIO, INC.
    Grand Rapids, Michigan
art director, designer, calligrapher
  KEVIN BUDELMANN
editor
  DICK HOLM
photographer
  BOB NEUMANN
copywriter
  KATE CONVISSOR
client
  HERMAN MILLER INC.

PENGUIN books

January to April

2(000)

creative firm
PENGUIN PUTNAM, INC.
New York, New York

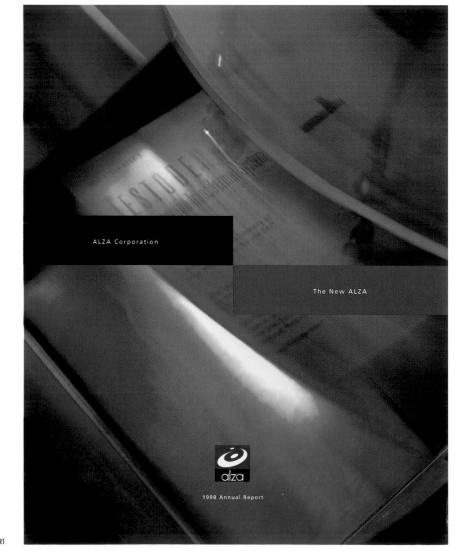

ALZA Corporation

The New ALZA

alza

1998 Annual Report

creative firm
CASPER DESIGN GROUP
Berkeley, California
creative director
BILL RIBAR
designer
CHRISTOPHER BUEHLER
photographer
DAVID POWERS
client
ALZA CORPORATION 1998 ANNUAL REPORT

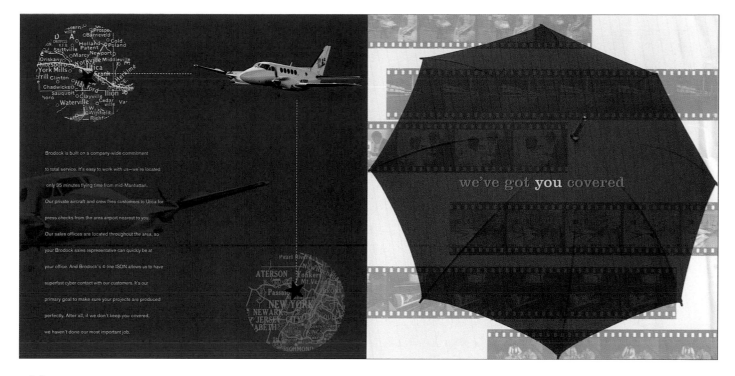

we've got **you** covered

creative firm
   PLATINUM DESIGN, INC.
   New York, New York
art director
   VICTORIA STAMM
designers
   KELLY HOGG, MIKE JOYCE
photographer
   BART GORIM
copywriter
   ARTHUR LEBOW
client
   BRODOCK PRESS

coolsavings com

creative firm
   PARAGRAPHS DESIGN
   Chicago, Illinois
designer
   JENNIFER ESPOSITO
client
   COOL SAVINGS

creative firm
   PARAGRAPHS DESIGN
   Chicago, Illinois
designer
   SCOTT HICKMAN
client
   CSC

69

creative firm
DESIGN GUYS
Minneapolis, Minnesota
art director
STEVEN SIKORA
designer
JAY THEIGE
client
TARGET STORES

herbasis™

creative firm
SIGN KOMMUNIKATION GMBH
Frankfurt, Germany
creative director
KARL W. HENSCHEL
client
DEBIS SYSTEMHAUS

debis
Systemhaus

IT services on
an international
scale

ROMA
LONDON
TOKYO
BERLIN
NEW YORK
PARIS
BRUXELLES

Keller
and
Heckman LLP

Business
law+science℠

creative firm
JILL TANENBAUM GRAPHIC DESIGN & ADVERTISING
Bethesda, Maryland
creative director
JIM TANENBAUM
senior designer
LEAH GERMANN
client
KELLERT HECKMAN

People

The people of Harb, Levy & Weiland are working for you. We carefully select a service team comprised of HLW people with experience and expertise tailored to the needs of each client. The service team is headed by an engagement partner who is directly involved with every aspect of your account.

The experience and specialized knowledge of everyone at HLW is available for assistance as needed, while the combined resources of Nexia International, the twelfth largest accounting organization in the world, are available to serve your international needs and to extend our accounting, tax and consulting capability.

Our partners average more than twenty years of public accounting experience, including many years with international accounting firms. This combined experience includes substantial work in most industries and functional specialties in all aspects of audit, accounting and taxation, and many elements of consulting.

HLW people have the highest academic and professional credentials, and we expect a work ethic and spirit committed to quality and timely service. Our formal training typically exceeds the forty hours per year required for CPA licensing. Additional training allows our firm's professionals to update and expand their skills to better serve our clients.

Audit
&
Accounting

creative firm
STRATFORD DESIGN ASSOCIATES
Brisbane, California
designer
G.W. STRATFORD, SR.
photographers
GERALD L. FRENCH,
KERRICK JAMES
client
HARB LEVY & WEILAND

BIKING 1999

Butterfield & Robinson

The World's Great Biking Journeys

creative firm
VIVA DOLAN COMMUNICATIONS AND DESIGN, INC.
Toronto, Canada
designer
FRANK VIVA
illustrator
DOUG ROSS
photographer
ED CHIN
editor
DALI CASTRO
production artist
SONJA KLOSS
client
BUTTERFIELD & ROBINSON

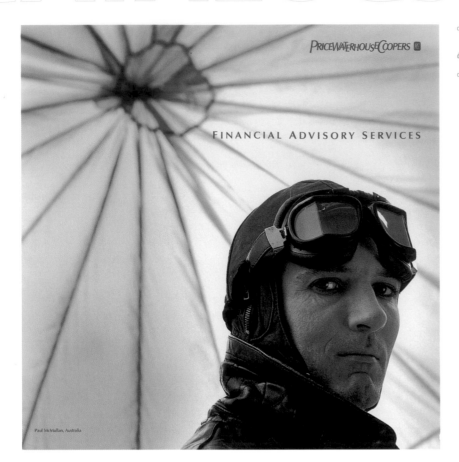

Paul McMullan, Australia

FINANCIAL ADVISORY SERVICES

PRICEWATERHOUSECOOPERS

creative firm
EDWARD WALTER DESIGN
New York, New York
designer
MARTIN BRYNELL
client
PRICEWATERHOUSECOOPERS

GAUDNEK
MUSEUM &
SAMMLUNG

creative firm
CHAVDA GRAPIX
Oviedo, Florida
designer
JAGDISH J. CHAVDA
client
DR. WALTER GAUDNEK

creative firm
FROST DESIGN LTD
London, England
creative director
VINCE FROST
client
PHOTONICA

creative firm
A TO Z COMMUNICATIONS, INC.
Pittsburgh, Pennsylvania
senior graphic designer
JOE TOMKO
client
PERSAD

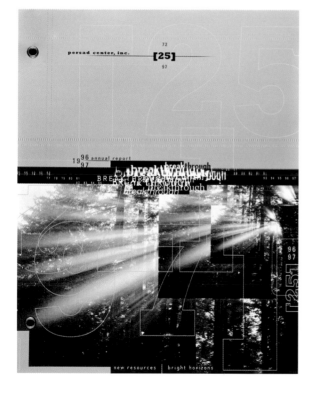

creative firm
HARPER & CASE LTD
New York, New York
creative director
LISSA TOOLE
designer
JEANNE McMANAMAN
client
CHILDREN'S AID SOCIETY

RENEWING A BLOCK IN HARLEM

PHASE II — AFTER THE RENOVATIONS

The Children's Aid Society/
Carmel Hill Project: Years 5 and 6

Photographs by Bill Foley
Text by Terry Quinn

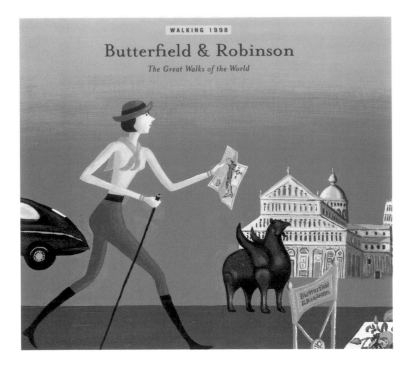

creative firm
  VIVA DOLAN COMMUNICATIONS AND DESIGN, INC.
  Toronto, Canada
art director, designer
  FRANK VIVA
illustrator
  MALCOLM HILL
photographers
  RON BAXTER SMITH, MacDUFF EVERTON,
  HILL PEPPARD, STEVEN ROTHFELD
copywriter
  DOUG DOLAN
client
  BUTTERFIELD & ROBINSON

creative firm
  WPA PINFOLD
  Leeds, Yorks, United Kingdom
art director
  MYLES PINFOLD
design manager
  ANDY PROBERT
designer
  PHIL MOMSON
client
  JOHN SMITH'S LTD

creative firm
  EMERSON, WAJDOWICZ STUDIOS
  New York, New York
creative director
  JUREK WAJDOWICZ
senior art director
  LISA LaROCHELLE
client
  DOMTAR, EDDY SPECIALTY PAPERS

BENDING STEEL

with your bare hands is strictly optional, but it couldn't hurt.

Building new competencies in your organization is always a super smart move. Expectations among stakeholders are universally rising, and the pressure is on to achieve truly cosmic outcomes and results.

New ways to get things done smarter, faster and better can generate the momentum you need to take giant leaps ahead. Because those who stand still in business today may not be still standing tomorrow.

For savvy, fast-growing organizations like yours that know the value of moving decisively to seize opportunities and dodge speeding bullets, SportsMind has a promise:

We'll help build powerful new competencies throughout your organization — from the boardroom to the backroom. And we'll help your super men and women take new action that can lead to some very attractive, long-term outcomes:

- **Reduced cycle times** and increased attention to detail that boost productivity.
- **Enhanced organization-wide morale** that reduces turnover and fuels loyalty.
- **Expanded accountability and reliability** that generate project success.
- **Increased customer satisfaction** that builds profitability.
- **Open communication channels** that power cooperation and collaboration.

SportsMind. We can help you fly past the competition.

SPEED AND AGILITY

Faster than a speeding bullet...

Able to leap tall buildings in a single bound. Getting your organization to the top in today's competitive business environment requires cohesive, super-scale effort. Not to mention real-time decision making, nimble strategies and operational agility.

IT'S ABOUT BUILDING NEW COMPETENCIES TO GENERATE NEW OUTCOME!

creative firm
KLUNDT HOSMER DESIGN
Spokane, Washington
designers
JUDY DAVIS-HEGGEM,
DAREN KLUNDT,
RICK HOSMER
client
SPORTS MIND

WALKING 1999

Butterfield & Robinson
The Great Walks of the World

creative firm
VIVA DOLAN COMMUNICATIONS AND DESIGN, INC.
Toronto, Canada
designer
FRANK VIVA
illustrator
DOUG ROSS
photographer
ED CHIN
copywriter
DOUG DOLAN
editor
DALI CASTRO
production artist
SONJA KLOSS
client
BUTTERFIELD & ROBINSON

 (catalog spread)

LEMONGRASS & LIMELEAF / WHITE GINGER AROMATIC CANDLE

Fill any room with the ambience of a walk in the tropics. These quality candles are formulated with perfume-quality fragrance, for a true island signature. The frosted glass container is a classic addition to any decor. Allow yourself to be renewed, surrounded by enticing touches of your favorite Island Thymes fragrance.

APPROX. 40 HOURS

03532   LEMONGRASS & LIMELEAF
03531   WHITE GINGER

WHITE GINGER VOTIVE CANDLES

These richly scented votives are perfect for refilling the Aromatic Candle or any standard-size votive container. Light one or more to gently fill the room with captivating notes of Hawaiian White Ginger.

03501   3 VOTIVES – APPROX. 15 HOURS EACH

LEMONGRASS & LIMELEAF BURNING STICKS

On a terrace, balcony or backyard deck, the open air turns to the tropics with wisps of Lemongrass & Limeleaf, carried beautifully in these potent Burning Sticks.

03632   20 BURNING STICKS

LEMONGRASS & LIMELEAF / WHITE GINGER REFRESHER OIL

Add a few drops of Refresher Oil to Potpourri or Scented Stones to revive their tropical fragrance, or use it with a lamp ring or aromatherapy diffuser to create a fragrant aura.

15 ML. / 0.5 FL OZ

03592   LEMONGRASS & LIMELEAF
03591   WHITE GINGER

LEMONGRASS & LIMELEAF / WHITE GINGER HOME FRAGRANCE MIST

An abundant burst of Home Fragrance Mist adds an immediate ambience to your surroundings.

85 G / 3 OZ

03562   LEMONGRASS & LIMELEAF
03561   WHITE GINGER

LEMONGRASS & LIMELEAF POTPOURRI

Indonesian lemongrass infused with West Indian lime creates an energetic potpourri, harvested from the tropical hills.

03602   LEMONGRASS & LIMELEAF

LEMONGRASS & LIMELEAF / WHITE GINGER SCENTED STONES

Smooth, fragrant stones and colorful botanicals presented in a wooden treasure box make an unusual home accent.

03622   LEMONGRASS & LIMELEAF
03621   WHITE GINGER

1-800-366-4071   19

creative firm
  DESIGN GUYS
  Minneapolis, Minnesota
creative director
  LYNETTE ERICKSON-SIKORA
art director
  STEVEN SIKORA
designers
  GARY PATCH , JAY THEIGE
photographer
  PATRICK FOX
client
  THYMES LIMITED

MOLD MAKING

creative firm
  KLUNDT HOSMER DESIGN
  Spokane, Washington
designers
  BRIAN GAGE,
  DARIN KLUNDT
client
  ALTEK

creative firm
  GREENFIELD/BELSER LTD
  Washington D.C.
art director, designer
  BURKEY BELSER
copywriter
  LISEANNE SCHWARTZ
client
  WILLIAMS & JENSEN

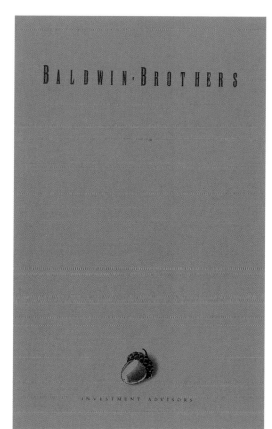

creative firm
  ROSE SREBRO DESIGN
  Waban, Massachusetts
creative director, designer
  ROSE SREBRO
illustrator
  CHRIS GALL
client
  BALDWIN BROTHERS

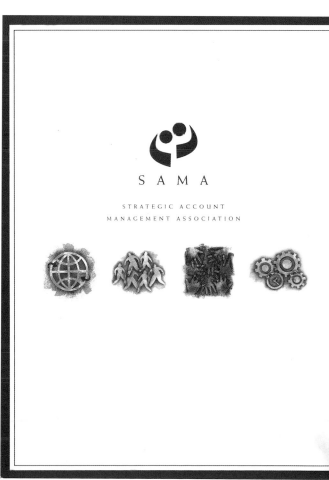

creative firm
  HARPER + CASE, LTD
  New York, New York
creative director, designer
  LISSA TOOLE
client
  SAMA

The synergy of materials Sophisticated strength. Subtle softness.

Styling substance. The synergistic interplay of

materials—whether natural or manufactured—

creates visual and tactile excitement.

Elegant arcs of
wood and Corian®
in Black Pearl create
a classic console.

creative firm
  REESE, TOMASES, & ELLICK
  Wilmington, Delaware
creative director
  RICK CLEMONS
designer
  CINDY DUMONT
client
  DUPONT CORIAN

creative firm
  WAGES DESIGN
  Atlanta, Georgia
designer
  MATT TAYLOR
photographer
  RALPH DANIELS
copywriter
  PAT WAGES
client
  SWARTZ INSTITUTIONAL FINANCE

PRIVATE
PLACEMENT
FUNDING
for the NEXT MILLENNIUM

What will the next 100 years bring for your company? As the 21st
century unfolds, no doubt it will present unique situations and unexpected
opportunities. Imagine facing those years with the confidence your
capital requirements will be met thoroughly and swiftly, allowing your
management team to stay focused on its core competencies. With the right
partner, private equity financing can strengthen your position in the
competitive business environment. With our history of pioneering private
equity instruments, Swartz is uniquely positioned to be a vital resource,
leveraging your growth potential throughout the critical years to come.
Now small and mid-cap companies have access to big financial resources.

*"With the right partner, private equity financing can strengthen
your position in the competitive business environment."*

trip guide 2000

creative firm
  VIVA DOLAN COMMUNICATIONS AND DESIGN
  Toronto, Canada
art director, designer
  FRANK VIVA
illustrators
  FRANK VIVA, TERRY SHOFFNER
photographers
  ROB HOWARD, ED CHIN, MacDUFF EVERTON, JOHN KANE,
  KINDRA CLINEFF, TOM KIRKENDALL, ROB CRANDELL, HOWARD GARETT,
  CHARLIE SCOTT, DAVID SWALES, DENIS PAGÉ, PHILIPPE BROWN,
  ROBERT MINNES, MICHAEL LISS
copywriter
  DOUD DOLAN
editor
  DALI CASTRO
production artist
  SONJA KLOSS
client
  BUTTERFIELD & ROBINSON

creative firm
  DISNEYLAND CREATIVE SERVICES
  Anaheim, California
creative director
  SCOTT STARKEY
photographer
  WALTER URIE
copywriter
  TONY SERNA
client
  DISNEYLAND COMMUNITY AFFAIRS-BILL ROSS

THE MAGIC OF SHARING

THE Disneyland RESORT

creative firm
  HORNALL ANDERSON DESIGN WORKS
  Seattle, Washington
art director
  JACK ANDERSON
designers
  JACK ANDERSON, BELINDA BOWLING,
  ANDREW SMITH, ED LEE
client
  STREAMWORKS

WHY JACK CHARLTON IS NOT A BIG BELIEVER IN FRICTION

Reels

[Some say obsession can create perfection. We tend to agree.] -- Jack Charlton has run every type of test on his fly reels that you can possibly imagine -- structural, hydraulic, thermal, metallurgical, composite -- even airflow analysis. And because of those tests, we've been able to arrive at a reel that can stop fish with [no breakaway friction, jerks or surprises.] Plus, it can make it through season upon season of wet, cold, sand, salt, and "forgotten-in-the-back-of-the-truck" abuse. Charlton reel customers claim they can find [no better reel at any price.] We think they're right.

Charlton offers a wide range of reels from the simplest, lightweight S3500 trout model to the air-vortex-cooled S600A offshore reel. We'll put each and every one of these reels up against any other reel available.

Charlton. A reel for every situation...

79

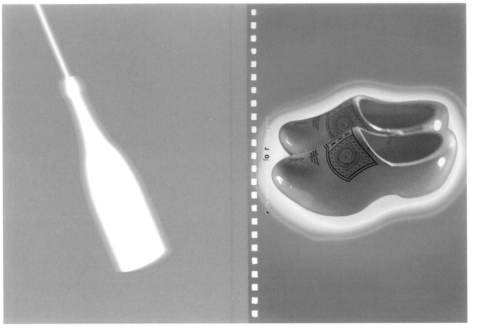

creative firm
  TRICKETT & WEBB LTD
  London, England
designers
  LYNN TRICKETT,
  BRIAN WEBB,
  MARCUS TAYLOR
photographer
  ANDREW HALL
copywriter
  NEIL MATTINGLEY
client
  ISTD FINE PAPER LTD

creative firm
  PLATINUM DESIGN, INC.
  New York, New York
art director
  MIKE JOYCE
designer
  MIKE JOYCE
copywriter
  PAMELA COOK
client
  ENTERCOM

creative firm
  DOTZLER CREATIVE ARTS
  Omaha, Nebraska
client
  THE CREATIVE CENTER

creative firm
  KLUNDT HOSMER DESIGN
  Spokane, Washington
designers
  JUDY HEGGEM-DAVIS,
  DARIN KLUNDT
client
  ICM MANAGEMENT, INC.

creative firm
  HORNALL ANDERSON
  DESIGN WORKS
  Seattle, Washington
art director
  JACK ANDERSON
designers
  JACK ANDERSON, KATHY SAITO,
  JULIE LOCK, ED LEE,
  HEIDI FAVOUR, VIRGINIA LE
client
  GROUND ZERO

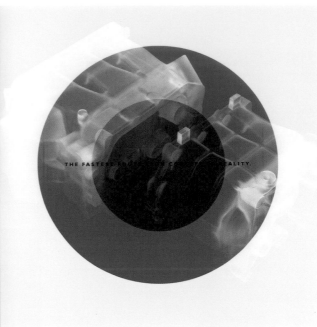

THE FASTEST ROUTE FROM CONCEPT TO REALITY.

creative firm
DOUGLAS JOSEPH PARTNERS
Los Angeles, California
art director
DOUG JOSEPH
designer
JULIE SLOTO-MELLEN
copywriter
MARK SCAPICCHIO
client
3D SYSTEMS CORPORATION

4 | SMALL SLENDER CABINET (1 bottom shelf) *Also available as...*
TALL SLENDER CABINET (2 bottom shelves)

SLENDER FLOOR CABINET | 5

creative firm
AIRE DESIGN COMPANY
Tucson, Arizona
creative director
CATHARINE M. KIM
art director
SHARI RYKOWSKI
client
KNF DESIGNS

Vol. 18
number 1
1998

sonorensis
Wildlife Rehabilitation

ARIZONA – SONORA DESERT MUSEUM

creative firm
AIRE DESIGN COMPANY
Tucson, Arizona
creative director
CATHARINE M. KIM
art director
SHARI RYKOWSKI
client
ARIZONA-SONORA DESERT MUSEUM

creative firm
TANGRAM STRATEGIC DESIGN
Novara, Italy
creative director, art director, designer
ENRICO SEMPI
client
RIBES

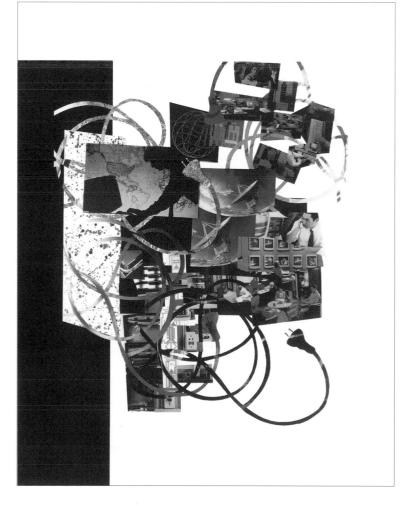

creative firm
BBK STUDIOS INC.
Grand Rapids, Michigan
designer
MICHAEL BARILE
illustrators
MICHAEL BARILE,
ALLEN McKINNEY
copywriter
BOB TORIN
client
STEELCASE, INC.

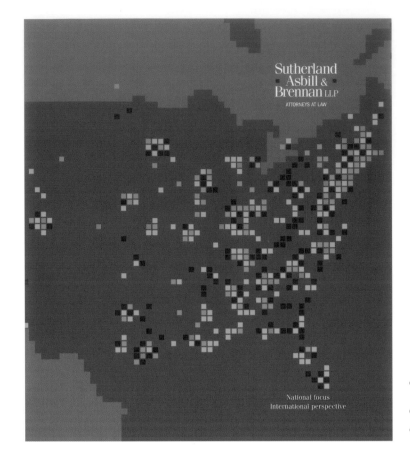

creative firm
GREENFIELD/BELSER LTD
Washington, D.C.
art director, designer
BURKEY BELSER
client
SUTHERLAND ASBILL & BRENNAN

creative firm
VIVA DOLAN COMMUNICATIONS AND DESIGN
Toronto, Canada
art director, designer
FRANK VIVA
illustrator
MALCOLM HILL
photographers
RON BAXTER SMITH. MacDUFF EVERTON,
HILL PEPPARD, STEVEN ROTHFELD
copywriter
DOUG DOLAN
client
BUTTERFIELD & ROBINSON

creative firm
WPA PINFOLD
Leeds, England
design manager
ANDY PROBERT
designer
PHIL MOMSON
client
WINPAC GROUP

creative firm
BBK STUDIO INC.
Grand Rapids, Michigan
creative director
KEVIN BUDELMANN
designer
ALLISON POPP
illustrators, photographers
NICK MERRICK, BOB NEUMANN, SUSAN CARR
copywriter
DEB WIERENGA
client
HERMAN MILLER INC.

creative firm
THE WYANT SIMBOLI GROUP
Norwalk, Connecticut
creative director
JULIE WYANT
production manager
KAREN OLENSHI
designers
PAUL M. NEEL, SHERI CIFALDI, LANCE HERTZBACH
client
GE CAPITAL

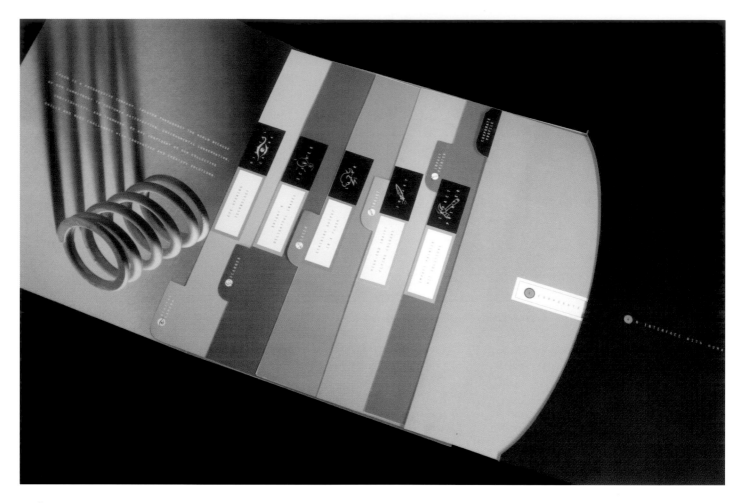

creative firm
UKULELE DESIGN CONSULTANTS PTE LTD
Singapore
design director
KIM CHUN-WEI
designer
LYNN LIM
copywriter
EVELYN TENG
client
EPSON SINGAPORE PTE LTD

creative firm
HORNALL ANDERSON DESIGN WORKS
Seattle, Washington
art directors
JACK ANDERSON, LISA CERVENY
designers
LISA CERVENY, DAVID BATES, ALAN FLORSHEIM
client
LEATHERMAN TOOL GROUP

creative firm
KINETIK COMMUNICATION GRAPHICS, INC.
Washington, D.C.
designers
BETH CLAWSON,
JEFFREY FABIAN,
SCOTT RIER,
KAMOMI SOLIDUM
client
SMITHSONIAN INSTITUTION

creative firm
HORNALL ANDERSON DESIGN WORKS
Seattle, Washington
art directors
JOHN HORNALL, KATHA DALTON
designers
JOHN HORNALL, KATHA DALTON,
MARY HERMES, STEPHANIE LORIG,
ALAN COPELAND, MICHAEL BRUGMAN
client
FOSTER PEPPER SHEFELMAN

creative firm
WATERSDESIGN.COM
  New York, New York
creative director
  JOHN WATERS
content
  JACQUELINE STOLTE
designer
  LAURA SAUTER
client
  WALTER P. SAUER

creative firm
  5D STUDIO
  Malibu, California
art director
  JANE KOBAYASHI
designer
  ANNE COATES
client
  WALKER ZANGER

creative firm
KLUNDT HOSMER DESIGN
Spokane, Washington
designer
DARIN KLUNDT
client
COPELAND DESIGN & CONSTRUCTION

creative firm
SQUARE ONE DESIGN
Grand Rapids, Michigan
art director
MIKE GORMAN
designer
ELENA TISLEVICS
client
JOHN WIDDICOMB

creative firm
WATERSDESIGN.COM
New York, New York
creative director
JOHN WATERS
producer
SUSAN DeMIRJIAN
content director
ANDY AUSTIN
designers
DIRK ROWNTREE, SUSAN HILDEBRAND
client
WESTVACO

YOUR READERS WILL DEMAND A SEQUEL...   STERLING® ULTRA 80lb Web Dull   STERLING® ULTRA 80lb Web Matte

STORIES. Because there's nothing like a story well told, your next pictorial deserves nothing less than Westvaco's Sterling® Ultra Web Dull, with its bright, clean white finish. And when it comes time for reprints, Sterling Ultra sets the stage for the words and images that tell all our stories over and over again.

89

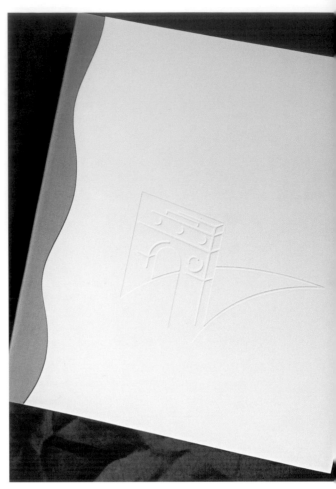

creative firm
3OSIXTY DESIGN, INC.
Los Angeles, California
creative director
HENRY VIZCARRA
art director, illustrator
PÄR LARSSON
designers
**RICKARD OLSSON, PÄR LARSSON,
PEGGY MARTIN, SUPPASAK VIBOONLARP**
client
VIACOM CONSUMER PRODUCTS

creative firm
O&J DESIGN INC.
New York, New York
art director
ANDRZEJ J. OLEJNICZAK
designer
LESLIE NAYMAN
client
NEW YORK UNIVERSITY SCHOOL OF CONTINUING AND PROFESSIONAL STUDIES

creative firm
ROLF HARDER & ASSOC. INC.
Beaconsfield, Canada
designer
ROLF HARDER
client
ENGLISH MONTREAL SCHOOL BOARD

creative firm
OH&CO
IN COLLABORATION WITH
IDEO
New York, New York
creative director
BRENT OPPENHEIMER
strategy director
ROBIN HAUETER
designer
ROBERT HOMACK
client
AMTRAK

creative firm
MORTENSEN DESIGN
Mountain View, California
art director
GORDON MORTENSEN
designers
GORDON MORTENSEN, PJ NIDECKER
client
HANDSPRING, INC

creative firm
O&J DESIGN INC.
New York, New York
art director
ANDRZEJ J. OLEJNICZAK
designers
LIA CAMARA-MARISCAL,
CHRISTINA MUELLER,
SASHA SWETSCHINSKI
client
AVON PRODUCTS INC.

creative firm
  LARSEN DESIGN
  + INTERACTIVE
    Minneapolis, Minnesota
creative director, designer
  TODD MANNES
client
  MINNESOTA PARKS &
  TRAILS COUNCIL

creative firm
    McELVENEY + PALOZZI DESIGN GROUP, INC.
    Rochester, New York
creative director
    WILLIAM McELVENEY
art director
    ELLEN JOHNSON
client
    THE LODGE AT WOODCLIFF

HORIZONS
THE LODGE AT WOODCLIFF

creative firm
    MICHAEL COURTNEY DESIGN
    Seattle, Washington
art director, designer
    MICHAEL COURTNEY
illustrator
    DENISE WEIR
client
    EVERGREEN PRINTING

creative firm
    McELVENEY + PALOZZI
    DESIGN GROUP, INC.
    Rochester, New York
creative director
    WILLIAM McELVENEY
art director
    ELLEN JOHNSON
client
    THE LODGE AT WOODCLIFF

THE LODGE AT
Woodcliff

93

G-FORCE
COLLABORATIONS

creative firm
  McELVENEY + PALOZZI
  DESIGN GROUP, INC.
  Rochester, New York
creative director
  WILLIAM McELVENEY
art director
  MATT NOWICKI
designer
  DILLON CONSTABLE
client
  G-FORCE COLLABORATIONS

creative firm
  BUTLER KEMP DESIGN
  North Adelaide, Australia
art director
  DEREK BUTLER
designer
  HELLEN KIPRIZLOGLOV
client
  DAISHSAT

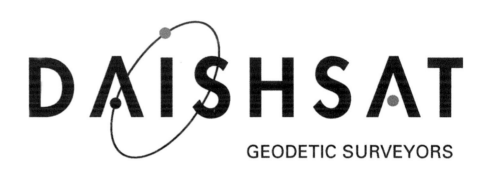

DAISHSAT
GEODETIC SURVEYORS

GNIBUS
PUBLIC RELATIONS

creative firm
  THE WECKER GROUP
  Monterey, California
designer
  MATT GNIBUS
client
  GNIBUS PUBLIC RELATIONS

the
Children's
Museum

creative firm
BIG CAT MARKETING COMM.
Colorado Springs, Colorado
designer
NORMANDINA SNOW
client
THE CHILDREN'S MUSEUM

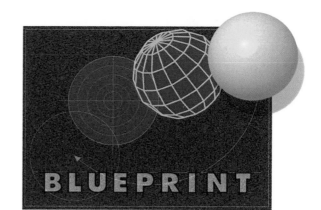

BLUEPRINT

creative firm
SIBLEY PETEET DESIGN
Dallas, Texas
designer
BRENT McMAHAN
client
SABRE GROUP

IM

AQUAFUTURE

creative firm
THE WECKER GROUP
Monterey, California
designers
ROBERT WECKER, MATT GNIBUS
client
AQUA FUTURE, INC.

AUREA

creative firm
KEVIN AKERS
—DESIGNER
San Rafael, California
designer
KEVIN AKERS
client
AUREA HEADSET
MANUFACTURER

creative firm
ARNOLD SAKS ASSOCIATES
New York, New York
designer
ARNOLD SAKS
client
ALCOA

creative firm
McMILLIAN DESIGN
Woodside, New York
art director
WILLIAM McMILLIAN
client
DR. RICHARD BELLI

creative firm
DEVER DESIGNS
Laurel, Maryland
art director
JEFFREY L. DEVER
designers
JEFFREY L. DEVER, EMILY KENDALL
client
CARNEGIE ENDOWMENT FOR INTERNATIONAL PEACE

creative firm
HORNALL ANDERSON DESIGN WORKS
Seattle, Washington
art director
JACK ANDERSON
designers
MARGARET LONG, JASON HICKNER
client
GETTUIT

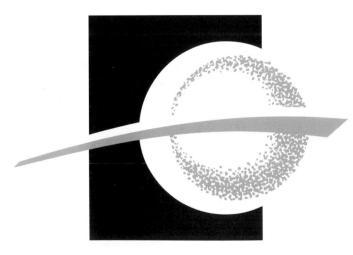

gettuit.com™

creative firm
MIRIELLO GRAFICO, INC.
San Diego, California
designers
CHRIS KEENEY, DENNIS GARCIA
client
NEWPORT COMMUNICATIONS

creative firm
ROBERT MEYERS DESIGN
Fairlawn, Ohio
designer
ROBERT MEYERS
client
PITTSBURGH ST. PATRICK'S DAY

creative firm
KEVIN AKERS—DESIGNER
San Rafael, California
designer
KEVIN AKERS
client
SUSAN SARGENT
(textile designer)

creative firm
HORNALL ANDERSON DESIGN WORKS
Seattle, Washington
art director
JACK ANDERSON
designers
JACK ANDERSON, KATHY SAITO,
GRETCHEN COOK, JAMES TEE,
JULIE LOCK, HENRY YIU
client
GETTUIT (WORKENGINE)

workengine™

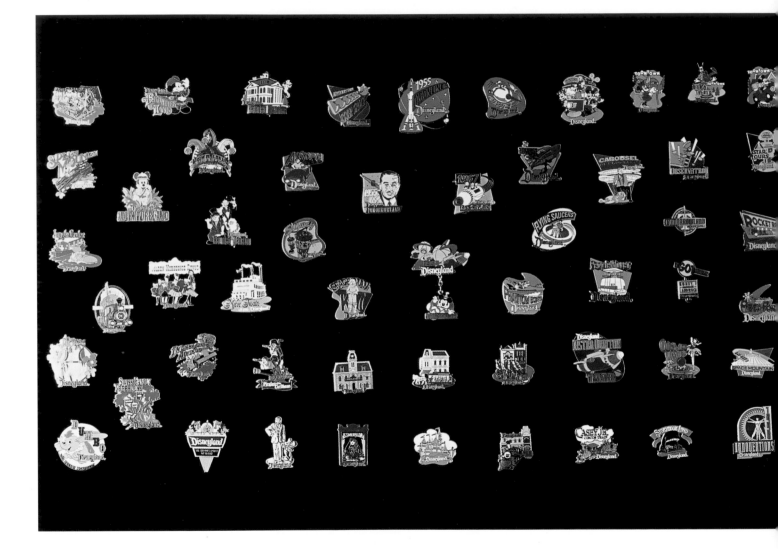

creative firm
DISNEYLAND CREATIVE SERVICES
Anaheim, California
creative director
SCOTT STARKEY
designers
MIKE PUCHALSKI, DATHAN SHORE,
DAVID RILEY & ASSOCATES, BARTON/KOMAI/DUNNAHOE
client
DISNEYLAND MERCHANDISE

creative firm
THE RIORDON DESIGN GROUP
Oakville, Canada
art director
RIC RIORDON
designer, illustrator
DAN WHEATON
client
CHUCK GAMMAGE ANIMATION

creative firm
ROBERT MEYERS DESIGN
Fairlawn, Ohio
designer
ROBERT MEYERS
client
SHADYSIDE CHAMBER OF COMMERCE

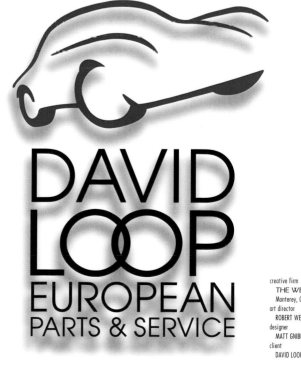

creative firm
SAYLES GRAPHIC DESIGN
Des Moines, Iowa
art director, illustrator
JOHN SAYLES
client
MEREDITH CORPORATION

creative firm
THE WECKER GROUP
Monterey, California
art director
ROBERT WECKER
designer
MATT GNIBUS
client
DAVID LOOP EUROPEAN

99

creative firm
  BECKER DESIGN
  Milwaukee, Wisconsin
designer
  NEIL BECKER
client
  MILWAUKEE BALLET NUTCRACKER

creative firm
  SHOOK DESIGN GROUP, INC.
  Charlotte, North Carolina
graphic designer
  JEFF CAMILLO
client
  BACK TO THE FIFTIES SODA SHOPPE

creative firm
  WAGES DESIGN
  Atlanta, Georgia
designer
  MATT TAYLOR
client
  UTILITIES PROTECTION CENTER

creative firm
  SHIELDS DESIGN
  Fresno, California
designer
  CHARLES SHIELDS
client
  FRESNO METROPOLITAN MUSEUM

creative firm
  SQUIRES & COMPANY
  Dallas, Texas
designer
  CHRISTIE GROTHEIM
client
  DEEP ELLUM DASH '98

creative firm
  SHIELDS DESIGN
  Fresno, California
designer
  CHARLES SHIELDS
photographer
  CAMERAD,INC.
client
  CHARLES SHIELDS

creative firm
  BRYNELL DESIGN
  New York, New York
designer
  MARTIN BRYNELL
client
  WHERE

creative firm
  SHIELDS DESIGN
  Fresno, California
designer
  CHARLES SHIELDS
photographer
  PHIL RUDY
client
  PHIL RUDY PHOTOGRAPHY

One Hilton
One Place to Stay

creative firm
  KEVIN AKERS—DESIGNER
  San Rafael, California
designer
  KEVIN AKERS
client
  HILTON HOTELS

creative firm
  BOBCO DESIGN, INC.
  Irvine, California
designer
  ROBERT S. NENNINGER
client
  THE GOLDEN GATE BREAD CO.
  (sourdough bread exporter)

About Face
Salon & Boutique

creative firm
  BECKER DESIGN
  Milwaukee, Wisconsin
designer
  NEIL BECKER
client
  ABOUT FACE

DakotaCom.net

creative firm
AIRE DESIGN COMPANY
Tucson, Arizona
creative director
CATHARINE M. KIM
art director
SHARI RYKOWSKI
client
DAKOTACOM.NET

NAPA VALLEY CELEBRATES

CLIMB AGAINST THE ODDS

AN ASSAULT ON BREAST CANCER

creative firm
DESIGN SOLUTIONS
Napa, California
art director, designer
DEBORAH MITCHELL
client
THE BREAST CANCER FUND

creative firm
BRYNELL DESIGN
New York, New York
designer
MARTIN BRYNELL
client
WHERE

creative firm
MacVICAR DESIGN + COMMUNICATIONS
Arlington, Virginia
senior designer
WILLIAM A. GORDON
client
IDS—INTERACTIVE DIGITAL SYSTEMS

BAR
CENTRO
Madrid
©European Bar

ids

creative firm
SAYLES GRAPHIC DESIGN
Des Moines, Iowa
art director, illustrator
JOHN SAYLES
client
VINO VICCINO'S RISTORANTE

r i s t o r a n t e

innoVisions™

creative firm
HORNALL ANDERSON
DESIGN WORKS
Seattle, Washington
art director
JACK ANDERSON
designers
JACK ANDERSON, KATHY SAITO, ALAN COPELAND
client
WELLS FARGO (INNOVISIONS)

creative firm
    THE WECKER GROUP
    Monterey, California
designers
    ROBERT WECKER, MATT GNIBUS
client
    DOUBLETREE MONTEREY

creative firm
    BRUNAZZI & ASSOCIATI/
    IMAGE + COMMUNICATION
    Turin, Italy
art director
    GIOVANNI BRUNAZZI
designer
    ADA BRUNAZZI
client
    AUGUSTA BAGIENNORUM

creative firm
    THE WECKER GROUP
    Monterey, California
designer
    ROBERT WECKER
client
    THE HEARTH SHOP

creative firm
    INTERBRAND
    GERSTMAN ı MEYERS
    New York, New York
creative director
    JEFF ZACK
client
    KELLOGG'S

creative firm
  GARDNER DESIGN
  Wichita, Kansas
designers
  BILL GARDNER, BRIAN MILLER
client
  TALLGRASS BEEF

creative firm
  SAYLES GRAPHIC DESIGN
  Des Moines, Iowa
art director, illustrator
  JOHN SAYLES
client
  THE POWER TEAM

creative firm
  THE RIORDON DESIGN GROUP INC.
  Oakville, Canada
art director
  RIC RIORDON
designer
  DAN WHEATON
client
  FREE T.V.

creative firm
  McMILLIAN DESIGN
  Woodside, New York
art director
  WILLIAM McMILLIAN
client
  McMILLIAN DESIGN

S U S H I   N I G H T S

creative firm
SQUIRES & COMPANY
Dallas, Texas
designer
CHRISTIE GROTHEIM
client
SUSHI NIGHTS

creative firm
BOBCO DESIGN, INC.
Irvine, California
designer
ROBERT S. NENNINGER
client
THE CRAZY HORSE STEAKHOUSE RESTAURANT

CRAZY HORSE STEAKHOUSE

creative firm
KEVIN AKERS—DESIGNER
San Rafael, California
designer
KEVIN AKERS
client
SAVE HEADWATERS FOREST

creative firm
GARDNER DESIGN
Wichita, Kansas
designers
BILL GARDNER, BRIAN MILLER
client
COWLEY COUNTY COMMUNITY COLLEGE

HEARTLAND ARTS SERIES

The JOURNEY is ABOUT to BEGIN

creative firm
 PRIMO ANGELI INC.
 San Francisco, California
creative director
 CARLO PAGODA
project director
 RICH SCHEVE
senior designer
 TERRENCE TONG
illustrator
 MARK JONES
client
 SILICON GAMING (ODYSSEY)

creative firm
 McGAUGHY DESIGN
 Falls Church, Virginia
designer
 MALCOLM McGAUGHY
client
 McGAUGHY DESIGN

creative firm
 DOTZLER CREATIVE ARTS
 Omaha, Nebraska
client
 HOPE CENTER

creative firm
 WALLACE CHURCH ASS. INC.
 New York, New York
designers
 STAN CHURCH, CRAIG SWANSEN
client
 LYCOS

creative firm
SABINGRAFIK, INC.
Carlsbad, California
art director
MARILEE BANKERT
designer, illustrator
TRACY SABIN
client
OLIVER McMILLIN

creative firm
SHOOK DESIGN GROUP, INC.
Charlotte, North Carolina
graphic designer
JEFF CAMILLO
client
THE SUNSET CLUB

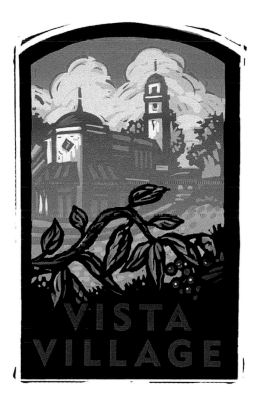

creative firm
GARDNER DESIGN
Wichita, Kansas
designer
BILL GARDNER
client
KANSAS JOINT REPLACEMENT INSTITUTE

creative firm
THE WECKER GROUP
Monterey, California
designer
ROBERT WECKER
client
UNIVERSAL INTERNET

creative firm
GARDNER DESIGN
Wichita, Kansas
designers
BILL GARDNER, KAREN HOGAN
client
GLORY

G L O R Y

creative firm
ROSS ADVERTISING
Peoria, Illinois
creative directors
BRIAN BRUSH, SKIP DAMPIER
designer
BRIAN BRUSH
client
WAHL

creative firm
AIRE DESIGN COMPANY
Tucson, Arizona
creative director
CATHARINE M. KIM
art director
SHARI RYKOWSKI
client
COMMUNITY FOUNDATION FOR SOUTHERN ARIZONA

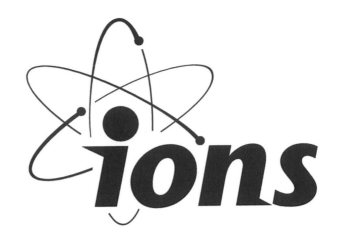

creative firm
  TELMET DESIGN ASSOCIATES
  Toronto, Canada
designer
  TIIT TELMET
client
  IONS WORLD CORP

creative firm
  HORNALL ANDERSON DESIGN WORKS
  Seattle, Washington
art director
  JACK ANDERSON
designers
  JACK ANDERSON, MIKE CALKINS
illustrator
  MIKE CALKINS
client
  HAMMERQUIST & HALVERSON

creative firm
  MADDOCKS & CO.
  Carlsbad, California
art director
  CLAIRE SEBENIUS
illustrator
  TRACY SABIN
client
  EL CHOLO

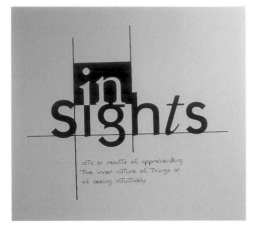

creative firm
  MICHAEL NIBLETT DESIGN
  Fort Worth, Texas
designer
  MICHAEL NIBLETT
client
  J.M. MOUDY EXHIBITION HALL

creative firm
  MICHAEL COURTNEY DESIGN
  Seattle, Washington
art director
  MICHAEL COURTNEY
designers
  MICHAEL COURTNEY, DAN HOANG, HEIDI FAVOUR, BRIAN O'NEILL
client
  FLEISCHMANN OFFICE INTERIORS

creative firm
  KEVIN AKERS—DESIGNER
  San Rafael, California
designer
  KEVIN AKERS
client
  SAN FRANCISCO SYMPHONY
  (Grateful Dead Members SFS Concert t-shirt logo)

PALMER | GOLF
BUILT TO HIT IT

creative firm
  MIRIELLO GRAFICO, INC.
  San Diego, California
designers
  CHRIS KEENEY, COURTNEY MEYER
client
  ARNOLD PALMER GOLF

creative firm
  KEVIN AKERS—DESIGNER
  San Rafael, California
designer
  KEVIN AKERS
client
  SAN FRANCISCO SYMPHONY
  (Grateful Dead Members SFS Concert t-shirt logo)

creative firm
  SHOOK DESIGN
  GROUP, INC.
  Charlotte, North Carolina
graphic designer
  JEFF CAMILLO
client
  THE TOWN OF CORNELIUS, NC

creative firm
  DEVER DESIGNS
  Laurel, Maryland
art director, designer
  JEFFREY L. DEVER
client
  DEVER DESIGNS

creative firm
    ROSS ADVERTISING
    Peoria, Illinois
senior art director
    NICK JIBBEN
client
    UPPER LIMITS TEAM CHALLENGE

creative firm
    THE WECKER GROUP
    Monterey, California
designer
    ROBERT WECKER
client
    SAN JUAN BAUTISTA CHAMBER OF COMMERCE

creative firm
    McELVENEY + PALOZZI
    DESIGN GROUP, INC.
    Rochester, New York
creative director
    STEVE PALOZZI
client
    SPRING STREET SOCIETY

creative firm
    TIM SMITH DESIGN
    Loveland, Ohio
designers
    TIM SMITH, LESLIE BURNS
client
    BURNS AUTO PARTS

creative firm
  SIBLEY PETEET DESIGN
  Dallas, Texas
designer
  BRENT McMAHAN
client
  JOHN HUTTON

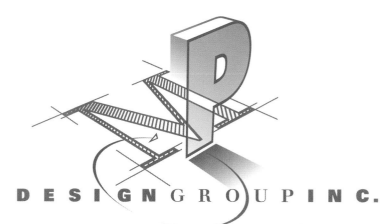

DESIGN GROUP INC.

creative firm
  McELVENEY + PALOZZI
  DESIGN GROUP, INC.
  Rochester, New York
creative directors
  WILLIAM McELVENEY, STEVE PALOZZI
senior art director
  JON WESTFALL
client
  McELVENEY + PALOZZI DESIGN GROUP, INC.

LeRoy Village Green
RESIDENTIAL HEALTHCARE FACILITY

creative firm
  McELVENEY + PALOZZI DESIGN GROUP, INC.
  Rochester, New York
creative director
  WILLIAM McELVENEY
art director
  LISA PARENTI
designer
  JAN MARIE GALLAGHER
client
  LEROY VILLAGE GREEN

creative firm
  DEUTSCH DESIGN WORKS
  San Franicsco, California
creative director
  BARRY DEUTSCH
senior designer
  LORI WYNN
client
  BELLAGIO RESORT & HOTEL, LAS VEGAS

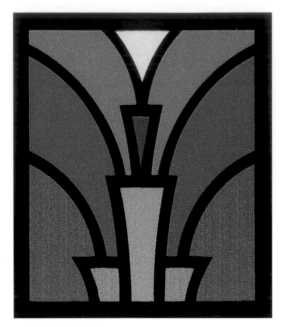

creative firm
  THE WECKER GROUP
    Monterey, California
designer
  ROBERT WECKER
client
  BLUE FIN BILLIARDS

creative firm
  KEVIN AKERS—DESIGNER
    San Rafael, California
designer
  KEVIN AKERS
client
  MONACO COSMETICS

creative firm
  ROSS ADVERTISING
    Peoria, Illinois
creative directors
  BRIAN BRUSH, SKIP DAMPIER
client
  ARCHER DANIELS MIDLAND

creative firm
  GARDNER DESIGN
    Wichita, Kansas
designer
  CHRIS PARKS
client
  SAFETEMP

creative firm
  TYLER BLIK DESIGN
  Carlsbad, California
art director, designer
  RON FLEMING
illustrator
  TRACY SABIN
client
  OTAY RANCH

creative firm
  KEVIN AKERS—DESIGNER
  San Rafael, California
designer
  KEVIN AKERS
client
  INKWELL
  (print brokers)

creative firm
  KEVIN AKERS—DESIGNER
  San Rafael, California
designer
  KEVIN AKERS
client
  COUNTRY GROWERS
  (nursery)

creative firm
  HORNALL ANDERSON DESIGN WORKS
  Seattle, Washington
art directors
  JACK ANDERSON, LISA CERVENY
designers
  JACK ANDERSON, LISA CERVENY, SONJA MAX, MARY HERMES
illustrator
  MARY HERMES
client
  TIGERLILY

creative firm
GARDNER DESIGN
Wichita, Kansas
designer
CHRIS PARKS
client
CARLOS O'KELLYS

ILI◁D ᴿᴹ

creative firm
SIBLEY PETEET DESIGN
Dallas, Texas
designer
TOM HOUGH
client
CHASE BANK

HAUTe DECOR .COM

creative firm
TOM FOWLER, INC.
Stamford, Connecticut
art directors, designers
THOMAS G. FOWLER, ELIZABETH P. BALL
client
HAUTE DECOR.COM

creative firm
COMPASS
DESIGN
Minneapolis, Minnesota
designers
MITCHELL LINDGREN,
TOM ARTHUR,
RICH McGOWEN
client
SUNRISE GOURMET

SUNRISE GOURMET™

creative firm
THE WECKER GROUP
Monterey, California
designer
ROBERT WECKER
client
DOUBLETREE MONTEREY

creative firm
GREENFIELD/BELSER LTD
Washington, D.C.
art director, designer
BURKEY BELSER
client
MORRIS JAMES

garbs
clothing   accessories   jewelry

creative firm
BECKER DESIGN
Milwaukee, Wisconsin
designer
NEIL BECKER
client
GARBS

creative firm
COMPASS DESIGN
Minneapolis, Minnesota
designers
MITCHELL LINDGREN, TOM ARTHUR, RICH McGOWEN
client
NIKOLA'S SPECIALTY FOODS

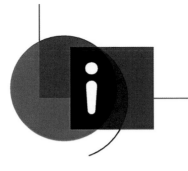

INTELLIGENT/DIGITAL

creative firm
  WAGES DESIGN
  Atlanta, Georgia
designer
  DOMINGA LEE
client
  INTELLIGENT DIGITAL

MIRAPOINT

creative firm
  MORTENSEN DESIGN
  Mountain View, California
art director
  GORDON MORTENSEN
designer
  PJ NIDECKER
client
  MIRAPOINT, INC.

CENTRE EUROPEEN LASER

creative firm
  TANGRAM STRATEGIC DESIGN
  Novara, Italy
creative director
  ENRICO SEMPI
art director, designer
  ANTONELLA TREVISAN
client
  CENTRE EUROPEEN DU LASER

SwiftTouch

creative firm
  GILL FISHMAN ASSOCIATES, INC.
  Cambridge, Massachusetts
creative director
  GILL FISHMAN
designer, illustrator
  ALICIA OZYJOWSKI
client
  SWIFT TOUCH CORP.

creative firm
  THE WECKER GROUP
  Monterey, California
designer
  ROBERT WECKER
client
  THE WECKER GROUP

creative firm
  BRYNELL DESIGN
  New York, New York
designer
  MARTIN BRYNELL
client
  WHERE

creative firm
  MINALE TATTERSFIELD + PARTNERS
  Richmond, England
creative director
  MARCELLO MINALE
client
  SAN PELLEGRINO

conversā

creative firm
  HORNALL ANDERSON DESIGN WORKS
  Seattle, Washington
art director
  JACK ANDERSON
designers
  JACK ANDERSON, KATHY SAITO, ALAN COPELAND
client
  CONVERSĀ

LINKS FOR LIFE

creative firm
McMILLIAN DESIGN
Woodside, New York
art director
WILLIAM McMILLIAN
client
GOLF DIGEST MAGAZINE

Center Trust

creative firm
JAMES ROBIE DESIGN ASSOCIATES
Los Angeles, California
creative director, designer
JAMES ROBIE
client
CENTER TRUST, INC.

creative firm
GARDNER DESIGN
Wichita, Kansas
designer
BRIAN MILLER
client
BALANCE

creative firm
COMPASS DESIGN
Minneapolis, Minnesota
designers
MITCHELL LINDGREN,
TOM ARTHUR, RICH McGOWEN
client
WORLD WIDE SPORTS

123

creative firm
FIVE VISUAL COMMUNICATION & DESIGN
West Chester, Ohio
designers
DENNY FAGAN, RONDI TSCHOPP
client
DOUBLE TREE HOTEL DAYTON DOWNTOWN

creative firm
BRUCE YELASKA DESIGN
San Francisco, California
art director, designer
BRUCE YELASKA
client
BIKRAM'S YOGA COLLEGE

creative firm
GARDNER DESIGN
Wichita, Kansas
designers
CHRIS PARKS, BILL GARDNER
client
SERGEANT'S

creative firm
HORNALL ANDERSON DESIGN WORKS
Seattle, Washington
art director
JACK ANDERSON
designers
JACK ANDERSON, BELINDA BOWLING, ANDREW SMITH, ED LEE
client
STREAMWORKS

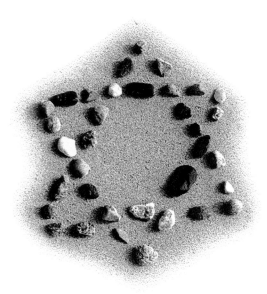

WRIGHT
WILLIAMS
& KELLY

creative firm
GILL FISHMAN ASSOCIATES, INC.
Cambridge, Massachusetts
creative director
GILL FISHMAN
designer
TAMMY TORREY
photographer
THOMAS TORREY
client
ISRAEL'S 50TH BIRTHDAY CELEBRATION

creative firm
THE WECKER GROUP
Monterey, California
designers
ROBERT WECKER, MATT GNIBUS
client
WRIGHT WILLIAMS & KELLY

The Refinery

creative firm
MINALE TATTERSFIELD + PARTNERS
Richmond, England
creative director
DIMITRI KARAVIAS
designer
LEE NEWHAM
client
THE REFINERY
(grooming emporium for men)

creative firm
MULLER + CO.
Kansas City, Missouri
creative director
JOHN MULLER
art director, designer
MARK VOSS
client
KANSAS CITY BLUES & JAZZ FESTIVAL

creative firm
  PEG FAIMON DESIGN
  Oxford, Ohio
designer
  PEG FAIMON
client
  MIAMI UNIVERSITY

creative firm
  KEVIN AKERS—DESIGNER
  San Rafael, California
designer
  KEVIN AKERS
client
  CHRISTIAN TEEN MAGAZINE

creative firm
  SAYLESS GRAPHIC DESIGN
  Des Moines, Iowa
art director, designer, illustrator
  JOHN SAYLES
client
  GLAZED EXPRESSIONS

SOUTHWEB PRINTING

creative firm
  BUTLER KEMP DESIGN
  North Adelaide, Australia
art director
  DEREK BUTLER
designer
  HELLEN KIPRIZLOGLOV
client
  SOUTHWEB PRINTING
  (web printers)

ORGANIC
SYSTEMS

creative firm
  GILL FISHMAN ASSOCIATES, INC.
  Cambridge, Massachusetts
creative director
  GILL FISHMAN
designer
  TAMMY TORREY
client
  ORGANIC SYSTEMS, INC.

creative firm
  GILL FISHMAN ASSOCIATES, INC.
  Cambridge, Massachusetts
creative director
  GILL FISHMAN,
designer
  TAMMY TORREY
client
  OPTEON

A RESTAURANT

creative firm
  THE WECKER GROUP
  Monterey, California
art director
  ROBERT WECKER
designers
  RUTH MINERVA, CRAIG RADER
client
  MICHAELS

creative firm
  GILL FISHMAN ASSOCIATES, INC.
  Cambridge, Massachusetts
creative director
  GILL FISHMAN
designer, illustrator
  ALICIA OZYJOWSKI
client
  LOGAL.NET

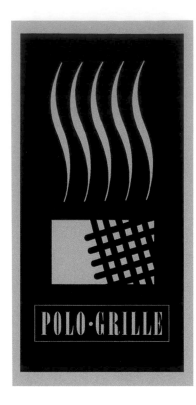

creative firm
   FIVE VISUAL COMMUNICATION & DESIGN
   West Chester, Ohio
designers
   DENNY FAGAN, RONDI TSCHOPP
client
   DOUBLETREE HOTEL DAYTON DOWNTOWN

creative firm
   DESIGN SOLUTIONS
   Napa, California
designer
   DEBORAH MITCHELL
client
   LIGHTHOUSE RELOCATION SYSTEMS

creative firm
   DOTZLER CREATIVE ARTS
   Omaha, Nebraska
client
   CHRIST FOR THE CITY

creative firm
   SAYLES GRAPHIC DESIGN
   Des Moines, Iowa
art director, illustrator
   JOHN SAYLES
client
   MEREDITH CORPORATION "INDUSTRIAL REVOLUTION"

creative firm
  AIRE DESIGN COMPANY
  Tucson, Arizona
creative director
  CATHARINE M. KIM
art director
  SHARI RYKOWSKI
client
  SOLUTIONS

creative firm
  HORNALL ANDERSON DESIGN WORKS
  Seattle, Washington
art director
  JACK ANDERSON
designers
  JACK ANDERSON, KATHY SAITO, ALAN COPELAND
client
  WELLS FARGO (ATRéVA)

personify

creative firm
  HORNALL ANDERSON DESIGN WORKS
  Seattle, Washington
art director
  JACK ANDERSON
designers
  JACK ANDERSON, DEBRA McCLOSKEY, HOLLY CRAVEN
client
  PERSONIFY

OGOS

creative firm
THE WECKER GROUP
Monterey, California
designer
ROBERT WECKER
client
GREAT EXPECTATIONS LIGHTING

GREAT EXPECTATIONS
LIGHTING Co.

creative firm
PRIMO ANGELI, INC.
San Francisco, California
creative director
CARLO PAGODA
project director
RICH SCHEVE
senior designer
KELSON MAU
client

AVON
the company for women

ristorante

creative firm
  O&J DESIGN, INC.
  New York, New York
art director
  ANDRZEJ OLEJNICZAK
designer
  HEISHIN RA
client
  AVON PRODUCTS, INC.

creative firm
  SAYLES GRAPHIC DESIGN
  Des Moines, Iowa
art director, illustrator
  JOHN SAYLES
client
  BASIL PROSPERI

creative firm
  BIG CAT MARKETING COMM
  Colorado Springs, Colorado
designer
  ANNA BARNES
client
  SKYLANDS MUSIC & ARTS ALLIANCE

creative firm
  TOR PETTERSEN & PARTNERS
  London, England
designer
  JEFF DAVIS
client
  MAP COMMUNICATIONS

131

creative firm
  LOVE PACKAGING GROUP
  Wichita, Kansas
designers
  BRIAN MILLER, CHRIS WEST
client
  THE FANTASTIC WORL OF GOURMET CHOCOLATE
  (chocolate manufacturer)

creative firm
  COMPASS DESIGN
  Minneapolis, Minnesota
designers
  MITCHELL LINDGREN, TOM ARTHUR, RICH McGOWEN
client
  GREAT WATERS BREWING CO.

creative firm
  TANGRAM STRATEGIC DESIGN
  Novara, Italy
creative director
  ENRICO SEMPI
art director, designer
  ANTONELLA TREVISAN
illustrator
  GUIDO ROSA
client
  CAMERA DI COMMERCIO DI VICENEA

creative firm
  WAGES DESIGN
  Atlanta, Georgia
designer
  DOMINGA LEE
client
  AIGA (BIG NIGHT)

creative firm
  HORNALL ANDERSON DESIGN WORKS
  Seattle, Washington
art directors
  JACK ANDERSON, LARRY ANDERSON
designers
  JACK ANDERSON, LARRY ANDERSON, MARY HERMES,
  MIKE CALKINS, MICHAEL BRUGMAN
client
  U.S. CIGAR

creative firm
  ADKINS/BALCHUNAS
  Providence, Rhode Island
creative director
  JERRY BALCHUNAS
designers
  SUSAN DE ANGELIS, JERRY BALCHUNAS
client
  SBARRO

creative firm
  DESIGN GUYS
  Minneapolis, Minnesota
art director
  STEVEN SIKORA
designers
  AMY KIRKPATRICK, ANNE PETERSON
letterer
  TODD AP JONES
client
  TARGET STORES

THE SAINT JOHN'S BIBLE

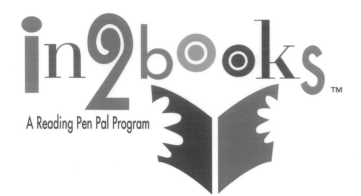

A Reading Pen Pal Program

creative firm
GREENFIELD/BELSER LTD.
Washington, D.C.
art director
BURKEY BELSER
designer
JANET MORALES
client
IN2BOOKS

OCEANPLACE

creative firm
SABINGRAFIK, INC.
Carlsbad, California
art director
MARILEE BANKERT
designer, illustrator
TRACY SABIN
client
OLIVER McMILLIN

MONTEREY SPORTS CENTER

creative firm
THE WECKER GROUP
Monterey, California
designer
ROBERT WECKER
client
MONTEREY SPORTS CENTER

creative firm
McELVENEY + PALOZZI
DESIGN GROUP, INC.
Rochester, New York
creative director
WILLIAM McELVENEY
art director
LISA PARENTI
client
ABBOTTS FROZEN CUSTARD

creative firm
TELMET DESIGN ASSOCIATES
Toronto, Canada
art director
TIIT TELMET
designers
JOSEPH GAULT, MARKO BARAC
illustrator
JOSEPH GAULT
client
EVERYWARE DEVELOPMENT CORP.

™

creative firm
THE WECKER GROUP
Monterey, California
designer
ROBERT WECKER
client
DELTA POINT, INC.

creative firm
GILL FISHMAN ASSOCIATES, INC.
Cambridge, Massachusetts
creative director
GILL FISHMAN
designer
MICHAEL PERSONS
client
ORIDION MEDICAL

creative firm
DEVER DESIGNS
Laurel, Maryland
art director, designer
JEFFREY L. DEVER
client
DIAMANTI, INC.

135

creative firm
GARDNER DESIGN
Wichita, Kansas
designer
BILL GARDNER
client
BUZZCUTS MAXIMUM LAWNCARE

creative firm
SIBLEY PETEET DESIGN
Dallas, Texas
designer
DONNA ALDRIDGE
client
CATHEDRAL OF HOPE

< P O P U L I >

creative firm
SQUIRES & COMPANY
Dallas, Texas
designers
BRANDON MURPHY, AMY CHANG
client
POPULI

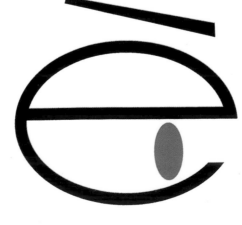

creative firm
KEVIN AKERS—DESIGNER
San Rafael, California
designer
KEVIN AKERS
client
BILL EMBERLEY
(video producer)

MUSIC PUBLISHING

going strong at No. 1

THE FULL MONTY

THE ONLY THING TO BE...

1,000,000+
of the world's most
popular
songs

On-line
customers
wax
lyrical

creative firm
TOR PETTERSEN & PARTNERS
London, England
designers
JEFF DAVIS, JIM ALLSOPP
client
THE EMI GROUP

---

creative firm
DEVER DESIGNS
Laurel, Maryland
art director, designer
JEFFREY L. DEVER
photographer
TIM BARNWELL
client
THE ROSEN GROUP/AMERICANSTYLE

NATURAL ReSOURCES

BY SUE WASSERMAN

Mornings in Penland, N.C., are filled with moments of quiet lingering, watching the sunlight play softly against the subtle bluegray shadows of the vast Blue Ridge mountain range; or waving casual greetings to the conductor as the first train of the day chugs slowly past the shore of the gurgling Toe River. The richness of this rural community's natural resources first attracted computer consultant Mignon Durham, who loved exploring the wealth of hiking trails and fishing holes, finding it the perfect weekend escape from never-ending phone calls and faxes. Before long, however, the Winston-Salem native discovered that the region's finest natural resources aren't the rivers and mountains but the local artists who have forged a small, tightly knit community around the prestigious Penland School of Crafts.

MIGNON DURHAM finds countless treasures right in her own backyard

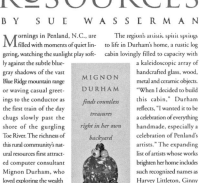

The region's artistic spirit springs to life in Durham's home, a rustic log cabin lovingly filled to capacity with a kaleidoscopic array of handcrafted glass, wood, metal and ceramic objects. "When I decided to build this cabin," Durham reflects, "I wanted it to be a celebration of everything handmade, especially a celebration of Penland's artists." The expanding list of artists whose works brighten her home includes such recognized names as Harvey Littleton, Ginny Ruffner, Jon Kuhn, Rob Levin, Marvin Jensen and Ed and Philip Moulthrop.

The cabin itself is a marvel, the result of Durham's impassioned efforts to restore and join three pre-Civil War cabins while incorporating the finest elements of contemporary craft. "My challenge and joy was in commissioning artists to do work they had never done before," she says.

PHOTOGRAPHY BY TIM BARNWELL

Sue Wasserman is a freelance writer specializing in the arts and design. She is based in Asheville, Ga.

137

creative firm
  THE OBSERVER
  London, England
art director
  WAYNE FORD
photographer
  FRANCESCA SORRENTI
fashion editor
  JO ADAMS
editor
  SHERYL GARRATT
client
  THE OBSERVER LIFE MAGAZINE

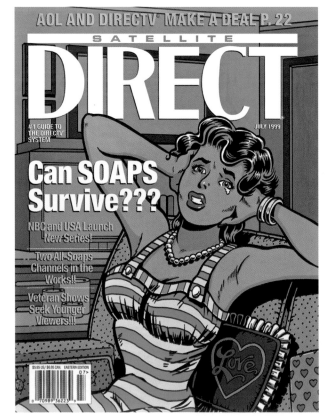

creative firm
  COMMTEK COMMUNICATIONS CORPORATION
  Fairfax, Virginia
art director
  LIZ RICHARDS
illustrator
  GEORGE TOOMER
client
  SATELLITE DIRECT

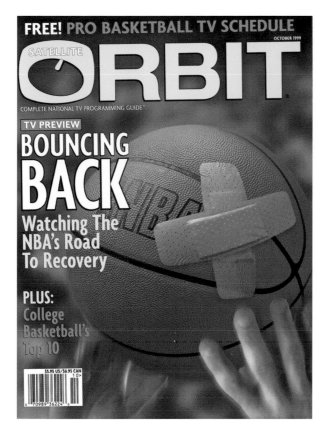

FREE! PRO BASKETBALL TV SCHEDULE

OCTOBER 1999

SATELLITE
ORBIT.

COMPLETE NATIONAL TV PROGRAMMING GUIDE

TV PREVIEW
**BOUNCING
BACK**
Watching The
NBA's Road
To Recovery

PLUS:
College
Basketball's
Top 10

$5.95 US/$6.95 CAN

creative firm
   COMMTEK COMMUNICATIONS CORP.
   Fairfax, Virginia
design director
   POLLY JOHNSON
illustrator
   STUART SIMONS
client
   SATELLITE ORBIT

creative firm
   THE OBSERVER
   London, England
art director
   WAYNE FORD
photographer
   HEATHER FAVELL
fashion editor
   JO ADAMS
editor
   SHERYL GARRATT
client
   THE OBSERVER LIFE MAGAZINE

Fashion editor **Jo Adams** Photographs **Heather Favell**

Sequin dress, £39.99,
from Rays Catalogue
(inquiries 00800 601689).
Cream jacket, De La Guarda
costume wardrobe.
Shoes, £69.95, by Rockport,
from Selfridges, 400 Oxford
Street, London W1 (stockist
inquiries 01524 580480).

Swinging in
the rain

High-flying performance group De La Guarda, whose act is a mix of trapeze, dancing,
drumming and dramatics, has been enthralling audiences since it opened this summer
at the Roundhouse, in London's Camden. The costumes – everyday clothes that make the
performers look as if they have been pulled out of the audience – are customised to allow
total freedom of movement. To spruce up the act, we raided the stores in search of
relaxed suits for men, mismatched skirts and tops, a bit of sparkle, and some good old,
practical Rockport shoes – an eclectic blend of the sensible and the frivolous...

139

W.Y.S.I.W.Y.G.

|| || ||| || ||| || |||| || |||
(what you see is what you get)

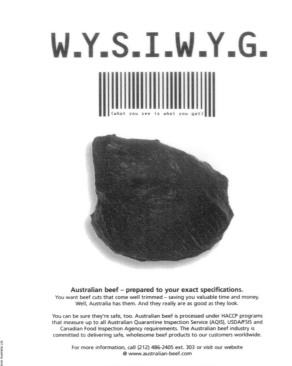

Australian beef – prepared to your exact specifications.
You want beef cuts that come well trimmed – saving you valuable time and money.
Well, Australia has them. And they really are as good as they look.

You can be sure they're safe, too. Australian beef is processed under HACCP programs
that measure up to all Australian Quarantine Inspection Service (AQIS), USDA/FSIS and
Canadian Food Inspection Agency requirements. The Australian beef industry is
committed to delivering safe, wholesome beef products to our customers worldwide.

For more information, call (212) 486-2405 ext. 303 or visit our website
@ www.australian-beef.com

australian beef The highest standards. Worldwide.

creative firm
RISE AGENCY, INC.
New York, New York
art director, creative director
CAROLINA RODRIGUEZ
designer
ROBERT ZWASCHKA
copywriter
CATHERINE PENFOLD
client
AUSTRALIAN BEEF

creative firm
BOLDRINI & FICCARDI
Mendoza, Argentina
art director
LEONARDO FICCARDI
designer
VICTOR BOLDRINI
client
REVISTA

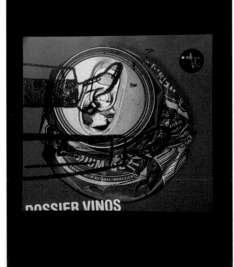

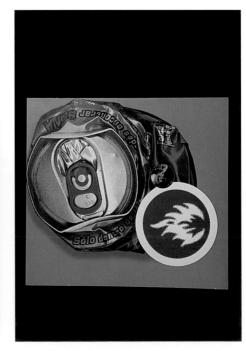

Pastor Bill Oudemolen of the Foothills Bible Church, in Littleton, gave the sermon at the funeral of 16-year-old John Tomlin. 'What happened at Columbine High School was the work of Satan,' he said

PRAY FOR HEALING

A sign in Littleton in response to the tragedy

My son Daniel died at Columbine. He'd expect me to be here today.

SHAME

Tom Mauser, whose son Daniel was shot dead at Columbine High, addresses an 8,000-strong crowd on the steps of the Denver State Capitol Building. The protest condemned the timing of the National Rifle Association's annual meeting in Denver only a week and a half after the killings

Ten days after the shooting, the victims' cars remain in the school car park, piled high with wilting flowers. The vehicles became shrines to their young owners

A day after the shooting, a television journalist in the grounds of Columbine High reports to camera. In the background, shocked students wander across the school playing fields

Jason Horn, 25, (above, right) buys a handgun at the Firing Line gun store in Aurora, Colorado, one week after the massacre. He chose a Kimber .45 calibre compact, and in the while-you-wait background check, he explained it was for 'home defence'. He left the store with the gun. His friend Kirk Smith, 19, accompanied him. Both are from Littleton

Charlton Heston, president of the National Rifle Association, addresses a crowd of 2,000 pro-gun members at a meeting in Denver on 1 May. Responding to calls for tighter gun control after the tragedy at Columbine High School, he said: 'Those who would give up their freedom to purchase a little security... deserve neither freedom nor security'

Posters advertising military-designed assault weapons in the window of Paladin Arms. For local gun stores, it's business as usual

creative firm
THE OBSERVER
London, England
art director
WAYNE FORD
photographer
ZED NELSON
picture editor
JENNIE RICKETTS
editor
SHERYL GARRATT
client
THE OBSERVER LIFE MAGAZINE

creative firm
COMMITER COMMUNICATIONS CORP
Fairfax, Virginia
art director
LIZ RICHARDS
client
SATELLITE DIRECT

ALFRED HITCHCOCK'S IMPOSING FIGURE IS AS FAMILIAR TO MOVIEGOERS AS IMAGES FROM *PSYCHO* (TOP) AND *VERTIGO* (RIGHT).

THE MASTER OF SUSPENSE WAS BORN 100 YEARS AGO THIS MONTH, BUT THE SHADOW HE HAS CAST OVER AMERICAN FILMS WILL LAST MUCH LONGER.

The Hitchcock Legacy
BY PAT DOWELL

MOVIE THRILLERS were being made before Alfred Hitchcock first sat in the director's chair in 1925, but nearly 75 years later his name still defines the ultimate in big-screen excitement. It comes in many shadings—the sheer terror of *Psycho* as meek Anthony Perkins unravels; the sleek, sophisticated thrill of Cary Grant landing just one graceful step ahead of pursuers across half a continent in *North by Northwest*; the gathering doom of James Stewart's dark obsession with a woman he must bring back to life in *Vertigo*.

Hitchcock's thrillers were so unforgettable that "Hitchcockian" is just about the nicest word any critic can apply to a movie that keeps you guessing, not about whodunit but rather how and why, and will they get caught? That's the difference between a mystery, which Hitchcock disdained, and suspense, which he understood like no other filmmaker before or since.

Hitchcock was born on August 13, 1899, and to mark his centennial Encore (ch. 526) has created an original documentary, *Dial H for Hitchcock: The Genius Behind the Showman*, which airs at 8 p.m. ET on his birthday. It anchors a 24-hour festival of some of Hitchcock's greatest hits, including *Shadow of a Doubt*, *The Trouble With Harry*, *Vertigo* and *Psycho*. (Check the daily listings for show times.) →

143

While a student at the University of Alabama in 1952, I interned with a national public accounting firm in Atlanta. On my way to work I sometimes passed what was probably the first "adult" store I had ever seen. I remember a large sign out front with quotes from opinions of U.S. Supreme Court associate justice Hugo L. Black. In recent years my office has been in the Hugo L. Black U.S. Courthouse in Birmingham, Alabama. The foyer walls have bronze plaques, also containing quotes from Justice Black.

I have often wondered what made Justice Black tick. I realize that he is an icon to many in law, the media, and academia,* but my study of his career and his judicial reasoning raises questions about the First Amendment jurisprudence that he is significantly credited with establishing. "Expedience" is a continuous theme in his career.

The Pre-Court Years

After he became a lawyer in Birmingham, Alabama, Black joined the Ku Klux Klan. In the early 1920s he represented a preacher charged with murdering a Catholic priest who had married the defendant's daughter to a Puerto Rican. Black appealed to both the religious and racial prejudices of the jury (he gave the Klan members on the jury the Klan sign), which acquitted the defendant. He had similar success in less notorious but similar cases.

In 1924, when U.S. senator Oscar W. Underwood from Alabama denounced the Ku Klux Klan, he knew that he could not retain his seat in 1926. John F. Kennedy's book *Profiles in Courage* recognizes Underwood's courage. Kennedy's book quotes another writer: "Had Senator Underwood played the game in Alabama in accord with the sound political rule of seeming to say something without doing so, there would have been no real opposition to his remaining in the Senate for the balance of his life." Black did not denounce the Klan, but joined it instead and was given a lifetime membership. He gave a letter of resignation to be disclosed when convenient. The oath he took included a promise to "preserve by any and all justifiable means and methods . . . white supremacy" (Roger K. Newman, *Hugo Black, A Biography*, pp. 91, 92). He made open appeals to its members and received its support when he ran for and was elected to the U.S. Senate, taking Underwood's position in 1926. During the campaign he addressed nearly all the 148 Klan Klaverns in Alabama (*Ibid.*, p. 104). His total votes received closely paralleled the total Alabama Klan membership (*Ibid.*, p. 115). He acknowledged that he owed his victory to the Klan. To a Klan gathering he stated: "I desire to impress upon you as representatives of

Robert B. Propst is a senior U.S. district judge in Alabama.

A U.S. District Judge From Alabama Takes On Justice Hugo Black, Liberty Magazine, and Judicial Activism

KU·KLUX ICON

By Robert B. Propst

ILLUSTRATION BY MARC BURCKHARDT

creative firm
DEVER DESIGNS
Laurel, Maryland
art director, designer
JEFFREY L. DEVER
illustrator
MARC BURCKHARDT
client
LIBERTY MAGAZINE

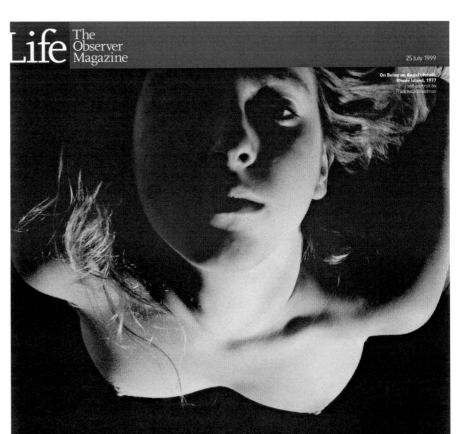

Life The Observer Magazine

25 July 1999

On Being an Angel (detail), Rhode Island, 1977
self-portrait by
Francesca Woodman

the woman who disappeared

the extraordinary art of Francesca Woodman

creative firm
THE OBSERVER
London, England
art director
WAYNE FORD
photographer
FRANCESCA WOODMAN
picture editor
JENNIE RICKETTS
editor
SHERYL GARRATT
client
THE OBSERVER LIFE MAGAZINE

creative firm
RISE AGENCY, INC.
New York, New York
creative director
CAROLINA RODRIGUEZ
art director, copywriter
CATHERINE PENFOLD
client
SWATCH U.S.

creative firm
THE OBSERVER
London, England
art director
WAYNE FORD
photographer
BEN INGHAM
fashion editor
JO ADAMS
editor
SHERYL GARRATT
client
THE OBSERVER LIFE MAGAZINE

creative firm
   COMMTEK COMMUNICATIONS CORP.
   Fairfax, Virginia
design director
   POLLY JOHNSON
client
   SATELLITE ORBIT

Thirty-six years after
making space history,
John Glenn still has
the right stuff |
By Art Durbano

RETURN OF THE
JEDI

18 • OCTOBER 1998 SATELLITE ORBIT

March/April 1999 $5.00 U.S./$6.00 Canada

FAMILY THERAPY
NETWORKER
Psychotherapy & Modern Life

The
Chemistry of
Sex
The Alchemy
of Love

AN EARLY WARNING SYSTEM FOR YOUR PRACTICE

creative firm
   DEVER DESIGNS
   Laurel, Maryland
art director, designer
   JEFFREY L. DEVER
client
   FAMILY THERAPY NETWORK

creative firm
   BIG CAT MARKETING COMMUNICATIONS
   Colorado Springs, Colorado
designer
   MATT DUNCAN
client
   THE CHRISTIAN MEDICAL + DENTAL SOCIETY

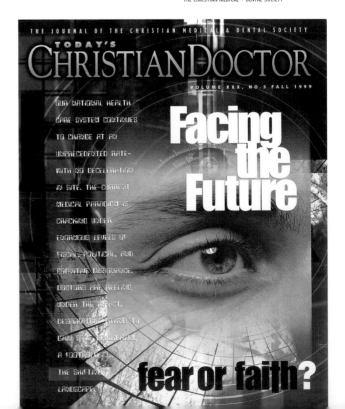

THE JOURNAL OF THE CHRISTIAN MEDICAL & DENTAL SOCIETY

TODAY'S
CHRISTIANDOCTOR

VOLUME XXX, NO.3 FALL 1999

OUR NATIONAL HEALTH
CARE SYSTEM CONTINUES
TO CHANGE AT AN
UNPRECEDENTED RATE—
WITH NO DECELERATION
IN SITE. THE CURRENT
MEDICAL PARADIGM IS
CRACKING UNDER
ENORMOUS LEVELS OF
FISCAL, POLITICAL, AND
COGNITIVE DISSONANCE.
DOCTORS ARE REELING
UNDER THE IMPACT,
DESPERATELY TRYING TO
GAIN SOME SEMBLANCE,
A FOOTHOLD IN
THE SHIFTING
LANDSCAPE.

Facing
the
Future

fear or faith?

creative firm
UKULELE DESIGN CONSULTANTS PTE LTD
Singapore
design director
KIM CHUN-WEI
designer
LYNN LIM
client
SINGAPORE TELEVISION TWELVE PTE LTD

making the difference with
on-target television

creative firm
DEVER DESIGNS
Laurel, Maryland
art director
JEFFREY L. DEVER
designer
AMY WHITE SUCHERMAN
illustrator
DAVID KLEIN
client
LIBERTY MAGAZINE

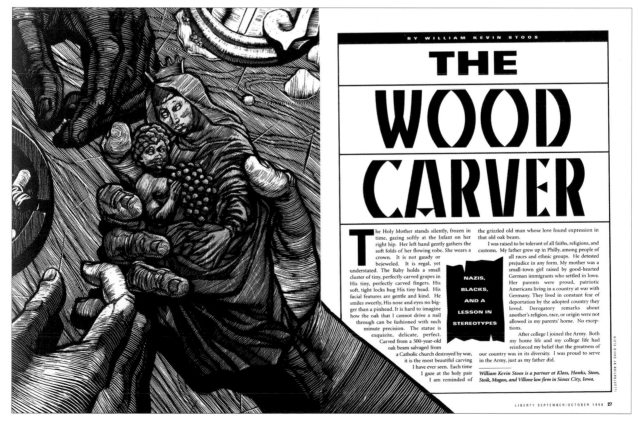

BY WILLIAM KEVIN STOOS

THE WOOD CARVER

The Holy Mother stands silently, frozen in time, gazing softly at the Infant on her right hip. Her left hand gently gathers the soft folds of her flowing robe. She wears a crown. It is not gaudy or bejeweled. It is regal, yet understated. The Baby holds a small cluster of tiny, perfectly carved grapes in His tiny, perfectly carved fingers. His soft, tight locks hug His tiny head. His facial features are gentle and kind. He smiles sweetly, His nose and eyes no bigger than a pinhead. It is hard to imagine how the oak that I cannot drive a nail through can be fashioned with such minute precision. The statue is exquisite, delicate, perfect. Carved from a 500-year-old oak beam salvaged from a Catholic church destroyed by war, it is the most beautiful carving I have ever seen. Each time I gaze at the holy pair I am reminded of

the grizzled old man whose love found expression in that old oak beam.

I was raised to be tolerant of all faiths, religions, and customs. My father grew up in Philly, among people of all races and ethnic groups. He detested prejudice in any form. My mother was a small-town girl raised by good-hearted German immigrants who settled in Iowa. Her parents were proud, patriotic Americans living in a country at war with Germany. They lived in constant fear of deportation by the adopted country they loved. Derogatory remarks about another's religion, race, or origin were not allowed in my parents' home. No exceptions.

After college I joined the Army. Both my home life and my college life had reinforced my belief that the greatness of our country was in its diversity. I was proud to serve in the Army, just as my father did.

NAZIS, BLACKS, AND A LESSON IN STEREOTYPES

William Kevin Stoos is a partner at Klass, Hanks, Stoos, Stoik, Mugan, and Villone law firm in Sioux City, Iowa.

creative firm
DEVER DESIGNS
Laurel, Maryland
art director, designer
JEFFREY L. DEVER
illustrator
JOEL SPECTOR
client
LIBERTY MAGAZINE

LIBERTY

Lessons From the Field of
Blackbirds
By
CÉLESTE PERRINO WALKER

Death came with a frigid dawn and the thump of mortar fire over the sleepy town of Prekez, Serbia. Marie Kodra, 38, fled with her five children as Serbs fired into the houses. Avoiding the streets that were crawling with police, Mrs. Kodra led the children into the hills. Seeing a police patrol and hoping for assistance, she ran up to them waving a white scarf. ◆ "I shouted, 'I am a woman with children!'" she said. "I heard the officer yell: 'Shoot! Kill them!' I pushed my children to the ground and an explosion went off near where we were lying." The family moved through the night until they reached an empty basement, where they hid until dawn. Mrs. Kodra said many families in houses they passed had been too frightened to let them in, fearing police retaliation. "It was not until I got out of the area where there was fighting that I learned that my husband was dead," she said, soon afterward collapsing into the arms of friends.' ◆ And so the stories go, chasing each other with the rapidity of the machine-gun fire that punctuates the tragic recountings. In the

The tragedy of Kosovo underscores the imperative of respect for other faiths and peoples.

Céleste perrino Walker, a much-published freelance journalist and book author, writes from Rutland, Vermont.

---

creative firm
DEVER DESIGNS
Laurel, Maryland
art director, designer
JEFFREY L. DEVER
client
THE ROSEN GROUP/AMERICANSTYLE

PHYSICISTS MAY NOT BE ABLE TO IDENTIFY THE HEART OF the Big Bang, but it doesn't take much to spot what sits at the core of one of the biggest explosions in the world of craft art: it's the pasta machine. Every dawn, artists wait, handles at the ready and rollers poised, for the day's

MOVERS&
by
LEE LAWRENCE
Shapers

Polymer clay artists are pushing beyond the ordinary into realms where imagination leads them.

selection of colors. Sporting brand names like Fimo, Primo and Sculpey, the little packets look like plastic but feel like clay.

"It's mud, but it's not," says Nan Roche, who first documented the polymer clay phenomenon in her 1991 book *The New Clay.* "On some deep level, polymer clay calls up that primeval response to mud. When you squish it, you regress to when you were 5 and you float, you dream ..."

There's no limit to what some people will try. When polymer clay hit the U.S. market in the early 1980s, caning became all the rage, with amateurs and artists turning out bright millefiori patterns. Today, artists twist, weave and laminate the clay. They paint it, carve it, sew it and print on it. And they are just as likely to capture the nuanced hues of amber or jade as they are to create colors so vibrant they pop into 3-D.

"Just when you think you've seen it all," says JoAnne Cooper, co-owner of

Lee Lawrence, a regular contributor to AMERICANSTYLE, *writes frequently on the arts for newspapers and magazines. She lives in Washington, D.C.*

With translucent clays, Kathleen Dustin's purse, left, achieves depth by overposing and adding layers of transparency to boldly drawn faces. In contrast, the colors in Rebecca Zimmerman's teapot, far left, are so bright they practically pop.

Color Fingo's bracelet combines fine silver with roller-printed polymer clay. She discovered the medium when a friend used her some buttons of the new material.

Borrowing a glassblowing technique, Pier Voulkos uses a puff of air to inflate "26 Purple Balloons," right. In baking, the hot air acts as the armature to hold the form in place.

96 • AMERICANSTYLE   SUMMER 1999

---

creative firm
TOR PETTERSEN & PARTNERS
London, England
designers
JEFF DAVIS, JIM ALLSOP
client
THE EMI GROUP

creative firm
 SAYLES GRAPHIC DESIGN
 Des Moines, Iowa
art director, illustrator
 JOHN SAYLES
client
 ALPHABET SOUP TOY STORE

creative firm
 BRUNAZZI & ASSOCIATI/IMAGE + COMMUNICATION
 Turin, Italy
art director
 ANDREA BRUNAZZI
designer
 SILVIA ZANETTI
client
 MONETTI

creative firm
 THE RIORDON DESIGN GROUP, INC.
 Oakville, Ontario, Canada
creative director
 DAN WHEATON
planet productions
 GARY CAPON
client
 IN-SPIRATION

creative firm
SPAGNOLA & ASSOCIATES
New York, New York
art director
TONY SPAGNOLA
designer
BOB CALLAHAN
architects
DAVIS BRODY BOND LLP
client
NEW YORK PUBLIC LIBRARY

creative firm
HORNALL ANDERSON DESIGN WORKS
Seattle, Washington
art director
CLIFF CHUNG
designers
CLIFF CHUNG, ALAN FLORSHEIM
client
NEXTRX CORPORATION

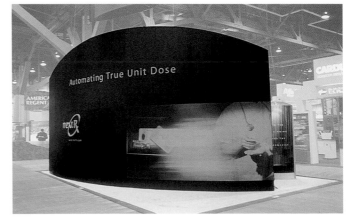

creative firm
HORNALL ANDERSON DESIGN WORKS
Seattle, Washington
art directors
JACK ANDERSON, CLIFF CHUNG
designers
CLIFF CHUNG, ALAN FLORSHEIM,
DAVID BATES, MIKE CALKINS
client
NOVELL, INC.

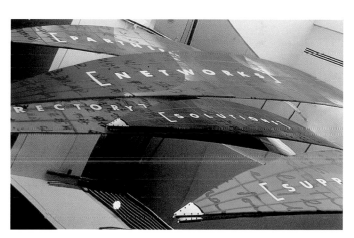

creative firm
SABINGRAFIK, INC.
Carlsbad, California
art director
LAURA BECKER
illustrator
TRACY SABIN
mosaicist
MIOTTE MOSAICS
marketing director
CHERI WALKER
client
UNIVERSITY TOWNE CENTRE

creative firm
MINALE TATTERSFIELD + PARTNERS
Richmond, Surrey, United Kingdom
creative director
BRIAN TATTERSFIELD
designer
PAUL ASTBURY
client
LONDON TRANSPORT

creative firm
TEAMWORK DESIGN LTD.
Hong Kong
design director
GARY TAM
senior designer
JOEL ONG
designers
ALEX CHAN, IVY WONG
client
PEAK TRAMWAYS CO. LTD.

creative firm
BLUMLEIN ASSOCIATES, INC.
Greenvale, New York
exhibit designers
WILLIAM ARBIZU, CHRIS LEONARDI
designer
MICHAEL KASE
client
SONY ELECTRONICS

creative firm
LORENC + YOO DESIGN
Roswell, Georgia
design director
JAN LORENC
project manager
DAVID PARK
designer
STEVE McCALL
client
FIRST UNION MANAGEMENT JOURNEY COMMUNICATIONS

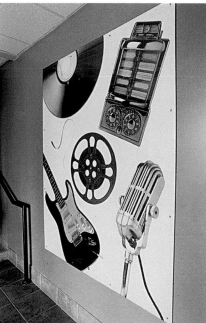

creative firm
  MICHAEL COURTNEY DESIGN
    Seattle, Washington
art director, designer
  MICHAEL COURTNEY
photographer
  J.F. HOUSEL
client
  ROSCHE SERVICES

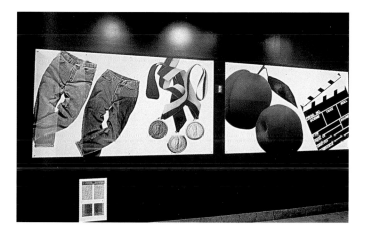

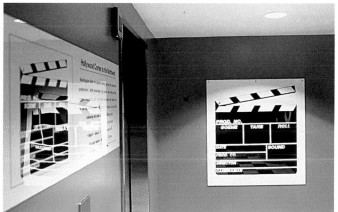

creative firm
  SQUARE ONE DESIGN
    Grand Rapids, Michigan
art directors
  MIKE GORMAN, LIN VERMEULEN
designer
  GRANT CARMICHAEL
fabrication
  BOB WARDLOW
client
  HERMAN MILLER, INC.

creative firm
  DESIGN GUYS
  Minneapolis, Minnesota
art director
  STEVEN SIKORA
designers
  DAWN SELG, AMY KIRKPATRICK
client
  TARGET STORES

creative firm
  DESIGN GUYS
  Minneapolis, Minnesota
art director
  STEVEN SIKORA
creative director
  LYNETTE ERICKSON-SIKORA
designer
  GARY PATCH
client
  TARGET STORES

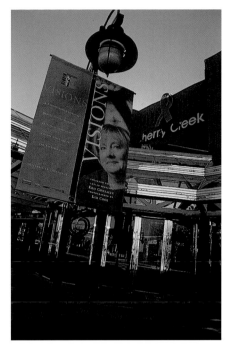

creative firm
ELLEN BRUSS DESIGN
Denver, Colorado
designers
ELLEN BRUSS,
CHARLES CARPENTER,
JASON C. OTERO
client
CHERRY CREEK SHOPPING CENTER
(RACE FOR THE CURE)

creative firm
SABINGRAFIK, INC.
Carlsbad, California
art directors
LAURA BECKER
marketing director
CHERI WALKER
illustrator
TRACY SABIN
client
UNIVERSITY TOWNE CENTRE

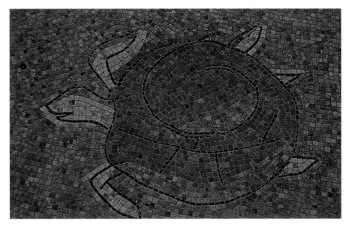

153

DON • IVAN • PUNCHATZ
ILLUSTRATION
A • TEXAS • TRADITION

DON IVAN PUNCHATZ RETROSPECTIVE EXHIBITION • FEBRUARY 15 THROUGH MARCH 10 • TCU MOUDY EXHIBITION HALL

creative firm
  WET PAPER BAG GRAPHIC DESIGN
   Fort Worth, Texas
art director, designer, copywriter
   LEWIS GLASER
illustrator
   DON IVAN PUNCHATZ
client
   TCU ART DEPARTMENT

creative firm
   CHAVDA GRAPIX
   Oviedo, Florida
designer
   JAGDISH J. CHAVDA
client
   UNIVERSITY OF CENTRAL FLORIDA PRESIDENT'S OFFICE

creative firm
  SELFRIDGE DESIGN, LTD.
  Plainfield, Illinois
art director
  SAM TAKAHASHI
illustrator
  M.C. SELFRIDGE
client
  NORTHEASTERN UNIVERSITY, BOSTON

creative firm
  CHAVDA GRAPIX
  Oviedo, Florida
designer
  JAGDISH J. CHAVDA
client
  UNIVERSITY OF CENTRAL FLORIDA PRESIDENT'S OFFICE

NEOS

Envision...

SUNGARD

creative firm
  GEORGOPULOS
  West Chester, Pennsylvania
designer
  JONATHAN GEORGOPULOS
client
  NEOS/SUNGARD PRODUCT

creative firm
  SABINGRAFIK, INC.
  Carlsbad, California
art director
  BLAIZE MEKINNA
illustrator
  TRACY SABIN
client
  SCRIPPS INSTITUTE OF OCEANOGRAPHY

creative firm
  SABINGRAFIK, INC.
  Carlsbad, California
art director
  JOHN BALL
illustrator
  TRACY SABIN
client
  INTEL

creative firm
  SELFRIDGE DESIGN, LTD.
  Plainfield , Illinois
illustrator
  M.C. SELFRIDGE
client
  SELFRIDGE DESIGN, LTD.

creative firm
  SABINGRAFIK, INC.
  Carlsbad, California
art director
  CHARLIE CARR
illustrator
  TRACY SABIN
client
  SANTANA MANAGEMENT

creative firm
  SABINGRAFIK, INC.
  Carlsbad, California
art directors
  TOM BURKE, TOM MORRISON
illustrator
  TRACY SABIN
client
  MORRISON AND BURKE

creative firm
  SABINGRAFIK, INC.
  Carlsbad, California
art directors
  TOM BURKE, TOM MORRISON
illustrator
  TRACY SABIN
client
  MORRISON AND BURKE

creative firm
  MIRES DESIGN
  Carlsbad, California
art director
  JOHN BALL
illustrator
  TRACY SABIN
client
  HARCOURT AND COMPANY

creative firm
  MIRES DESIGN
  Carlsbad, California
art director
  JOHN BALL
illustrator
  TRACY SABIN
client
  HARCOURT AND COMPANY

159

creative firm
  McELVENEY + PALOZZI DESIGN GROUP, INC.
  Rochester, New York
art director
  MATT GARRITY
creative director
  STEPHEN PALOZZI
illustrator
  MIKE JOHNSON
client
  GENESEE BREWING CO.

creative firm
  McELVENEY + PALOZZI DESIGN GROUP, INC.
  Rochester, New York
art director
  MATT GARRITY
creative director
  STEPHEN PALOZZI
illustrator
  NICK WOYCIESJES
client
  GENESEE BREWING CO.

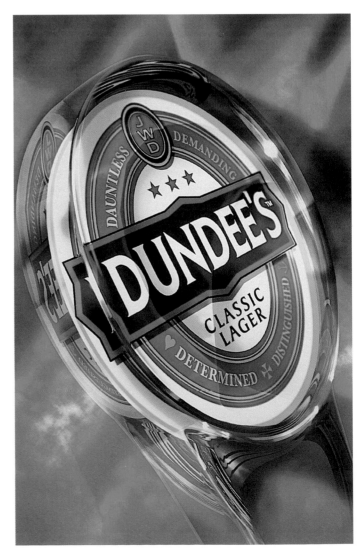

creative firm
  McELVENEY + PALOZZI DESIGN GROUP, INC.
  Rochester, New York
art director
  MATT GARRITY
creative director
  STEPHEN PALOZZI
illustrators
  MIKE JOHNSON, NICK WOYCIESJES
client
  GENESEE BREWING CO.

creative firm
  CYD DESIGN
  Milwaukee, Wisconsin
designer
  CORY DEWALT
illustrator
  DAVID WELKY
client
  STARK IMAGES

creative firm
BIG CAT MARKETING COMMUNICATIONS
Colorado Springs, Colorado
illustrator
PATER SPEACH
client
STERLING RESOURCES, INC.

creative firm
RAY BESSERDIN, PAPER SCULPTURE ARTIST
Mentone, Australia
art director
HENRY BIRMAN
designer
RAY BESSERDIN
client
BOOMERANG PAPER

creative firm
SELFRIDGE DESIGN, LTD.
Plainfield, Illinois
illustrator
M.C. SELFRIDGE
client
SELFRIDGE DESIGN, LTD.

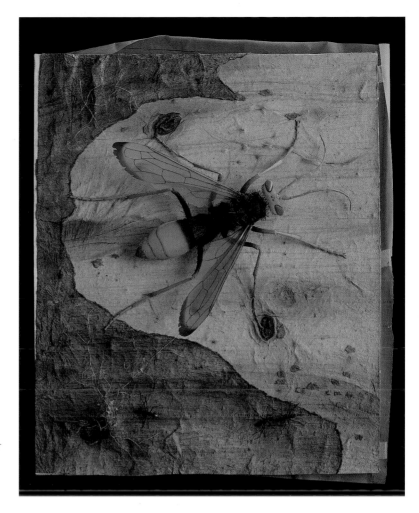

creative firm
  RAY BESSERDIN, PAPER SCULPTURE ARTIST
    Mentone, Australia
art director, designer
  RAY BESSERDIN
client
  RAY BESSERDIN

creative firm
  RAY BESSERDIN, PAPER SCULPTURE ARTIST
    Mentone, Australia
art director
  REBECCA LLOYD
designer
  RAY BESSERDIN
client
  BRW MEDIA/CPA MAGAZINE

creative firm
 ESTUDIO RAY
  Phoenix, Arizona
art directors
 CHRISTINE & JOE RAY
designers
 CHRISTINE RAY, JOE RAY, LESLIE LINK
illustrator
 JOE RAY
typographer
 LESLIE LINK
client
 AIGA ARIZONA

creative firm
 THE RIORDON DESIGN GROUP, INC.
  Oakville, Canada
illustrators
 DAN WHEATON, DAVID BATHURST
client
 FCB DIRECT/IBM B.A.N.D.

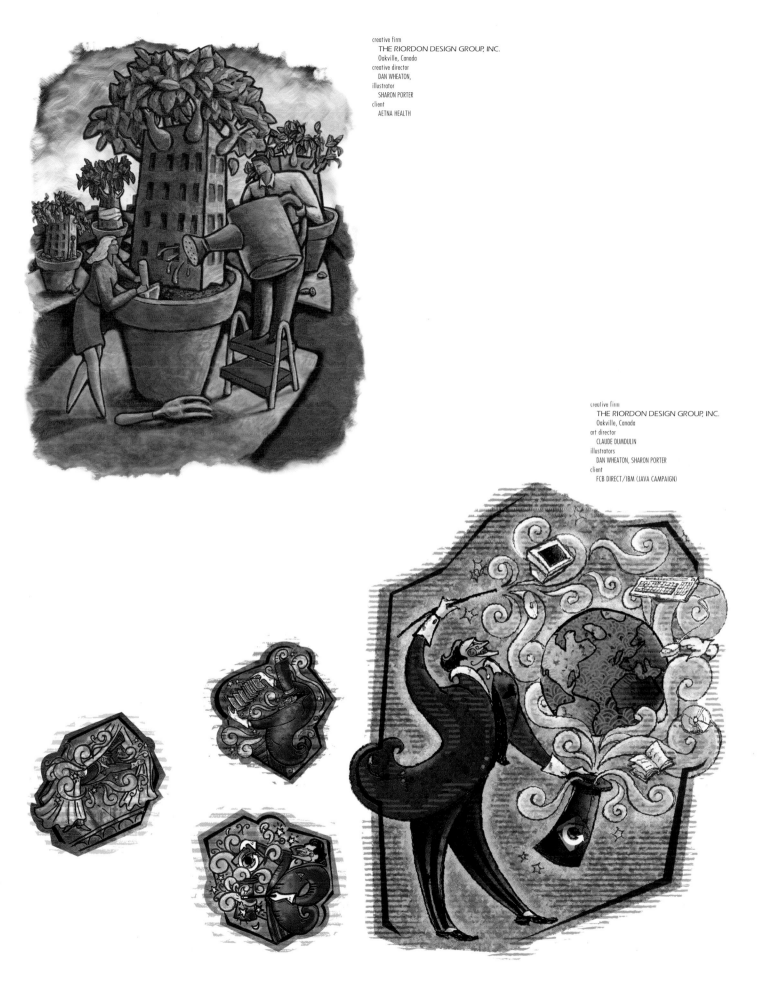

creative firm
 THE RIORDON DESIGN GROUP, INC.
 Oakville, Canada
creative director
 DAN WHEATON,
illustrator
 SHARON PORTER
client
 AETNA HEALTH

creative firm
 THE RIORDON DESIGN GROUP, INC.
 Oakville, Canada
art director
 CLAUDE DUMDULIN
illustrators
 DAN WHEATON, SHARON PORTER
client
 FCB DIRECT/IBM (JAVA CAMPAIGN)

creative firm
  SABINGRAFIK, INC.
  Carlsbad, California
art director
  SCOTT MIRES
illustrator
  TRACY SABIN
client
  INTEL

creative firm
  SABINGRAFIK, INC.
  Carlsbad, California
art director
  JOHN BALL
illustrator
  TRACY SABIN
client
  ANACOMP, INC.

creative firm
TELMET DESIGN ASSOCIATES
Toronto, Canada
design/production
MARKO BARAC
designer
TILT TELMET
client
CANADA POST CORPORATION

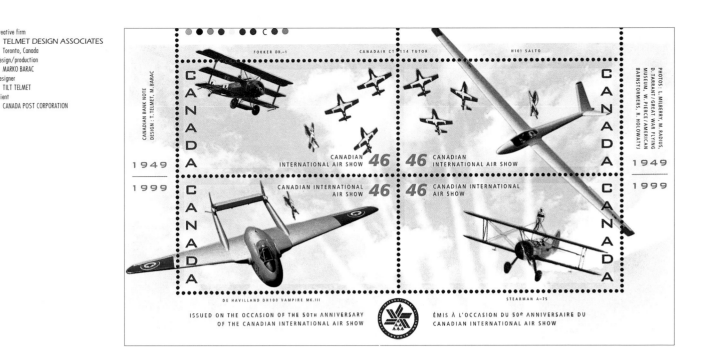

creative firm
TELMET DESIGN ASSOCIATES
Toronto, Canada
designer
TILT TELMET
illustrator
GARY LAY
design assistant
MARKO BARAC
client
CANADA POST CORPORATION

creative firm
  RAY BESSERDIN, PAPER SCULPTURE ARTIST
    Mentone, Australia
art director
  SQEEZ D'SOUZA
designer
  RAY BESSERDIN
client
  AUSTRALIAN GEOGRAPHIC MAGAZINE

creative firm
  RAY BESSERDIN, PAPER SCULPTURE ARTIST
    Mentone, Australia
art director, designer
  RAY BESSERDIN
client
  MacQUARIE BANK LTD

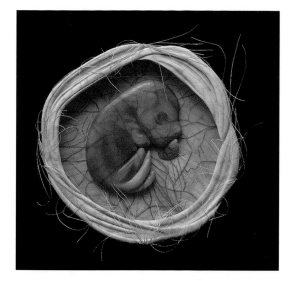

creative firm
   RAY BESSERDIN, PAPER SCULPTURE ARTIST
      Mentone, Australia
art director
   KARL ERIKOVIC
designer
   RAY BESSERDIN
client
   CROW MEDIA/TECHNICAL GROUP N.T.

creative firm
   RAY BESSERDIN, PAPER SCULPTURE ARTIST
      Mentone, Australia
art director
   KARL ERIKOVIC
designer
   RAY BESSERDIN
client
   CROW MEDIA/TECHNICAL GROUP N.T.

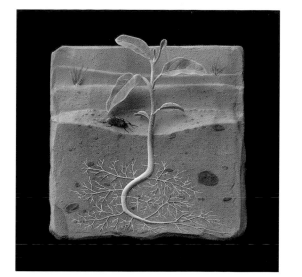

creative firm
   RAY BESSERDIN, PAPER SCULPTURE ARTIST
      Mentone, Australia
art director
   KARL ERIKOVIC
designer
   RAY BESSERDIN
client
   CROW MEDIA/TECHNICAL GROUP N.T.

creative firm
  TANGRAM STRATEGIC DESIGN
  Novara, Italy
art director, designer
  ANTONELLA TREVISAN
creative director
  ENRICO SEMPI
illustrator
  SERGIO QUARANTA
client
  STANDA

creative firm
  TANGRAM STRATEGIC DESIGN
  Novara, Italy
art directors
  ANTONELLA TREVISAN, ENRICO SEMPI
designer
  ANTONELLA TREVISAN
creative director
  ENRICO SEMPI
illustrator
  SERGIO QUARANTA
client
  E. VISHARA DI A. BIFFI ("SUGHI D'AUTORE")

creative firm
  HORNALL ANDERSON DESIGN WORKS
  Seattle, Washington
art directors
  JACK ANDERSON, JANA NISHI
designers
  JANA NISHI, BRUCE BRANSON-MEYER
client
  MOCAFE

creative firm
  LMS DESIGN
  Stamford, Connecticut
designers
  RICHARD SHEAR, ALEX WILLIAMS
client
  BC-USA

creative firm
McELVENEY + PALOZZI DESIGN GROUP, INC.
Rochester, New York
art director
GRETCHEN BYE
creative director
STEPHEN PALOZZI
client
CANANDAIGUA WINE CO.

creative firm
ANTISTA FAIRCLOUGH
Atlanta, Georgia
art directors
TOM ANTISTA, THOMAS FAIRCLOUGH
designers
TOM ANTISTA, THOMAS FAIRCLOUGH, JAMEY WAGNER
client
ANHEUSER, BUSCH, INC.

creative firm
McELVENEY + PALOZZI DESIGN GROUP, INC.
Rochester, New York
art director
DENNIS DeSILVA
creative directors
STEPHEN PALOZZI, WILLIAM McELVENEY
client
CANANDAIGUA WINE CO.

creative firm
BOLDRONI FICCARDI
Mendoza, Argentina
art director
VICTOR BOLDRINI
designer
LEONARDO FICCARDI
client
VINITERRA WINERY

creative firm
AFTER HOURS CREATIVE
Phoenix, Arizona
client
CLEARDATA.NET

creative firm
JAMES ROBIE DESIGN ASSOCIATES
Los Angeles, California
design director, designer
WAYNE FUJITA
creative director
JAMES ROBIE
client
BECKSON DESIGN ASSOCIATES

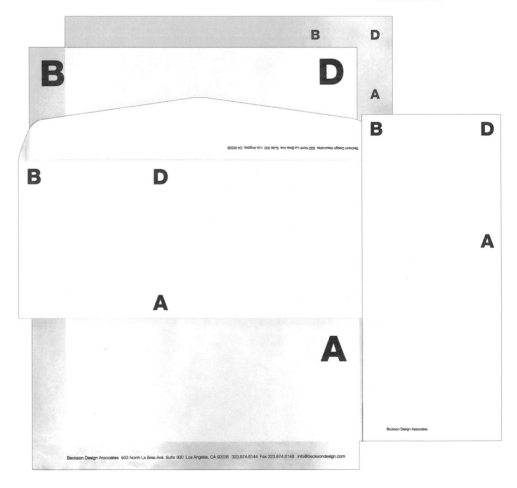

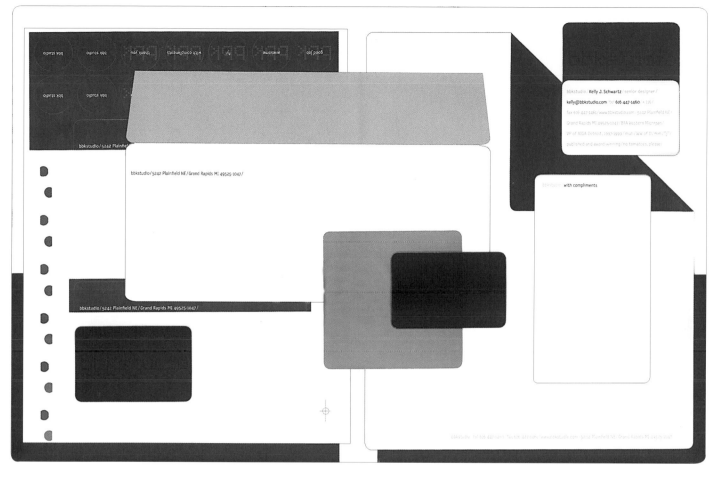

creative firm
BBK STUDIO INC.
Grand Rapids, Michigan
creative director, designer
YANG KIM
client
BBK STUDIO INC.

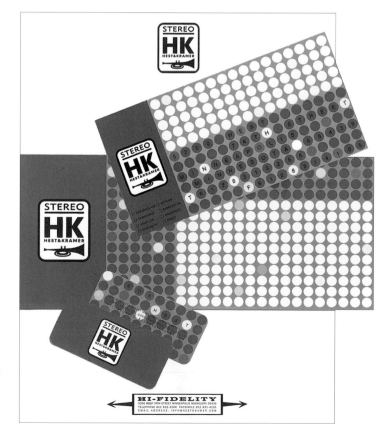

creative firm
DESIGN GUYS
Minneapolis, Minnesota
art director
STEVEN SIKORA
designer
SCOTT THARES
client
HEST & KRAMER

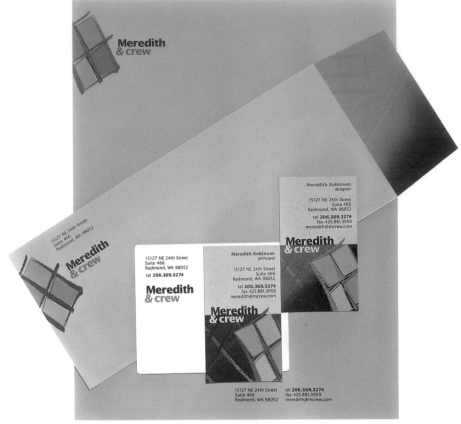

creative firm
  BELYEA
  Seattle, Washington
art director
  PATRICIA BELYEA
designer, illustrator
  NAOMI MURPHY
client
  MEREDITH & CREW

creative firm
  McELVENEY + PALOZZI DESIGN GROUP, INC.
  Rochester, New York
art director
  ELLEN JOHNSON
creative director
  WILLIAM McELVENEY
client
  THE LODGE AT WOODCLIFF

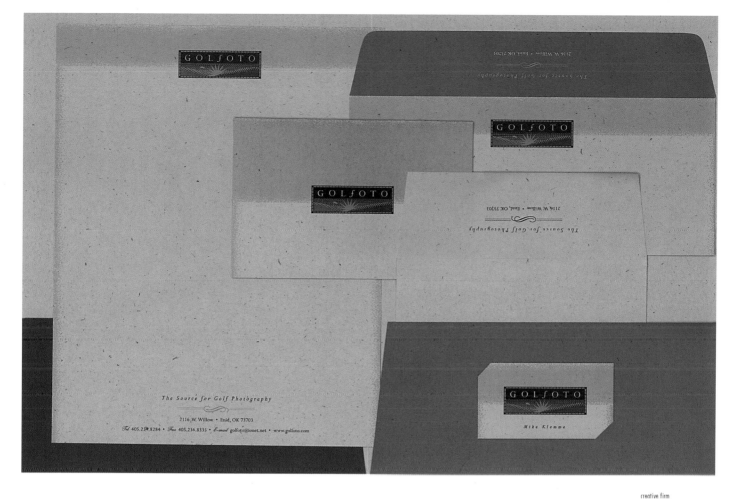

creative firm
GRETEMAN GROUP
Wichita, Kansas
art director, creative director
SONIA GRETEMAN
designer
JAMES STRANGE
client
GOLFOTO

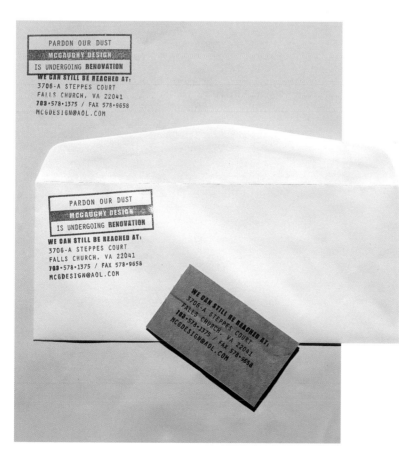

creative firm
McGAUGHY DESIGN
Falls Church, Virginia
designer
MALCOLM McGAUGHY
client
McGAUGHY DESIGN

175

creative firm
H2D
Milwaukee, Wisconsin
creative director
JOSEPH HAUSCH
client
CHRISTINE KEMPTER

creative firm
MULLER + CO.
Kansas City, Missouri
creative executive officer
JOHN MULLER
designer
JEFF MILLER
client
SURFACE DESIGN ASSOCIATION

creative firm
  BUTLER KEMP DESIGN
  North Adelaide, Australia
art director
  DEREK BUTLER
designer
  JULIE KEMP
client
  NOARUINGA LEISURE CENTRE

creative firm
  FIFTH STREET DESIGN
  Berkeley, California
designers
  J. CLIFTON MEEK,
  BRENTON BECK
client
  INDIAN ROCK IMAGESETTING

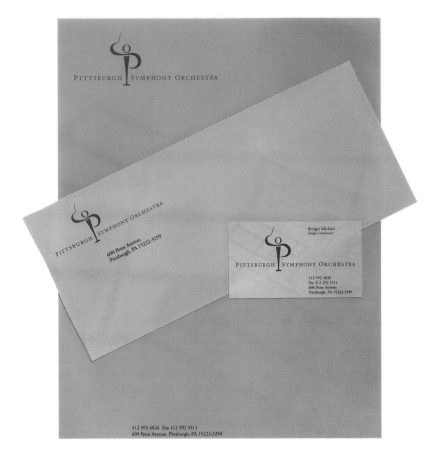

creative firm
ROBERT MEYERS DESIGN
  Fairlawn, Ohio
designer
ROBERT MEYERS
client
  PITTSBURGH SYMPHONY ORCHESTRA

creative firm
CHAVDA GRAPIX
  Oviedo, Florida
designer
JAGDISH J. CHAVDA
client
  DR. DEENDAYAL KHANDELWAL, FOUNDER

creative firm
  RANDI WOLF DESIGN, INC.
  Glassboro, New Jersey
graphic designer
  RANDI WOLF
client
  RANDI WOLF DESIGN

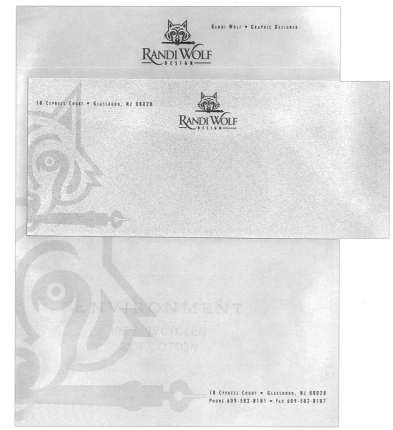

creative firm
  ROBERT MEYERS DESIGN
  Fairlawn, Ohio
designer
  ROBERT MEYERS
client
  INDIANER COMPUTER CORPORATION

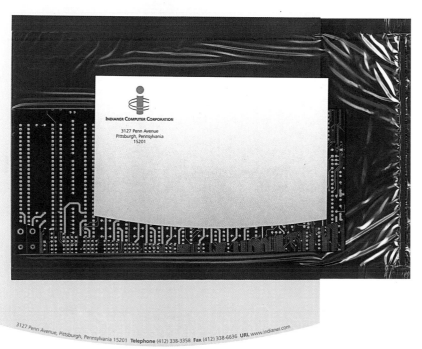

1779

creative firm
SQUIRES & COMPANY
Dallas, Texas
designer
CHRISTIE GROTHEIM
client
MacGUIFFIN MANAGEMENT

creative firm
GARDNER DESIGN
Wichita, Kansas
art director, designer
BILL GARDNER
client
GRIDER & CO.

creative firm
FROST DESIGN , LTD.
London, England
creative director
VINCE FROST
client
FOUR HUNDRED FILMS LTD

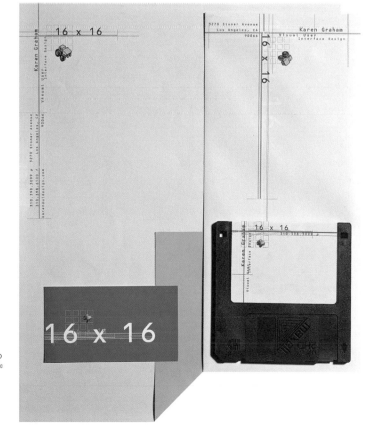

creative firm
5D STUDIO
Malibu, California
art director
JANE KOBAYASHI
designer
VICTOR CORPUZ
client
16 X 16

STREAMWORKS

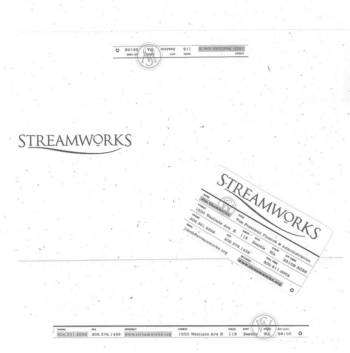

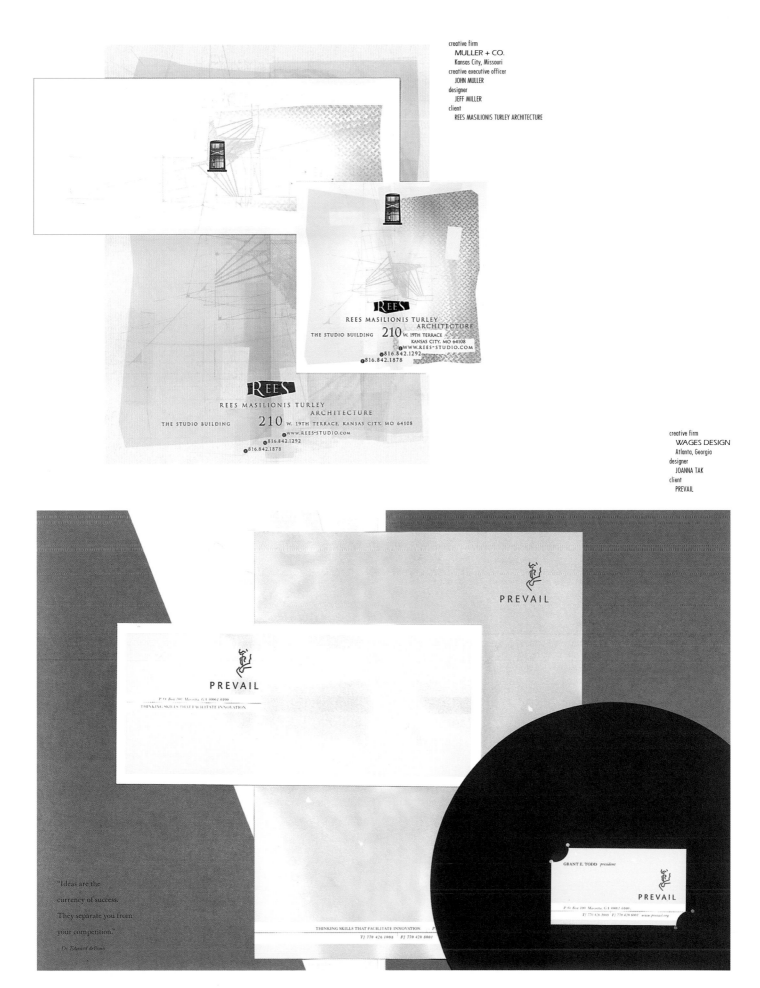

creative firm
  MULLER + CO.
  Kansas City, Missouri
creative executive officer
  JOHN MULLER
designer
  JEFF MILLER
client
  REES MASILIONIS TURLEY ARCHITECTURE

creative firm
  WAGES DESIGN
  Atlanta, Georgia
designer
  JOANNA TAK
client
  PREVAIL

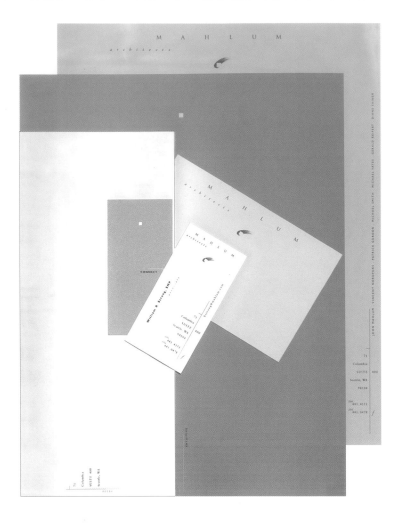

creative firm
HORNALL ANDERSON DESIGN WORKS
Seattle, Washington
art director
JACK ANDERSON
designers
JACK ANDERSON, HEIDI FAVOUR, MARGARET LONG
client
MAHLUM ARCHITECTS

creative firm
GARDNER DESIGN
Wichita, Kansas
art directors
BILL GARDNER, BRIAN MILLER
designer
BRIAN MILLER
client
BUTCHER & COOK'S

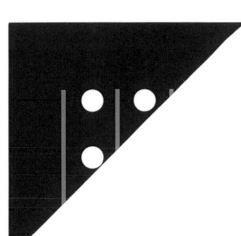

creative firm
  ELLEN BRUSS DESIGN
  Denver, Colorado
designer
  ELLEN BRUSS
client
  0.05 DESIGN · DAVID NICKEL

zero.zero five design
5354 Muirfield Court
Boulder Colorado 80301
p 303.530.5505
f 303.530.5504
zero.zerofivedesign@gte.net

creative firm
  GARDNER DESIGN
  Wichita, Kansas
art directors, designers
  BILL GARDNER, BRIAN MILLER
client
  TALLGRASS BEEF

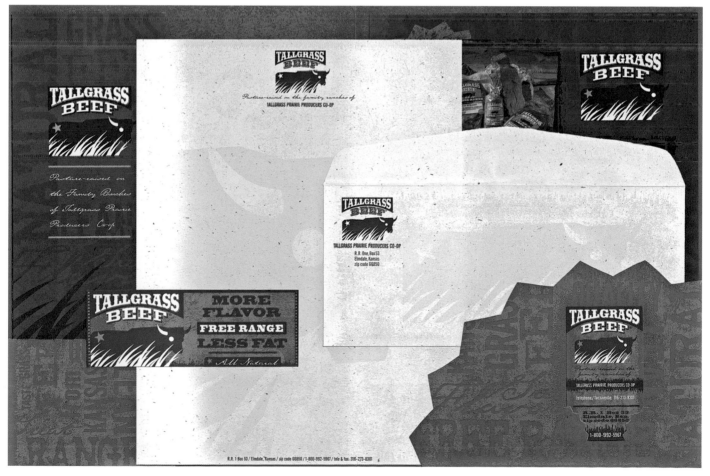

185

creative firm
  MULLER + CO.
  Kansas City, Missouri
creative director
  JOHN MULLER
art director, designer
  MARK VOSS
client
  KANSAS CITY BLUES + JAZZ FESTIVAL

creative firm
  RANDI WOLF DESIGN, INC.
  Glassboro, New Jersey
graphic designer, illustrator
  RANDI WOLF
client
  OLD STREET MARKET

creative firm
  NBBJ GRAPHIC DESIGN
  Seattle, Washington
designer
  PAM GILLIS
client
  NBBJ GRAPHIC DESIGN

creative firm
  TERRY M. ROLLER, GRAPHIC DESIGNER
  Hewitt, Texas
designer
  TERRY M. ROLLER
client
  ALLBRITTON ART INSTITUTE

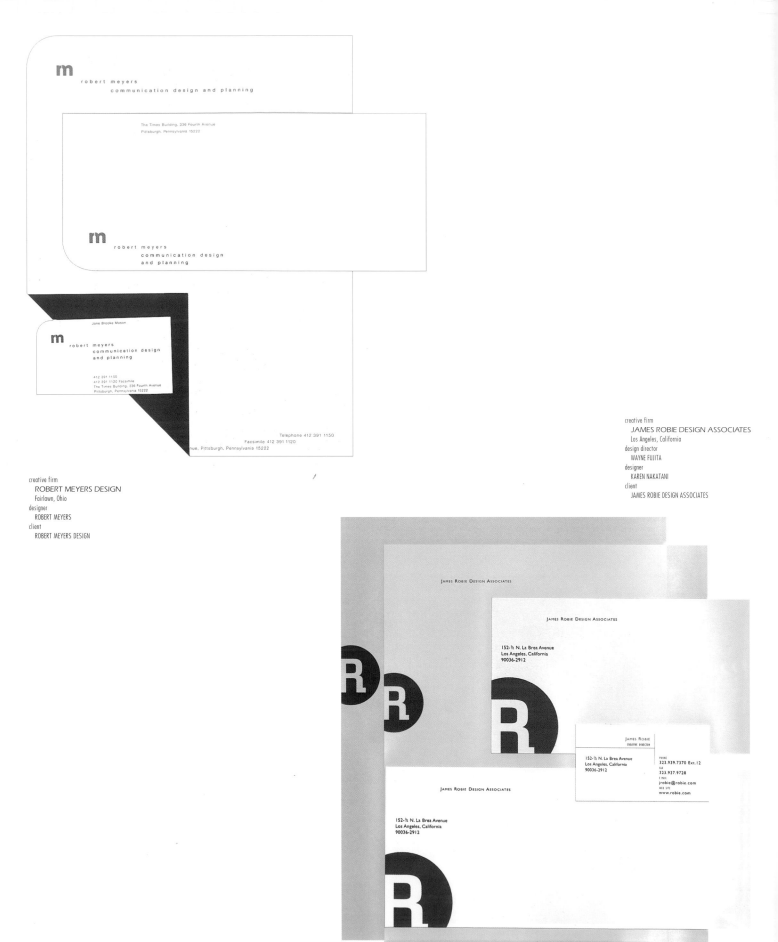

m
robert meyers
communication design and planning

The Times Building, 336 Fourth Avenue
Pittsburgh, Pennsylvania 15222

m
robert meyers
communication design
and planning

Jane Brooke Mason

m
robert meyers
communication design
and planning

412 391 1150
412 391 1120 Facsimile
The Times Building, 336 Fourth Avenue
Pittsburgh, Pennsylvania 15222

Telephone 412 391 1150
Facsimile 412 391 1120
nue, Pittsburgh, Pennsylvania 15222

creative firm
  ROBERT MEYERS DESIGN
    Fairlawn, Ohio
designer
  ROBERT MEYERS
client
  ROBERT MEYERS DESIGN

creative firm
  JAMES ROBIE DESIGN ASSOCIATES
    Los Angeles, California
design director
  WAYNE FUJITA
designer
  KAREN NAKATANI
client
  JAMES ROBIE DESIGN ASSOCIATES

JAMES ROBIE DESIGN ASSOCIATES

JAMES ROBIE DESIGN ASSOCIATES

152-½ N. La Brea Avenue
Los Angeles, California
90036-2912

JAMES ROBIE
CREATIVE DIRECTOR

152-½ N. La Brea Avenue
Los Angeles, California
90036-2912

PHONE
323.939.7370 Ext.12
FAX
323.937.9728
E MAIL
jrobie@robie.com
WEB SITE
www.robie.com

JAMES ROBIE DESIGN ASSOCIATES

152-½ N. La Brea Avenue
Los Angeles, California
90036-2912

152-½ N. La Brea Avenue Los Angeles, California 90036-2912 | PHONE 323.939.7370 FAX 323.937.9728 E.MAIL jrda@robie.com WEB SITE www.robie.com

creative firm
LOUEY/RUBINO DESIGN GROUP, INC.
Santa Monica, California
designer
ROBERT LOUEY
client
CALIFORNIA COUNCIL ON ECONOMIC EDUCATION

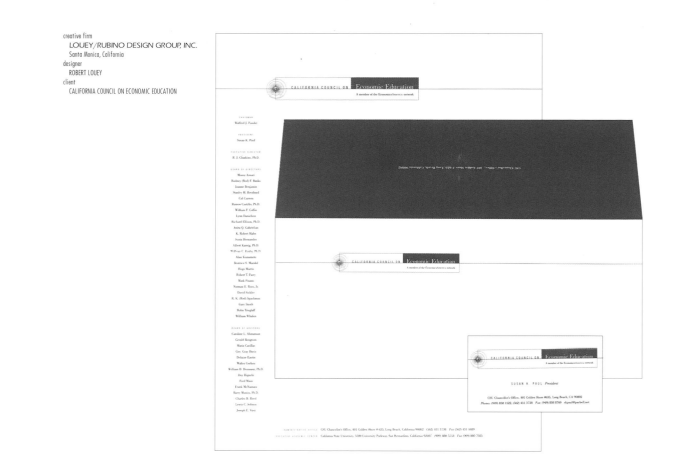

creative firm
TEIKNA GRAPHIC DESIGN INC.
Toronto, Canada
creative director, designer
CLAUDIA NERI
production
GARRY CAMPBELL
client
BUTTERFIELD & ROBINSON

189

creative firm
  FIFTH STREET DESIGN
  Berkeley, California
designers
  J. CLIFTON MEEK, BRENTON BECK
client
  COMPUTER ACCESS SYSTEMS

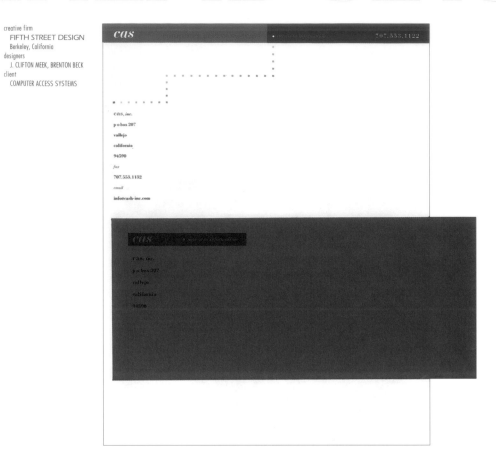

creative firm
  GARDNER DESIGN
  Wichita, Kansas
art director, designer
  BRIAN MILLER
client
  SCRIPT MASTER

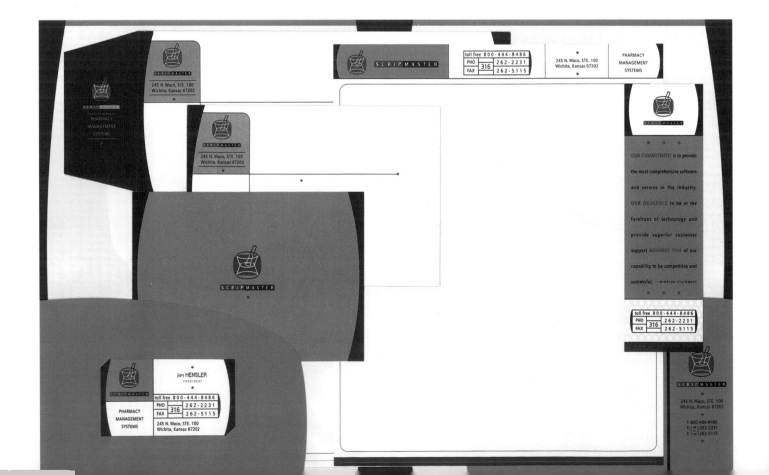

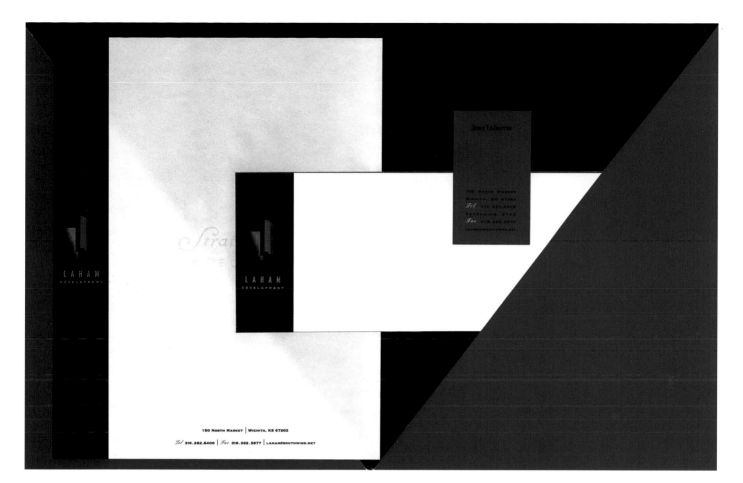

creative firm
  GRETEMAN GROUP
   Wichita, Kansas
creative director
  SONIA GRETEMAN
art directors
  SONIA GRETEMAN, JAMES STRANGE
designer
  JAMES STRANGE
client
  LAHAM DEVELOPMENT

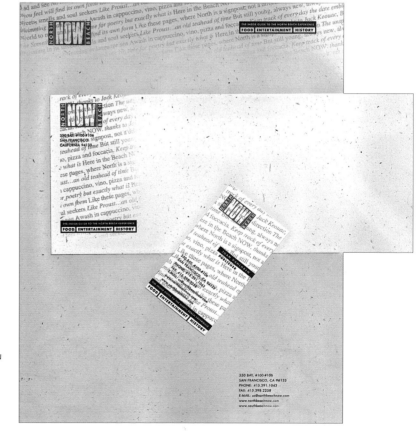

creative firm
  BRUCE YELASKA DESIGN
   San Francisco, California
art director
  BRUCE YELASKA
designers
  BRUCE YELASKA, KELLY LOW
writer
  JOAN DAULGREN

creative firm
  HORNALL ANDERSON DESIGN WORKS
    Seattle, Washington
art director
  JACK ANDERSON
designers
  KATHY DALTON, HOLLY CRAVEN
client
  TRANSPOINT

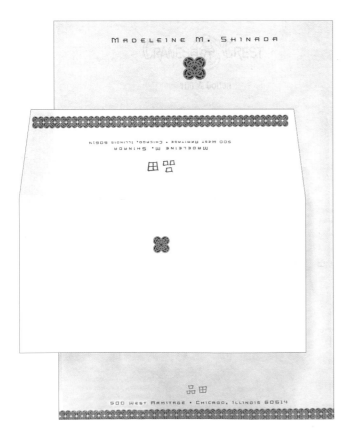

creative firm
  AIRE DESIGN COMPANY
    Tucson, Arizona
creative director
  CATHARINE M. KIM
art director
  SHARI RYKOWSKI
client
  MADELEINE M. SHINADA

creative firm
AIRE DESIGN COMPANY
Tucson, Arizona
creative director
CATHARINE M. KIM
art director
SHARI RYKOWSKI
client
AIRE DESIGN COMPANY

creative firm
SEWICKLEY GRAPHICS & DESIGN, INC.
Sewickley, Pennsylvania
graphic designer
STEVE CYPHER
client
AEROLINK INTERNATIONAL

193

creative firm
  HORNALL ANDERSON DESIGN WORKS
  Seattle, Washington
art directors
  JACK ANDERSON, LARRY ANDERSON
designers
  JACK ANDERSON, LARRY ANDERSON, MARY HERMES,
  MIKE CALKINS, MICHAEL BRUGMAN
client
  U.S. CIGAR

creative firm
  JOHN K. LANDIS GRAPHIC DESIGN
  Kutztown, Pennsylvania
art director
  JOHN K. LANDIS
client
  BARBARA SCHULMAN, FIBER ARTIST

creative firm
JULIA TAM DESIGN
Palos Verdes, California
designer
JULIA TAM
client
JANE BROWN INTERIORS

creative firm
PARAGRAPHS
Chicago, Illinois
client
ORCHESTRA 33

Jane Brown Interiors

Jane Brown Interiors

Jane Brown Interiors

32 Hillcrest Meadows ~ Rolling Hills Estates ~ California 90274

32 Hillcrest Meadows ~ Rolling Hills Estates ~ CA 90274

32 Hillcrest Meadows ~ Rolling Hills Estates, CA 90274 ~ 310.544.0625 ~ Fax 310.544.0635

orchestra
thirty three
entertainment

1135 sandburst lane carol stream illinois 60188-4350
orchestra thirty three entertainment inc.

PHYSIOTHERAPY

JULIE GUERIN

122 ELLIOT STREET, WHYALLA PLAYFORD SA 5600
ALL CORRESPONDENCE: PO BOX 162, WHYALLA SA 5600
TELEPHONE 8644 3444

PHYSIOTHERAPY

JULIE GUERIN

JULIE GUERIN

PHYSIOTHERAPY

122 ELLIOT STREET, WHYALLA PLAYFORD SA 5600
ALL CORRESPONDENCE: PO BOX 162, WHYALLA SA 5600
TELEPHONE 8644 3444

DOCTOR	
PATIENT NAME	DATE OF BIRTH
REASON FOR REFERRAL	
RELEVANT MEDICAL HISTORY	
SIGNATURE	DATE

creative firm
BUTLER KEMP DESIGN
North Adelaide, Australia
designers
DEREK BUTLER, HELLEN KIPRIZLOGLOU
client
JULIE GUERIN PHYSIOTHERAPY

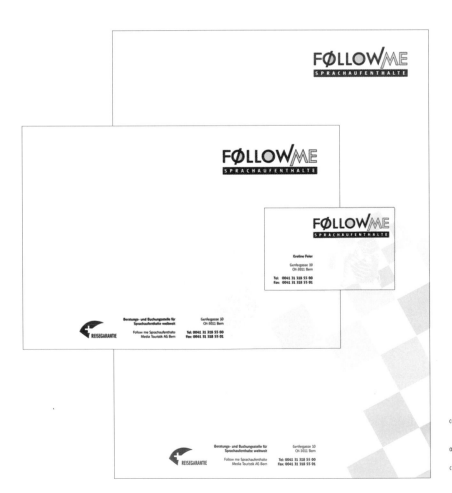

FØLLOWME
SPRACHAUFENTHALTE

FØLLOWME
SPRACHAUFENTHALTE

FØLLOWME
SPRACHAUFENTHALTE

Eveline Feier

Genfergasse 10
CH-3011 Bern

Tel: 0041 31 318 55 00
Fax: 0041 31 318 55 01

Beratungs- und Buchungsstelle für
Sprachaufenthalte weltweit

Follow me Sprachaufenthalte
Media Touristik AG Bern

Genfergasse 10
CH-3011 Bern

Tel: 0041 31 318 55 00
Fax: 0041 31 318 55 01

REISEGARANTIE

Beratungs- und Buchungsstelle für
Sprachaufenthalte weltweit

Follow me Sprachaufenthalte
Media Touristik AG Bern

Genfergasse 10
CH-3011 Bern

Tel: 0041 31 318 55 00
Fax: 0041 31 318 55 01

REISEGARANTIE

creative firm
REVOLUZION
Neuhausen do Eck, Germany
art director, designer
BERND LUZ DIPL
client
FOLLOW ME SPRACHREISEN

creative firm
BOLDRINI & FICCARDI
Mendoza, Italy
designers
VICTOR BOLDRINI, LEONARDO FICCARDI
photographer
CRISTIAN LAZZARI
client
GUILLERMO CORVALAN

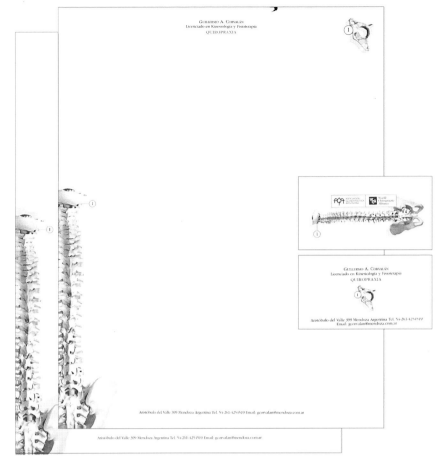

creative firm
H2D
Milwaukee, Wisconsin
creative director
JOSEPH HAUSCH
creative specialist
JENNIFER PECK
client
WISCONSIN HUMANE SOCIETY

TRiBE

Tribe pictures
244 Main
chatham, NJ 07928

[m o v i n g]
Pictures

creative firm
HORNALL ANDERSON DESIGN WORKS
Seattle, Washington
art director
JACK ANDERSON
designers
JACK ANDERSON, MIKE CALKINS
client
HAMMERQUIST & HALVERSON

creative firm
AERIAL VISUAL IDENTITY DESIGN
San Francisco, California
designers
TRACY MOON, STEPHANIE WEST, KIMBERLY GROSS
client
TRIBE PICTURES

HAMMERQUIST & HALVERSON

83 COLUMBIA ST. SUITE 400, SEATTLE, WA 98104

HAMMERQUIST & HALVERSON

83 COLUMBIA ST. SUITE 400, SEATTLE, WA 98104

HAMMERQUIST & HALVERSON

KAY WOOD

E-MAIL kay@hammerquist.net

HAMMERQUIST & HALVERSON

83 COLUMBIA ST. SUITE 400, SEATTLE, WA 98104 | TEL 206-682-3685 | FAX 206-682-3867 | E-MAIL info@hammerquist.net

creative firm
  FIFTH STREET DESIGN
  Berkeley, California
designers
  J. CLIFTON MEEK, BRENTON BECK
client
  POSTERDOCS

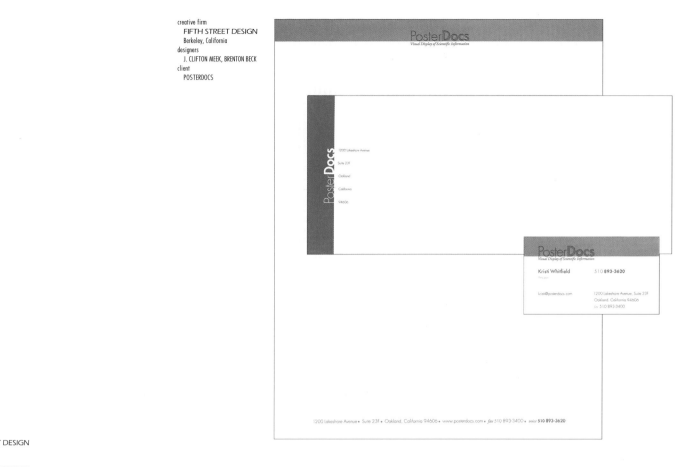

creative firm
  FIFTH STREET DESIGN
  Berkeley, California
designers
  J. CLIFTON MEEK, BRENTON BECK
client
  FIFTH STREET DESIGN

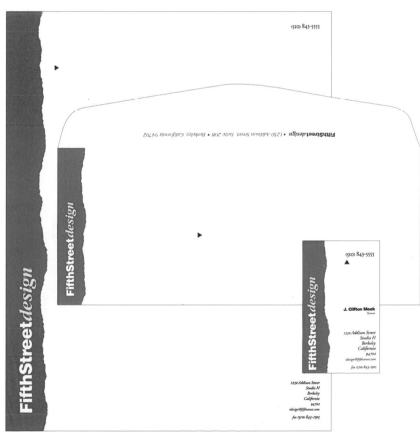

199

creative firm
  GARDNER DESIGN
  Wichita, Kansas
art directors
  BILL GARDNER, BRIAN MILLER
designer
  BRIAN MILLER
client
  PAUL CHAUNCEY PHOTOGRAPHY

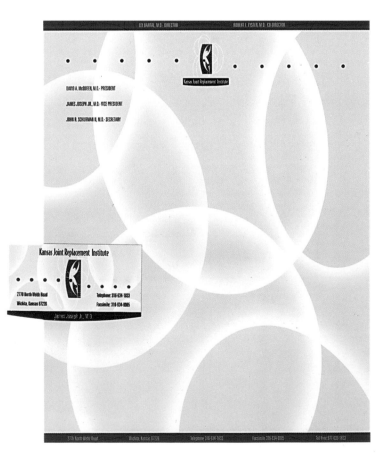

creative firm
  GARDNER DESIGN
  Wichita, Kansas
art directors
  TRAVIS BROWN, BRIAN MILLER
designer
  TRAVIS BROWN
client
  KANSAS JOINT REPLACEMENT INSTITUTE

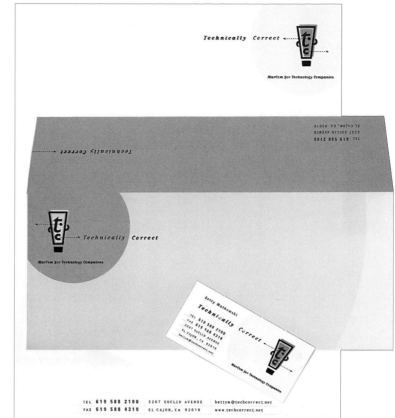

creative firm
  MIRIELLO GRAFICO INC.
  San Diego, California
designer
  DENNIS GARCIA
client
  TECHNICALLY CORRECT

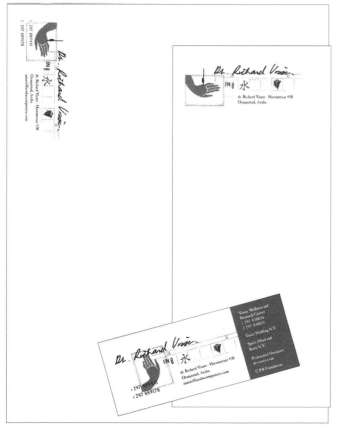

creative firm
  MIRIELLO GRAFICO INC.
  San Diego, California
designer
  CHRIS KEENEY
client
  DR. VISSER

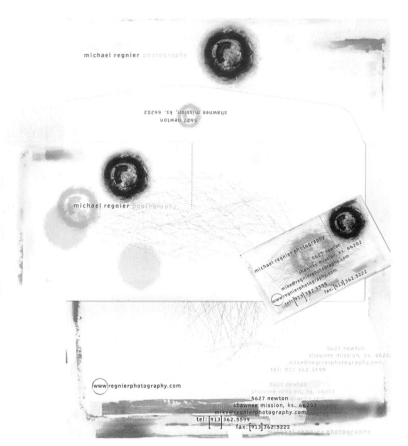

creative firm
MULLER + CO.
Kansas City, Missouri
creative director
JOHN MULLER
designer
JEFF MILLER
client
MICHAEL REGNIER PHOTGRAPHY

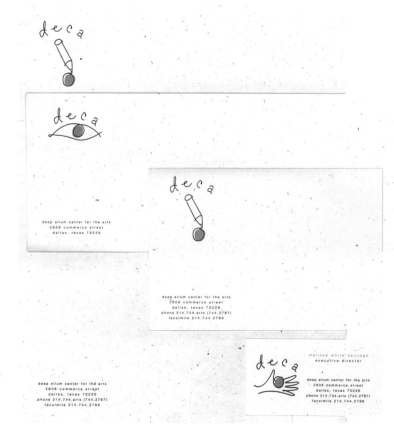

creative firm
SQUIRES & COMPANY
Dallas, Texas
designer
CHRISTIE GROTHEIM
client
DECA

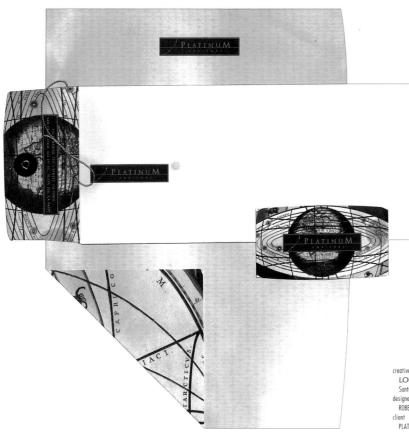

creative firm
  LOUEY/RUBINO DESIGN GROUP, INC.
  Santa Monica, California
designer
  ROBERT LOUEY
client
  PLATINUM ADVISORS

creative firm
  30 SIXTY DESIGN, INC.
  Los Angeles, California
creative director, art director
  HENRY VIZCARRA
designer
  ANNA KALINKA
photographer
  SCOTT HENSEL
copywriter
  HILLEL WASSERMAN
client
  30 SIXTY DESIGN, INC.

30sixty design, inc
2801 cahuenga boulevard west
los angeles ca 90068
ph 323 850 5311
fax 323 850 6638

creative firm
HORNALL ANDERSON DESIGN WORKS
Seattle, Washington
art directors
JOHN HORNALL, LARRY ANDERSON
designers
JOHN HORNALL, LARRY ANDERSON,
MARY CHIN HUTCHISON, BRUCE STIGLER
client
COPPER SKY GRILL

creative firm
HORNALL ANDERSON DESIGN WORKS
Seattle, Washington
art director
JACK ANDERSON
designers
JACK ANDERSON, MARY HERMES,
GRETCHEN COOK, JULIE LOCK
client
SPACE NEEDLE

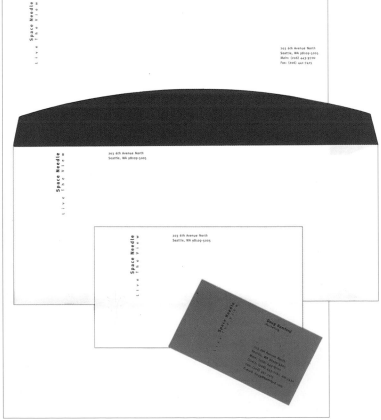

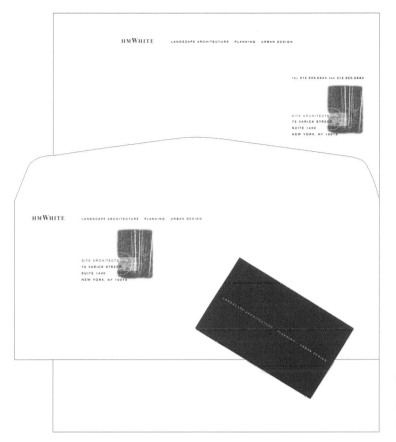

creative firm
SHOOK DESIGN GROUP, INC.
Charlotte, North Carolina
designer
STEVE FENTON
client
HM WHITE LANDSCAPE ARCHITECTS

creative firm
BRUCE YELASKA DESIGN
San Francisco, California
art director, designer
BRUCE YELASKA
client
BRUCE YELASKA DESIGN

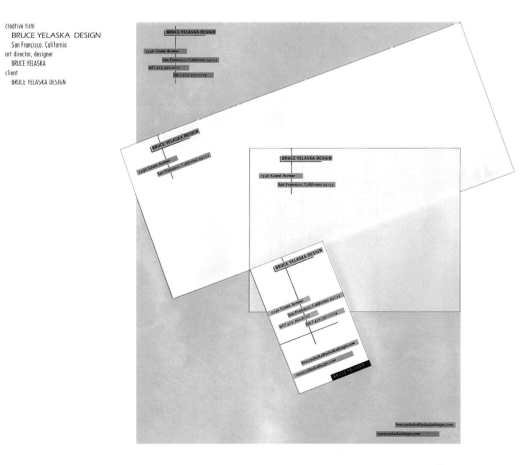

creative firm
BECKER DESIGN
Milwaukee, Wisconsin
designer
NEIL BECKER
client
HEIDI GILMORE

HEIDI GILMORE

343 North Broadway
Milwaukee, WI 53202

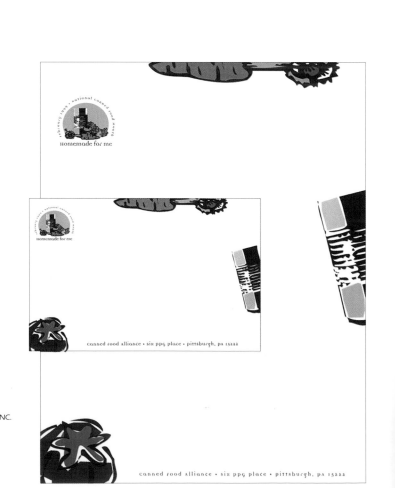

homemade for me

canned food alliance • six ppg place • pittsburgh, pa 15222

creative firm
A TO Z COMMUNICATIONS, INC.
Pittsburgh, Pennsylvania
creative director
ALAN BOARTS
designer
VONNIE HORNBURG
client
KETCHUM PR

creative firm
  ROSS ADVERTISING
  Peoria, Illinois
executive creative director
  SKIP DAMPIER
senior art director
  NICK JIBBEN
client
  GRIDIRON

creative firm
  HORNALL ANDERSON DESIGN WORKS
  Seattle, Washington
art director
  JACK ANDERSON
designers
  JACK ANDERSON, KATHY SAITO, JULIE LOCK,
  ED LEE, HEIDI FAVOUR, VIRGINIA LE
client
  GROUND ZERO

creative firm
DIRECTION DESIGN
Los Angeles, California
creative director, designer
ANJA MUELLER
managing director
TERESA A. LOPEZ

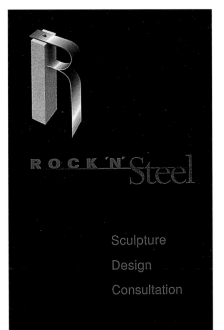

creative firm
GRETEMAN GROUP
Wichita, Kansas
creative director, art director
SONIA GRETEMAN
designers
SONIA GRETEMAN, CRAIG TOMSON
client
ROCK 'N' STEEL

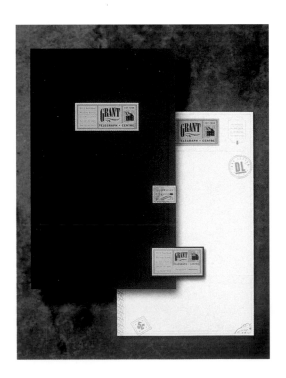

creative firm
GRETEMAN GROUP
Wichita, Kansas
creative director
SONIA GRETEMAN
art directors
SONIA GRETEMAN, JAMES STRANGE
designer
JAMES STRANGE
client
GRANT TELEGRAPH

creative firm
   GRETEMAN GROUP
   Wichita, Kansas
creative director
   SONIA GRETEMAN
art directors
   SONIA GRETEMAN, JAMES STRANGE
designers
   SONIA GRETEMAN, JAMES STRANGE, GARRETT FRESH
client
   HOTEL AT OLD TOWN

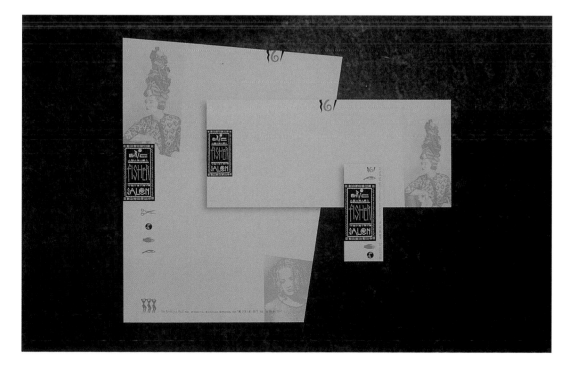

creative firm
   GRETEMAN GROUP
   Wichita, Kansas
creative director, art director
   SONIA GRETEMAN
designers
   SONIA GRETEMAN, JO QUILLIN
client
   ERIC FISHER SALON

creative firm
  BONNIE MATHER DESIGN
  Edmonds, Washington
designer
  BONNIE MATHER
client
  WYMAN PARK, SPECIALTY GIFTS

creative firm
  BONNIE MATHER DESIGN
  Edmonds, Washington
designer
  BONNIE MATHER
client
  BETH DUNTON, HAIR STYLIST

creative firm
  GRETEMAN GROUP
  Wichita, Kansas
creative director
  SONIA GRETEMAN
art directors
  SONIA GRETEMAN, JAMES STRANGE
designer
  JAMES STRANGE
client
  POLO CLUB

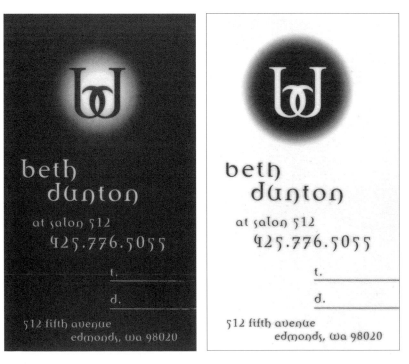

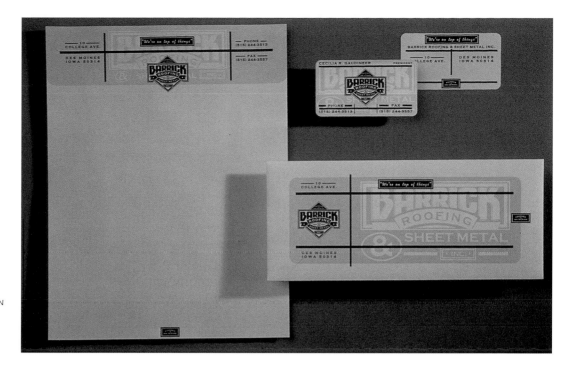

creative firm
SAYLES GRAPHIC DESIGN
Des Moines, Iowa
art director, illustrator
JOHN SAYLES
client
BARRICK ROOFING

Lewis Glaser
Coordinator of Graphic Design
Associate Professor

TEXAS CHRISTIAN UNIVERSITY
TCU Box 298000
Fort Worth, Texas 76129
817.257.7697 *voice* ★ 817.257.7780 *fax*
http://gamma.is.tcu.edu/~glaser
l.glaser@tcu.edu

creative firm
PIVOT DESIGN, INC.
Chicago, Illinois
creative director
BROCK HALDEMAN
designer
ELIZABETH JOHNSON
client
UPPERCASE BOOKS

creative firm
WET PAPER BAG GRAPHIC DESIGN
Fort Worth, Texas
art director, designer, illustrator, copywriter
LEWIS GLASER
client
TCU GRAPHIC DESIGN PROGRAM

UPPERCASE BOOKS, INC. 223 WEST ERIE STREET 4SW CHICAGO ILLINOIS 60610
TELEPHONE 312 280 3232 FACSIMILE 312 280 3233 WWW.UPPERCASEBOOKS.COM

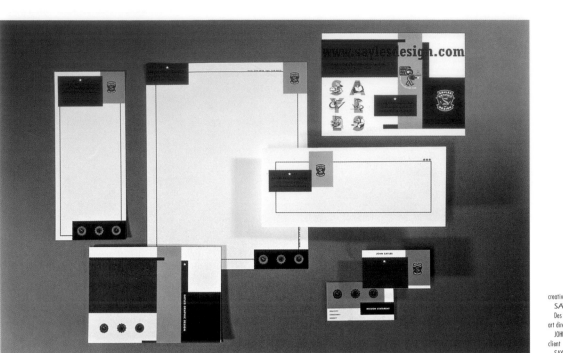

creative firm
SAYLES GRAPHIC DESIGN
Des Moines, Iowa
art director, illustrator
JOHN SAYLES
client
SAYLES GRAPHIC DESIGN

creative firm
SIBLEY PETEET DESIGN
Dallas, Texas
designer
TOM KIRSCH
client
AGI KLEARFOLD

creative firm
 SAYLES GRAPHIC DESIGN
 Des Moines, Iowa
art director, illustrator
 JOHN SAYLES
client
 CASA BONITA

creative firm
 SAYLES GRAPHIC DESIGN
 Des Moines, Iowa
art director, illustrator
 JOHN SAYLES
client
 CONSOLIDATED CORRECTIONAL FOOD SERVICES

creative firm
DEVER DESIGNS
Laurel, Maryland
art director, designer
JEFFREY L. DEVER
client
DEVER DESIGNS

christinemaclean@contentstudio.com
80 W. 13th St.   Holland MI 49423   616 393 0339   616 393 8914 fax

christinemaclean@contentstudio.com
80 W. 13th St.   Holland MI 49423

christinemaclean@contentstudio.com
80 W. 13th St.   Holland MI 49423   616 393 0339   616 393 8914 fax

creative firm
BBK STUDIO, INC.
Grand Rapids, Michigan
creative director, designer
YANG KIM
copywriter
CHRISTINE MacLEAN
client
CONTENT STUDIO

creative firm
  PARAGRAPHS DESIGN
  Chicago, Illinois
designer
  CRISPIN PREBYS
client
  PHYSICIANS INTERACTIVE

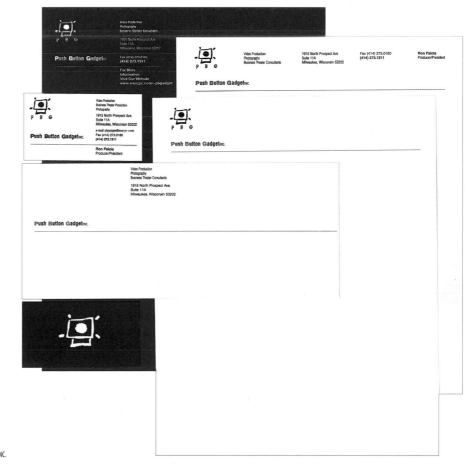

creative firm
  H2D
  Milwaukee, Wisconsin
creative director
  JOSEPH HAUSCH
client
  PUSH BUTTON GADGET, INC.

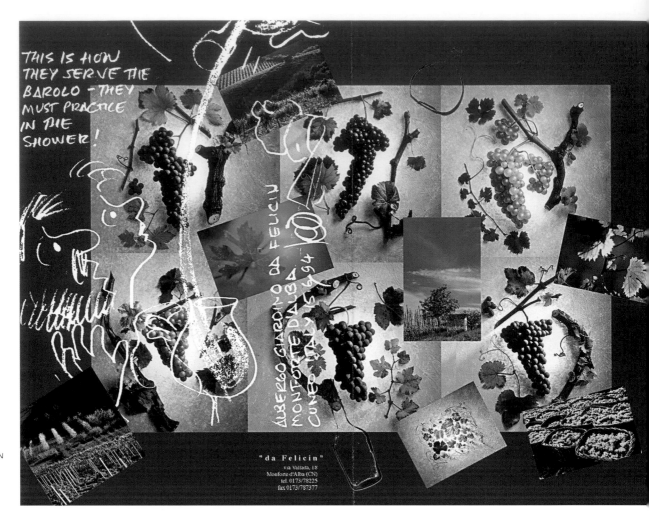

THIS IS HOW THEY SERVE THE BAROLO – THEY MUST PRACTICE IN THE SHOWER!

"da Felicin"
via Vallada, 18
Monforte d'Alba (CN)
tel. 0173/78225
fax 0173/787377

creative firm
BRUNAZZI & ASSOCIATI/
IMAGE + COMMUNICATION
Turin , Italy
designers
SILVIA ZANETTI, GIOVANNI BRUNAZZI
client
FELICIN

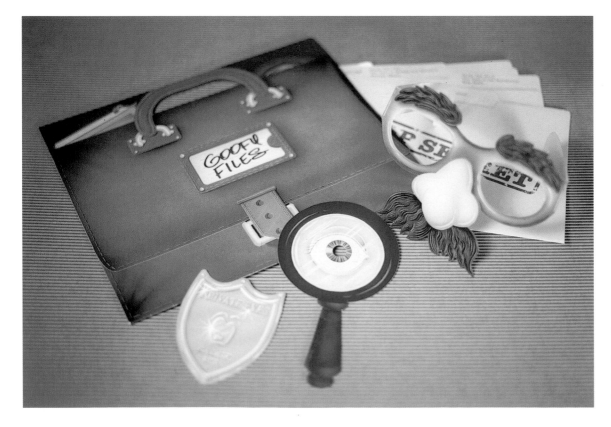

creative firm
DISNEY DESIGN GROUP
Lake Buena Vista, Florida
creative director
MICHELE KEATING
designer
MIKE WOOD
client
DISNEY CRUISE LINE

creative firm
JAMES ROBIE DESIGN ASSOCIATES
Los Angeles, California
creative director
JAMES ROBIE
designer
KAREN NAKATANI
client
THE HUMP SUSHI BAR & RESTAURANT

creative firm
DISNEY DESIGN GROUP
Lake Buena Vista, Florida
creative director
MICHELE KEATING
designer
MARK FRANKEL
illustrator
JOYCE STIGLICH
client
DISNEY CRUISE LINE

creative firm
CREATIVE SERVICES
New York, New York
art director, designer
GIULIO TURTURRO
client
SONY CLASSICAL

creative firm
THE RIORDON DESIGN GROUP, INC.
Oakville, Ontario, Canada
designer
SHIRLEY RIORDON
photographer
DAVID GRAHAM WHITE
client
TAMARA MORGAN CHAFFEE

creative firm
CREATIVE SERVICES
New York, New York
art director, designer
GIULIO TURTURRO
client
SONY CLASSICAL

creative firm
CREATIVE SERVICES
New York, New York
art director
ALLEN WEINBERG
designer
NICKY LINDEMAN
client
SONY CLASSICAL

creative firm
DISNEY CONSUMER PRODUCTS
Burbank, California
art director
LUIS M. FERNANDEZ
designers
TIFFANY CHON, MARCELLA WONG
client
THE DISNEY STORE

creative firm
THE RIORDON DESIGN GROUP, INC.
Oakville, Ontario, Canada
art director
TONI FITZPENN
designer
SHIRLEY RIORDON
illustrator
SHARON PORTER
client
VINEYARD MUSIC GROUP

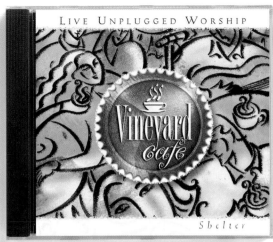

creative firm
CREATIVE SERVICES
New York, New York
art director
ALLEN WEINBERG
designer
RISA NOAH
photographer
CHRISTIAN MICHAELS/FPG INTERNATIONAL
client
SONY CLASSICAL

creative firm
CREATIVE SERVICES
New York, New York
art director, designer
GIULIO TURTURRO
illustrator
MATT MAHURIN
client
SONY CLASSICAL

You only live once.

175 value retailers.   5 minutes away.   Exit #155, Baseline Road.

ARIZONA MILLS

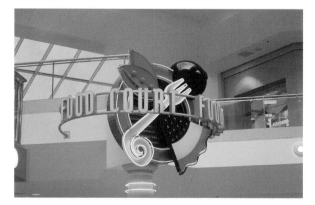

creative firm
GRETEMAN GROUP
Wichita, Kansas
creative directors, art directors
SONIA GRETEMAN, CHRIS BRUNNER
designers
SONIA GRETEMAN, CHRIS BRUNNER,
CRAIG TOMSON, JAMES STRANGE
client
CITY ARTS

creative firm
WAGES DESIGN
Atlanta, Georgia
designers
RANDY ALLISON, JOANNA TAK
client
GEORGIA STATE UNIVERSITY

creative firm
MULLER + CO.
Kansas City, Missouri
art director
JOANN OTTO
client
NORTH KANSAS CITY HOSPITAL DAY CARE CENTER

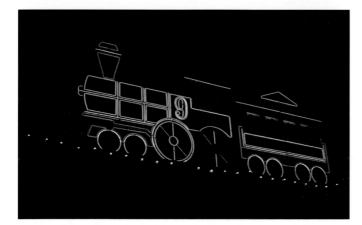

Hockey thure ith fun!

FOR TICKETS KC BLADES CALL 84-BLADE

Hockey ith my thport!

FOR TICKETS KC BLADES CALL 84-BLADE

Hockey ith a blatht!

FOR TICKETS KC BLADES CALL 84-BLADE

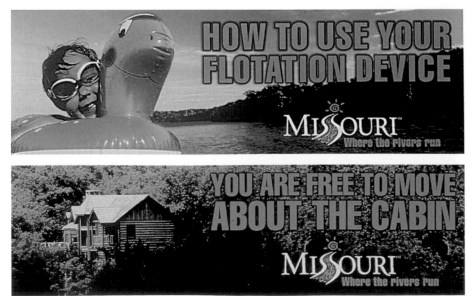

HOW TO USE YOUR
FLOTATION DEVICE

MISSOURI
Where the rivers run

YOU ARE FREE TO MOVE
ABOUT THE CABIN

MISSOURI
Where the rivers run

creative firm
  LORENC + YOO DESIGN
  Roswell, Georgia
design director
  JAN LORENC
designer
  STEVE McCALL
client
  HINES-COOL SPRINGS

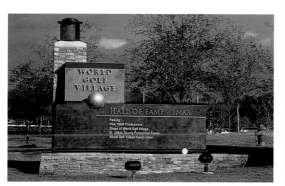

creative firm
  LORENC + YOO DESIGN
  Roswell, Georgia
design director
  JAN LORENC
designer
  STEVE McCALL
architect
  GARY FLESHER
client
  WORLD GOLF VILLAGE-DAVIDSON DEVELOPMENT

creative firm
  LORENC + YOO DESIGN
  Roswell, Georgia
design director
  JAN LORENC
designers
  STEVE McCALL, DAVID PARK
client
  GENERAL GROWTH PROPERTIES/JJR

creative firm
WPA PINFOLD
Leeds, England
designers
JAMES LITTLEWOOD, PAUL PHILLIPS
client
RANK HOLIDAYS

creative firm
MICHAEL COURTNEY DESIGN
Seattle, Washington
art director
MICHAEL COURTNEY
designers
MICHAEL COURTNEY, DAN HOANG
client
CORIXA CORPORATION

creative firm
DESIGN GUYS
Minneapolis, Minnesota
art director
STEVEN SIKORA
designers
GARY PATCH, ANNE PETERSON
client
TARGET STORES

creative firm
MULLER + CO.
Kansas City, Missouri
art director
JOANN OTTO
illustrator
JIM PAILLOT
writer
JEFF SOBUL
client
NORTH KANSAS CITY HOSPITAL DAY CARE CENTER

creative firm
SPENCER ZAHN & ASSOCIATES
Philadelphia, Pennsylvania
creative director
SPENCER ZAHN
designer
ED McHUGH
client
KEENAN MOTORS

creative firm
GREGORY GROUP
Dallas, Texas
creative director
JON GREGORY
client
EDS

creative firm
TANAGRAM, INC.
Chicago, Illinois
designer
LANCE RUTTER
client
NIKETOWN SEATTLE

creative firm
SQUIRES & COMPANY
Dallas, Texas
designer
THOMAS VASQUES
client
ST. PETE'S

225

creative firm
  SBG ENTERPRISE
  San Francisco, California
creative director
  THOMAS BOND
designer
  IRATXE MUMFORD
illustrator
  RIK OLSEN
client
  THE LEARNING COMPANY

creative firm
  DEUTSCH DESIGN WORKS
  San Francisco, California
creative director
  BARRY DEUTSCH
designers
  JOHN LUCAS, ERIC PINO, JACQUES ROSSOUW
client
  RED ORB DIVISION-BRODERBUND SOFTWARE AGES OF MYST

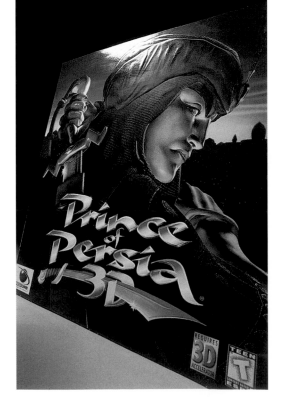

creative firm
  DEUTSCH DESIGN WORKS
  San Francisco, California
creative director
  BARRY DEUTSCH
designer
  JACQUES ROSSOUW
client
  RED ORB DIVISION-BRODERBUND SOFTWARE PRINCE OF PERSIA 3D

creative firm
  HUGHES DESIGN INC.
  Norwalk, Connecticut
client
  IBM VIAVOICE

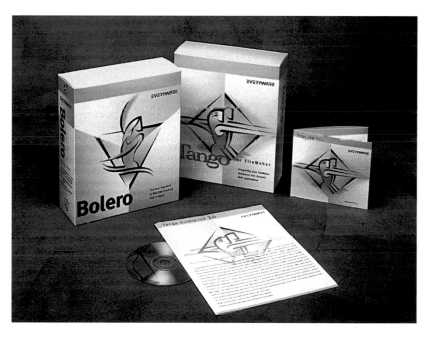

creative firm
  HORNALL ANDERSON DESIGN WORKS
  Seattle, Washington
art director
  JACK ANDERSON
designers
  JACK ANDERSON, KATHA DALTON,
  JANA WILSON ESSER, JANA NISHI,
  JULIE LOCK
client
  ADOBE

creative firm
  TELMET DESIGN ASSOCIATES
  Toronto, Canada
art director
  TIIT TELMET
designers
  JOSEPH GAULT, MARKO BARAC
client
  EVERYWARE DEVELOPMENT CORPORATION

creative firm
  LMS DESIGN
  Stamford, Connecticut
designers
  RICHARD SHEAR, ALEX WILLIAMS
client
  DELORME INC

creative firm
  BAILEY DESIGN GROUP, INC.
  Plymouth Meeting, Pennsylvania
creative director
  DAVID FIEDLER
designer
  LAURA MARKLEY
client
  C.F. MARTIN & COMPANY

creative firm
  BAILEY DESIGN GROUP, INC.
  Plymouth Meeting, Pennsylvania
creative director
  DAVID FIEDLER
designer
  LAURA MARKLEY
client
  C.F. MARTIN & COMPANY

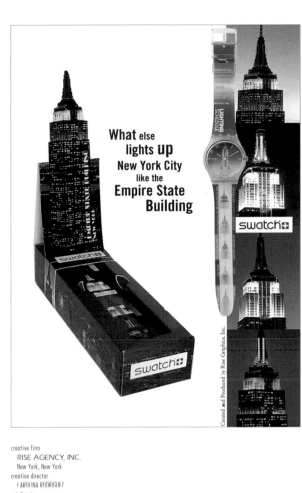

What else lights up New York City like the Empire State Building

swatch+

swatch

swatch+

Created and Produced by Rise Graphics, Inc.

creative firm
  RISE AGENCY, INC.
    New York, New York
creative director
  CAROLINA RODRIGUEZ
art director
  ROBERT ZWASCHKA
client
  SWATCH U.S.

creative firm
  FARENGA DESIGN GROUP
    New York, New York
designer
  ANTHONY FARENGA
client
  WATSON-GUPTILL PUBLICATIONS

creative firm
  VAN NOY GROUP
    Torrance, California
creative director
  BILL MURAWSKI
designer
  JOE HUIZAR
client
  PENTEL OF AMERICA, LTD.

229

creative firm
DEUTSCH DESIGN WORKS
San Francisco, California
creative director
BARRY DEUTSCH
senior designer
LORI WYNN
client
ANHEUSER-BUSCH MICHELOB HOLIDAY

creative firm
DEUTSCH DESIGN WORKS
San Francisco, California
creative director
BARRY DEUTSCH
senior designers
LORI WYNN, GREGG PERIN
client
ANHEUSER-BUSCH MILLENIUIM GIFT BOX

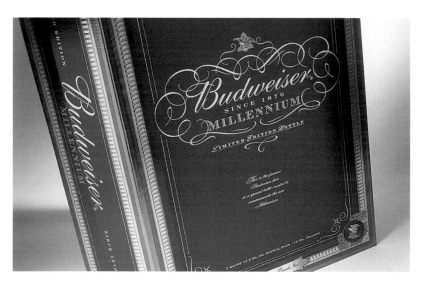

creative firm
DEUTSCH DESIGN WORKS
San Francisco, California
creative director
BARRY DEUTSCH
designer
JACQUES ROSSOUW
client
ANHEUSER-BUSCH MICHELOB MAPLE BROWN ALE

creative firm
   DEUTSCH DESIGN WORKS
   San Francisco, California
creative director
   BARRY DEUTSCH
designers,
   LORI WYNN, KATE GREENE
client
   ANHEUSER-BUSCH MILLENIUM TWELVE PACKS

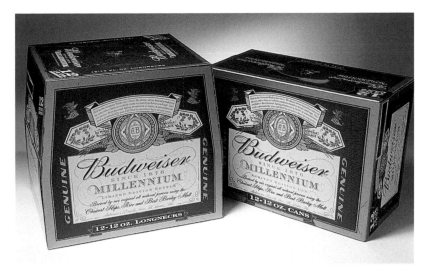

creative firm
   DEUTSCH DESIGN WORKS
   San Francisco, California
creative director
   BARRY DEUTSCH
senior designer
   LORI WYNN
client
   ANHEUSER-BUSCH MICHELOB SAMPLER PACK

creative firm
   COMPASS DESIGN
   Minneapolis, Minnesota
designers
   MITCHELL LINDGREN,
   TOM ARTHUR,
   RICH McGOWEN
client
   AUGUST SCHELL BREWING COMPANY

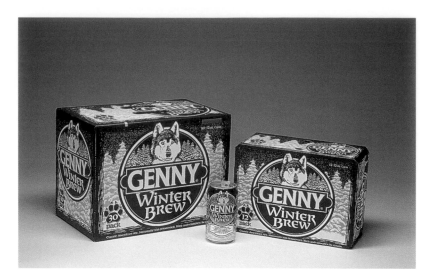

creative firm
McELVENEY + PALOZZI DESIGN GROUP, INC.
Rochester, New York
creative director
STEPHEN PALOZZI
art director
MATT GARRITY
client
GENESEE BREWING COMPANY

creative firm
ANTISTA FAIRCLOUGH
Atlanta, Georgia
art directors
TOM ANTISTA, THOMAS FAIRCLOUGH
designers
TOM ANTISTA, THOMAS FAIRCLOUGH,
JAMEY WAGNER
client
COCA-COLA (COOL NESTEA)

creative firm
KLIM DESIGN, INC.
Avon, Connecticut
creative director
MATT KLIM
client
CASA CUERVO, S.A. DE C.V.

creative firm
GARDNER DESIGN
Wichita, Kansas
art director, designer
BRIAN MILLER
client
HEMMEN WINES

creative firm
VAN NOY GROUP
Torrance, California
creative director
JIM VAN NOY
art director, designer
BILL MURAWSKI
illustrator
MIKE WEPLO
client
GAETANO SPECIALTIES, LTD.

creative firm
ANTISTA FAIRCLOUGH
Atlanta, Georgia
art directors, designers
TOM ANTISTA, THOMAS FAIRCLOUGH
client
FETZER VINEYARDS

235

creative firm
KLIM DESIGN, INC.
Avon, Connecticut
creative director
MATT KLIM
client
CASA CUERVO, S.A. DE C.V.

creative firm
BUTLER KEMP DESIGN
North Adelaide, Australia
art directors
DEREK BUTLER, JULIE KEMP
designer
HELLEN KIPRIZLOGLOU
client
BROWNS' OF PADTHAWAY

creative firm
WALLACE CHURCH ASSOCIATES INC.
New York, New York
designer
NIN GLAISTER
client
WALLACE CHURCH

creative firm
  BUTLER KEMP DESIGN
  North Adelaide, Australia
art director
  DEREK BUTLER
designers
  HELLEN KIPRIZLOGLOU, JULIE KEMP
client
  BROWNS' OF PADTHAWAY

creative firm
  DESIGN SOLUTIONS
  Napa, California
designer
  DEBORAH MITCHELL
Illustrator
  JOHN BURNS
client
  TREFETHEN VINEYARDS

creative firm
  McELVENEY + PALOZZI DESIGN GROUP, INC.
  Rochester, New York
creative directors
  STEPHEN PALOZZI, WILLIAM McELVENEY
art director
  GRETCHEN BYE
client
  CANANDAIGUA WINE COMPANY

creative firm
ANTISTA FAIRCLOUGH
Atlanta, Georgia
art directors, designers
TOM ANTISTA, THOMAS FAIRCLOUGH
client
BELL ARBOR VINEYARDS

creative firm
PEARLFISHER
London, England
creative director
JONATHAN FORD
designer
IAN CATLING
client
THE ABSOLUT COMPANY

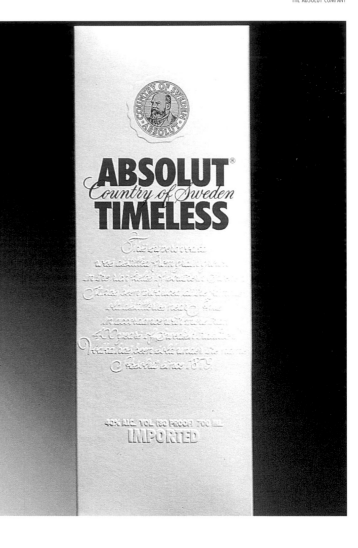

creative firm
PEARLFISHER
London, England
creative director
JONATHAN FORD
designer
SHAUN BOWEN
client
THE ABSOLUT COMPANY

creative firm
ESTUDIO RAY
Phoenix, Arizona
art directors
CHRISTINE RAY, JOE RAY
designers
CHRISTINE RAY, JOE RAY, LESLIE LINK
illustrator
JOE RAY
client
COFFEE PLANTATION

creative firm
ADKINS/BALCHUNAS
Providence, Rhode Island
creative director
JERRY BALCHUNAS
designers
MICHELLE PHANEUF, JERRY BALCHUNAS,
SUSAN DeANGELIS
client
AUTOCRAT, INC.

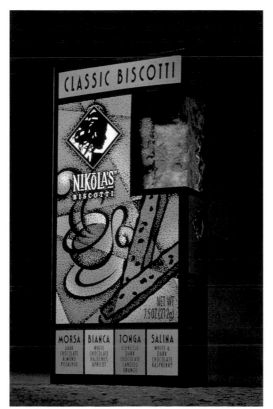

creative firm
COMPASS DESIGN
Minneapolis, Minnesota
designers
MITCHELL LINDGREN,
TOM ARTHUR,
RICH McGOWEN
client
NIKOLA'S SPECIALTY FOODS

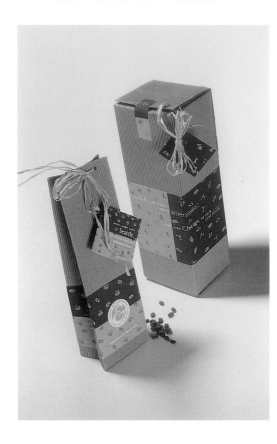

creative firm
   ROSS ADVERTISING
   Peoria, Illinois
creative directors
   SKIP DAMPIER, BRIAN BRUSH
designer
   BRIAN BRUSH
copywriter
   JOHN RUEBUSH
client
   ILLINOIS POWER

creative firm
   COMPASS DESIGN
   Minneapolis, Minnesota
designers
   MITCHELL LINDGREN,
   TOM ARTHUR,
   RICH McGOWEN
client
   AUNT GUSSIE'S COOKIES + CRACKERS

creative firm
   TANGRAM STRATEGIC DESIGN
   Novara, Italy
creative director, art director
   ENRICO SEMPI
designers
   ENRICO SEMPI, ANNA GRIHALDI
illustrator
   GUIDO ROSA
client
   STANDA

creative firm
ADKINS/BALCHUNAS
Providence, Rhode Island
creative director
JERRY BALCHUNAS
senior designer
MATTHEW FERNBERGER
client
BYBLOS

creative firm
THE WYANT SIMBOLI GROUP
Norwalk, Connecticut
creative director, designer
JULIA WYANT
illustrator
JULIE BERSON
client
PODS-OF-PLEASURE

creative firm
HORNALL ANDERSON DESIGN WORKS
Seattle, Washington
art director,
JANA NISHI
designers
JANA NISHI, SONJA MAX
client
STICKY FINGERS BAKERY

creative firm
  TANGRAM STRATEGIC DESIGN
  Novara, Italy
creative director
  ENRICO SEMPI
art directors
  ENRICO SEMPI, ANTONELLA TREVISAN
designer
  ANTONELLA TREVISAN
illustrator
  SERGIO QUARANTA
client
  E. VISMARA DI A. BIFFI ("CREME DI AUTORE")

creative firm
  TANGRAM STRATEGIC DESIGN
  Novara, Italy
creative director
  ENRICO SEMPI
art director, designer
  ANTONELLA TREVISAN
photographer
  STEFANACCI & CIARLO
client
  CONSILIA

creative firm
  PRIMO ANGELI INC.
  San Francisco, California
creative director
  CARLO PAGODA
designers
  HARUMI KUBO, SANDY RUSSELL, KOJI MIYAKE
client
  PARAMOUNT FARMS, INC.

creative firm
  SBG ENTERPRISE
  San Francisco, California
creative director
  MARK BERGMAN
illustrator
  JUSTIN CARROLL
photographer
  DAVID CAMPBELL
client
  DEL MONTE FOODS

creative firm
  BRUNAZZI & ASSOCIATI/IMAGE + COMMUNICATION
  Turin, Italy
creative director
  ANDREA BRUNAZZI
designer
  KATIA STABILE
client
  CRAI

creative firm
  RGB GRAPHIC DESIGN
  Rio De Janeiro, Brazil
designer
  MARIA LUIZA GONCALUES VEIGA BRITO
client
  DE MILLUS IND E COM. S.A.

creative firm
  SIBLEY PETEET DESIGN
  Dallas, Texas
designers
  DON SIBLEY, TOM HOUGH,
  DAVID BECK
client
  BELLAGIO HOTEL & CASINO

creative firm
  SAYLES GRAPHIC DESIGN
  Des Moines, Iowa
art director, illustrator
  JOHN SAYLES
client
  GIANNA ROSE "WATERCOLOUR"

creative firm
  BAILEY DESIGN GROUP, INC.
  Plymouth Meeting, Pennsylvania
creative director
  DAVID FIEDLER
designers
  LAUREN DUNOFF, TISHA ARMOUR,
  CHRISTIAN WILLIAMSON
client
  CULTIVATIONS

creative firm
  DISNEY DESIGN GROUP
  Lake Buena Vista, Florida
creative director
  MICHELE KEATING
designer
  THOMAS SCOTT
illustrator
  MICHAEL MOJHER
client
  DISNEY CRUISE LINE

creative firm
  PEARLFISHER
  London, England
creative director
  JONATHAN FORD
designer
  SARAH BUTLER
client
  SUPERDRUG STORES PLC

creative firm
  NAKATSUKA DAISUKE INC.
  Tokyo, Japan
designers
  SHU UEMURA, DAISUKE NAKATSUKA,
  KANNA NUMAJIRI
client
  SHU UEMURA COSMETICS INC.

creative firm
  NAKATSUKA DAISUKE INC.
  Tokyo, Japan
designers
  DAISUKE NAKATSUKA, JUNKO NAKATSUKA,
  TOMOKO KANOU, RYOKO YAGITA,
  KOICHIROU IKEDA, RYOKEI KURABA
client
  SHU UEMURA COSMETICS INC.

creative firm
 DESIGN GUYS
 MInneapolis, Minnesota
art director
 STEVEN SIKORA
designer
 JAY THEIGE
client
 BATH & BODY WORKS

creative firm
 LMS DESIGN
 Stamford, Connecticut
designers
 RICHARD SHEAR, RICK MAPES, ALEX WILLIAMS
client
 J.B. WILLIAMS

creative firm
 WALLACE CHURCH ASSOCIATES INC.
 New York, New York
creative director
 STAN CHURCH
designers
 WENDY CHURCH, PAULA BUNNY
client
 SCHROEDER & TREMAYNE

creative firm
NAKATSUKA DAISUKE INC.
Tokyo, Japan
designers
SHU UEMURA, DAISUKE NAKATSUKA,
JUNKO NAKATSUKA, TOM NAKATSUKA,
KANNA NUMAJIRI, OSAMU KUWATA
client
SHU UEMURA COSMETICS INC.

creative firm
SAYLES GRAPHIC DESIGN
Des Moines, Iowa
art director, illustrator
JOHN SAYLES
client
SUMER DISTRIBUTING

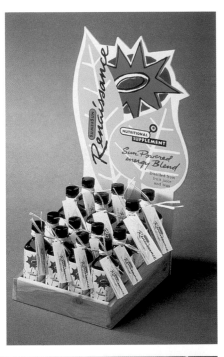

creative firm
SIBLEY PETEET DESIGN
Dallas, Texas
designer
JOY PRICE
client
SKIN CEUTICALS

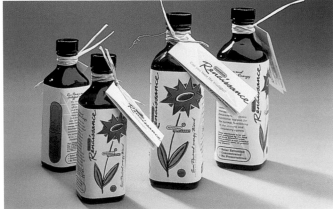

creative firm
  WALLACE CHURCH ASSOCIATES INC.
  New York, New York
creative director
  STAN CHURCH
designers
  WENDY CHURCH, DEREK SAMUEL
client
  INSTEAD

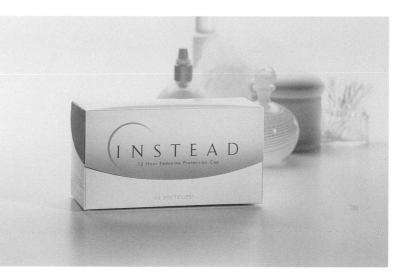

creative firm
  UKULELE DESIGN CONSULTANTS PTE LTD
  Singapore
design director
  KIM CHUN-WEI
designer
  LYNN LIM
client
  HIO SENG CO. PTE LTD

creative firm
  TANGRAM STRATEGIC DESIGN
  Novara, Italy
creative director, art director, designer
  ENRICO SEMPI
client
  GOLDEN LADY

creative firm
  INTERBRAND GERSTMAN + MEYERS
  New York, New York
creative director
  RAFAEL FELICIANO
client
  WHITEHALL ROBBINS

creative firm
  WALLACE CHURCH ASSOCIATES INC.
  New York, New York
creative director
  STAN CHURCH
designer
  JOE CUTICONE
illustrator
  LUCIAN TOMA
client
  GILLETTE

creative firm
  INTERBRAND GERSTMAN + MEYERS
  New York, New York
creative director
  CHRIS SANDERS
design director
  MICHAEL ENDY
senior designer
  MELISSA MULLIN
client
  PROCTOR & GAMBLE

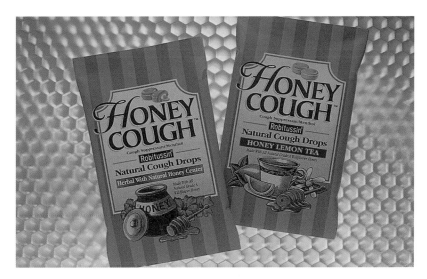

creative firm
INTERBRAND GERSTMAN + MEYERS
New York, New York
creative director
RAFAEL FELICIANO
client
WHITEHALL ROBINS

creative firm
INTERBRAND GERSTMAN + MEYERS
New York, New York
creative director
RAFAEL FELICIANO
client
LANDER COMPANY

creative firm
WALLACE CHURCH ASSOCIATES INC.
New York, New York
creative directors
STAN CHURCH, NIN GLAISTER
designer
PAULA BUNNY
client
TAYLOR MADE

creative firm
  INTERBRAND GERSTMAN + MEYERS
  New York, New York
creative directors
  JUAN CONCEPCION, MITCH GOTTLIEB
senior designer
  MELISSA MULLIN
client
  SCHERING PLOUGN

creative firm
  INTERBRAND GERSTMAN + MEYERS
  New York, New York
creative director
  JUAN CONCEPCION
client
  GENERAL MOTORS

creative firm
  INTERBRAND GERSTMAN + MEYERS
  New York, New York
creative director
  MITCH GOTTLIEB
client
  SHERWIN WILLIAMS

creative firm
  COMPASS DESIGN
  Minneapolis, Minnesota
designers
  MITCHELL LINDGREN, TOM ARTHUR, RICH McGOWEN
client
  TARGET STORES

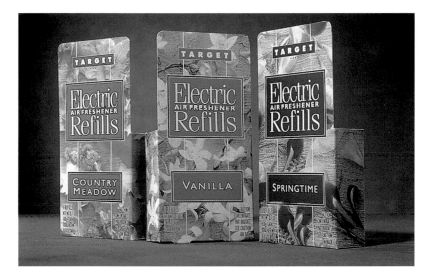

creative firm
  COMPASS DESIGN
  Minneapolis, Minnesota
designers
  MITCHELL LINDGREN, TOM ARTHUR, RICH McGOWEN
client
  TARGET STORES

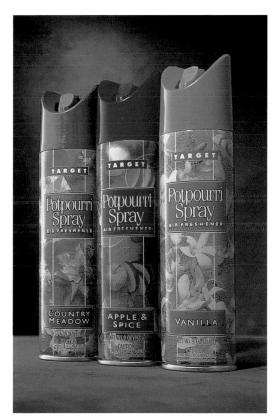

creative firm
  INTERBRAND GERSTMAN + MEYERS
  New York, New York
creative director
  RAFAEL FELICIANO
client
  MIRACLE GRO

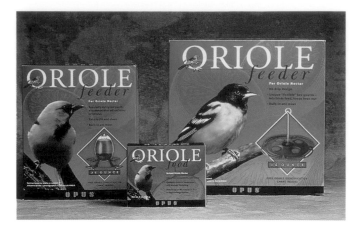

creative firm
PHILLIPS DESIGN GROUP
Boston, Massachusetts
creative director
STEVE PHILLIPS
senior designer
SUSAN LOGCHER
client
OPUS

creative firm
TANGRAM STRATEGIC DESIGN
Novara, Italy
creative director, art director
ENRICO SEMPI
designers
ENRICO SEMPI, ANTONELLA TREVISAN,
ANNA GRIMALDI
photographer
LA FOTOGRAPHIA DIE. MARI
client
BRICO

creative firm
ROSS ADVERTISING
Peoria, Illinois
executive creative director
SKIP DAMPIER
art directors
NICK JIBBEN, BRAD PASCUAL
copywriter
JOHN RUEBUSH
client
GRIDIRON

creative firm
TELMET DESIGN ASSOCIATES
Toronto, Ontario, Canada
designer
TILT TELMET
client
IONS WORLD CORPORATION

creative firm
THOMPSON & COMPANY
Memphis, Tennesee
creative director
TRACE HALLOWELL
art director
KENNY PATRICK
illustrator
ADAM McCAULEY
client
MEMPHIS REDBIRDS

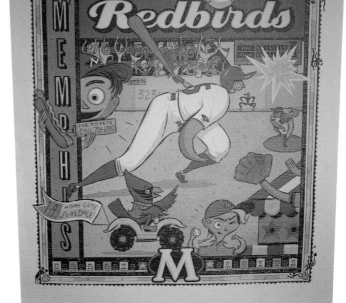

THE NEW ATTACK SUBMARINE. IT'S ALL COMING TOGETHER.

ELECTRIC BOAT CORPORATION
A GENERAL DYNAMICS COMPANY

creative firm
KEILER & COMPANY
Farmington, Connecticut
designer
JEFF LIN
client
ELECTRIC BOAT

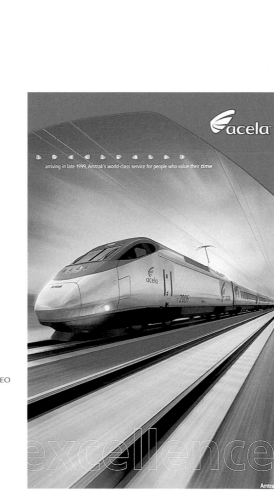

creative firm
OH&CO IN COLLABORATION WITH **IDEO**
New York, New York
creative director
BRENT OPPENHEIMER
strategy director
ROBIN HAUETER
design director
MARY ELLEN BUTTNER
copywriter
GINGER STRAND
client
AMTRAK

creative firm
  KIRK DESIGN
  Prescott, Arizona
designer
  MARY JO KIRK
client
  WHISKEY ROW MARATHON 1998

creative firm
  NAKATSUKA DAISUKE INC.
  Tokyo, Japan
designers
  DAISUKE NAKATSUKA, TOM NAKATSUKA,
  HIROMI YAMADA, SHOZO NAKAMURA
client
  YAMASA CORPORATION

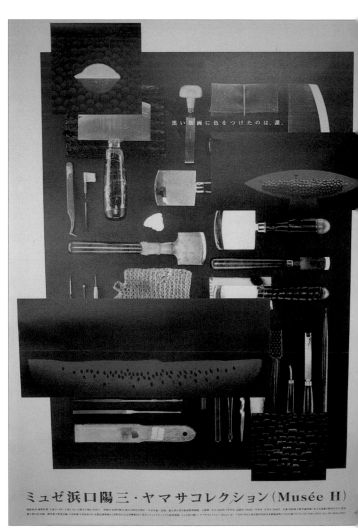

creative firm
 NESNADNY & SCHWARTZ
  Cleveland, Ohio
designer
 GREGORY OZNOWICH
client
 CLEVELAND ZOOLOGICAL SOCIETY

creative firm
 NIKE, INC.
  Beaverton, Oregon
designer
 JASON BACON
client
 NIKE EVENTS

creative firm
    NESNADNY & SCHWARTZ
    Cleveland, Ohio
designer
    TIMOTHY LACHINA
client
    ROCK AND ROLL HALL OF FAME MUSEUM

creative firm
    SAYLES GRAPHIC DESIGN
    Des Moines, Iowa
designer
    JOHN SAYLES
client
    ADVERTISING CLUB OF DELAWARE

creative firm
CREATIVE SERVICES
New York, New York
art director
GIULIO TURTURO
illustrator
MATT MAHURIN
client
SONY CLASSICAL

creative firm
BATEY ADS (PTE) LTD.
Singapore
designers
GARY KNIGHT, DARREN HOGAN
client
SINGAPORE ANTI-NARCOTICS ASSOCIATION

creative firm
  KEILER & COMPANY
  Farmington, Connecticut
designer
  JAMES PETTUS
client
  TOP FLITE GOLF

Study abroad at the Ichthus Hogeschool Rotterdam, University of Professional Education. Deadline for applications: April 7, 1998. Contact Jaye Crooks: CR100, tel: 410.837.6022, e-mail: jcrooks@ubmail.u

creative firm
  UNIVERSITY OF BALTIMORE
  Baltimore, Maryland
designers
  ED GOLD, DAN KRZEWICK
client
  UNIVERSITY OF BALTIMORE

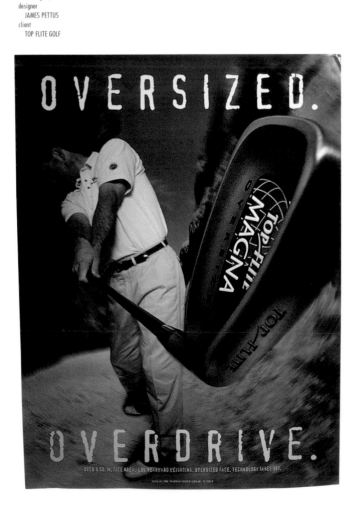

OVERSIZED.

OVERDRIVE.

OVER 5 SQ. IN. FACE AREA. LOW REARYARD WEIGHTING. OVERSIZED FACE. TECHNOLOGY TAKES OFF.

creative firm
THE RIORDON DESIGN GROUP INC.
Ontario, Canada
art director
RIC RIORDON
designer
GREER HUTCHISON
photography
DAVID GRAHAM WHITE
client
COMMUNITY FOUNDATION OF OAKVILLE

creative firm
AGNEW MOYER SMITH INC.
Pittsburgh, Pennsylvania
designers
JOHN SOTIRAKIS, GINA DATRES
client
PITTSBURGH DEPARTMENT OF CITY PLANNING

creative firm
CREATIVE SERVICES
New York, New York
art director, designer
GIULIO TURTURRO
client
SONY CLASSICAL

creative firm
GREG WALTERS DESIGN
Seattle, Washington
designers
GREG WALTERS, RICHARD HESS
client
SEATTLE DESIGN ASSOCIATION

creative firm
MITHOFF ADVERTISING INC.
El Paso, Texas
designer
CLIVE COCHRAN
illustrator
MELISSA GRIMES
client
GRAPHIC ARTS SOCIETY OF EL PASO
AND UNIVERSITY OF TEXAS AT EL PASO

creative firm
DESIGN MACHINE
New York, New York
creative director, art director, designer
ALEXANDER GELMAN
client
FIVE FIFTY FIVE GALLERY

creative firm
CAHAN & ASSOCIATES
San Francisco, California
designer
BOB DINETZ
client
WESTERN ART DIRECTORS CLUB

creative firm
ESTUDIO RAY
Phoenix, Arizona
art directors
CHRISTINE RAY, JOE RAY
designers
JOE RAY, LESLIE LINK
client
MARICOPA COMMUNITY COLLEGES

creative firm
  AFTER HOURS CREATIVE
  Phoenix, Arizona
client
  MARICOPA COMMUNITY COLLEGE DISTRICT

creative firm
  SAGMEISTER, INC.
  New York, New York
designer
  STEFAN SAGMEISTER
client
  AIGA

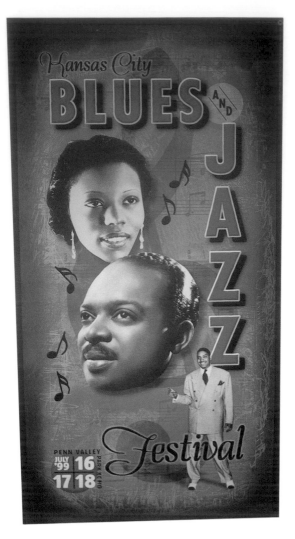

creative firm
CREATIVE SERVICES
New York, New York
art director, designer
GIULIO TURTURRO
photographer
EDWARD STEICHEN
client
SONY CLASSICAL

creative firm
MULLER + CO.
Kansas City, Missouri
creative director
JOHN MULLER
art director, designer
JANE HUSKEY
client
KANSAS CITY BLUES + JAZZ FESTIVAL

creative firm
  LEOPARD COMMUNICATIONS
  Boulder, Colorado
designers
  BRENDAN HEMP, RICH LOPEZ
client
  IBM PRINTING SYSTEMS COMPANY

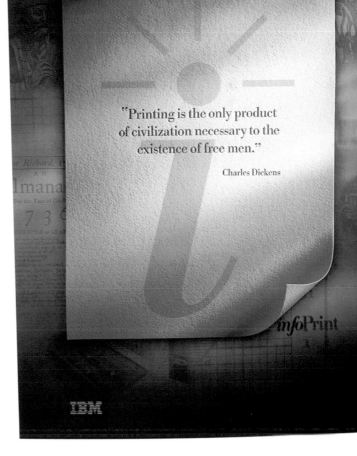

creative firm
  KEILER & COMPANY
  Farmington, Connecticut
designer
  JAMES PETTUS
client
  THEATERWORKS

creative firm
  SIBLEY PETEET DESIGN
  Dallas, Texas
designer
  DAVID BECK
photographer
  DUANE MICHAELS
client
  DUANE MICHAELS

creative firm
  TOM FOWLER, INC.
  Stamford, Connecticut
art director, designer, illustrator
  THOMAS G. FOWLER
client
  CONNECTICUT GRAND OPERA & ORCHESTRA

creative firm
ATLANTA COLLEGE OF ART
Atlanta, Georgia
designer
PETER WONG
client
ATLANTA COLLEGE OF ART

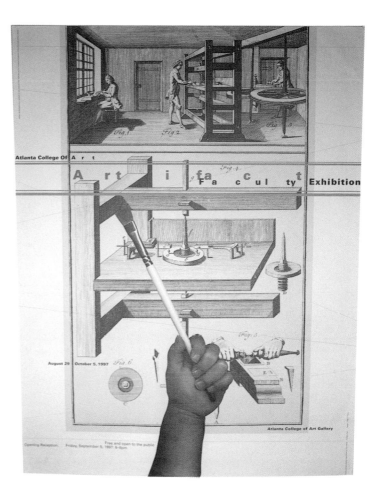

creative firm
SHIELDS DESIGN
Fresno, California
designer
CHARLES SHIELDS
photography
CAMERAD, INC.
client
FRESNO DESIGN COMMUNITY

creative firm
GARDNER DESIGN
Wichita, Kansas
art directors
BILL GARDNER, BRIAN MILLER
designer
BRIAN MILLER
client
KANSAS SPEECH-LANGUAGE-HEARING-ASSOCIATION

creative firm
FUSION ART INSTITUTE
Shizuoka-ken, Japan
art director
HYOMON FUMIHIKO ENOKIDO
designers
KOSHI OGAWA, HIDEAKI ENOKIDO
photographer
TORU KINOSHITA
client
SADOYA et Cie

creative firm
  GARDNER DESIGN
  Wichita, Kansas
art directors, designers
  BILL GARDNER, BRIAN MILLER
illustrator
  C.B. MORDAN
client
  SEDGWICK COUNTY ZOO

creative firm
  GARDNER DESIGN
  Wichita, Kansas
art director, designer
  BRIAN MILLER
client
  PRINTING HOUSE CRAFTSMAN

   MIRES DESIGN, INC.
   San Diego, California
designers
   SCOTT MIRES, DEBORAH HOM
illustrators
   SCOTT MIRES, DAVE ADEY, MIGUEL PEREZ
photographer
   CARL VANDERSCHUIT
client
   JABRA CORPORATION

creative firm
   MITHOFF ADVERTISING INC.
   El Paso, Texas
designer
   CLIVE COCHRAN
client
   EL PASO PRO-MUSICA

creative firm
    TOM FOWLER, INC.
        Stamford, Connecticut
art director, designer, illustrator
    THOMAS G. FOWLER
client
    CONNECTICUT GRAND OPERA & ORCHESTRA

creative firm
    WATT, ROOP & CO.
        Cleveland, Ohio
designers
    GREG OZNOWICH, JEFF PRUGH
client
    AIGA/CLEVELAND CHAPTER

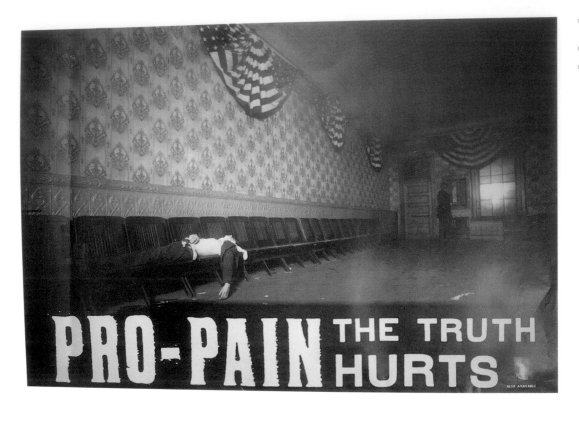

creative firm
SAGMEISTER INC.
New York, New York
designers
STEFAN SAGMEISTER, VERONICA OH
client
ENERGY RECORDS

creative firm
CAHAN & ASSOCIATES
San Francisco, California
designer
CRAIG CLARK
client
SAN FRANCISCO CREATIVE ALLIANCE

creative firm
  ASHER STUDIO
  Denver, Colorado
designers
  CONNIE ASHER, TRISH CUMMINGS
client
  MCI TELECOMMUNICATIONS

creative firm
  THE VISUAL MAFIA
  New York, New York
designers
  MATTHEW McGUINNESS, MORGAN SHEASBY,
  NICK BILTON, CHRIS GARVEY
client
  SOCIAL AWARENESS

creative firm
JOEL KATZ DESIGN ASSOCIATES
Philadelphia, Pennsylvania
creative director, designer
JOEL KATZ
client
CHEMICAL HERITAGE FOUNDATION

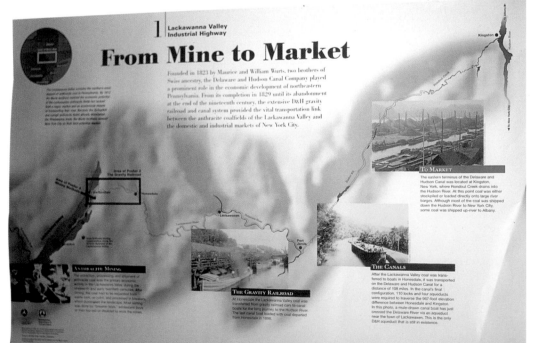

creative firm
JOEL KATZ DESIGN ASSOCIATES
Philadelphia, Pennsylvania
creative director
JOEL KATZ
designer, illustrator
DAVE SCHPOK
client
PENNSYLVANIA DEPARTMENT OF TRANSPORTATION

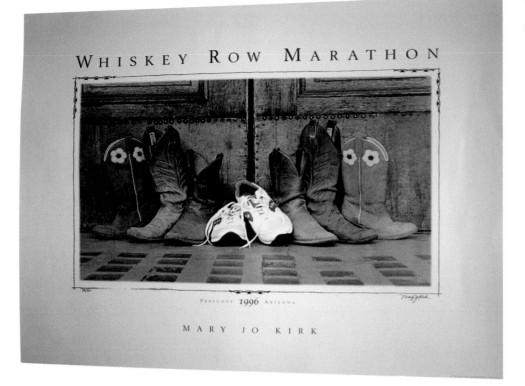

creative firm
  KIRK DESIGN
  Prescott, Arizona
designer
  MARY JO KIRK
client
  WHISKEY ROW MARATHON 1996

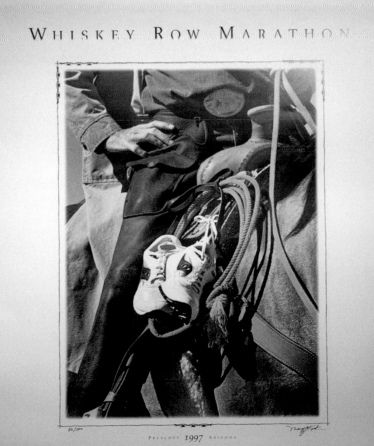

creative firm
  KIRK DESIGN
  Prescott, Arizona
designer
  MARY JO KIRK
client
  WHISKEY ROW MARATHON 1997

creative firm
POWELL TATE CREATIVE GROUP
Washington, D.C.
designers
LEE JENKINS, DAN CAVEY
client
NATIONAL PARK FOUNDATION

creative firm
SULLIVAN SCULLY DESIGN GROUP
Flagstaff, Arizona
designers
PJ NIDECKER, JULIE SULLIVAN
client
PETRIFIED FOREST NATIONAL PARK

creative firm
  MULLER + CO.
  Kansas City, Missouri
creative director
  JOHN MULLER
art director
  MARK BOTSFORD
designer
  JANE HUSKEY
illustrator
  MIKE REGNIER
copywriter
  ROB HOLMES
client
  MISSOURI DIVISION OF TOURISM

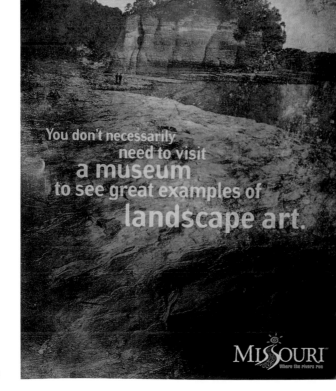

creative firm
  MULLER + CO.
  Kansas City, Missouri
creative director
  JOHN MULLER
art director
  MARK BOTSFORD
designer
  JANE HUSKEY
illustrator
  MIKE REGNIER
copywriter
  ROB HOLMES
client
  MISSOURI DIVISION OF TOURISM

277

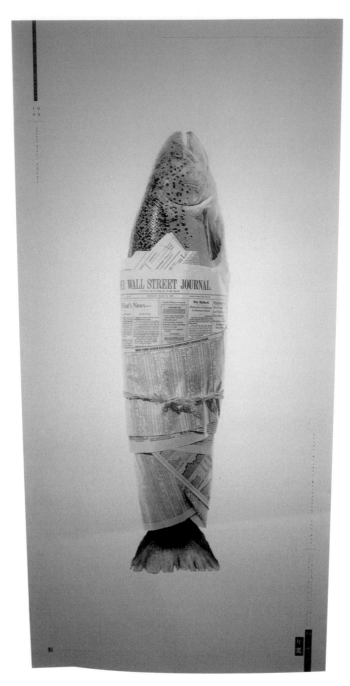

creative firm
   SQUIRES & COMPANY
   Dallas, Texas
designer
   BRANDON MURPHY
client
   SQUIRES & COMPANY

creative firm
   BBK STUDIO INC.
   Grand Rapids, Michigan
creative director
   KEVIN BUDELMANN
designer, typesetter
   ALISON POPP
photographer
   BILL LINDHOUT
calligrapher
   MATT RYZENGA
client
   BBK STUDIO INC.

creative firm
  KEITH WOOD PHOTOGRAPHY INC.
    Portland, Oregon
designers
  EISENBERG & ASSOCIATION
client
  KEITH WOOD PHOTOGRAPHY INC.

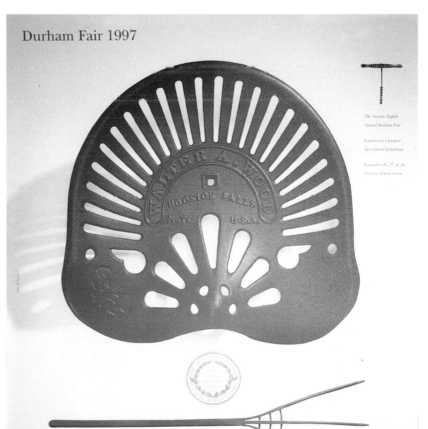

creative firm
  TED BERTZ GRAPHIC DESIGN, INC.
    Middletown, Connecticut
designers
  TED BERTZ, MARK TERRANOVA
photographers
  GLEN CURTIS, JOHN GIAMMATTEO
client
  THE DURHAM FAIR ASSOCIATION

creative firm
  WATT, ROOP + CO.
  Cleveland, Ohio
designer
  GREG OZNOWICH
client
  ROCK-N-ROLL HALL OF FAME GROUNDBREAKING

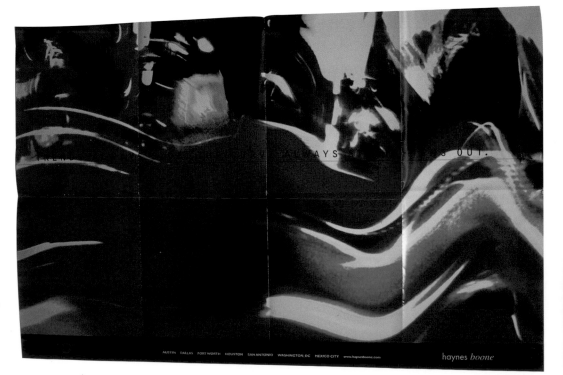

creative firm
  GREENFIELD/BELSER LTD
  Washington, D.C.
art director
  BURKEY BELSER
designer
  TOM CAMERON
client
  HAYNES AND BOONE

creative firm
  GRETEMAN GROUP
  Wichita, Kansas
creative director
  SONIA GRETEMAN
art directors
  SONIA GRETEMAN, JAMES STRANGE
designer
  JO QUILLIN
client
  WICHITA HUMANE SOCIETY

creative firm
  DESIGN TEAM ONE, INC.
  Cincinnati, Ohio
designer
  DAN BITTMAN
client
  THE CINCINNATI BALLET COMPANY

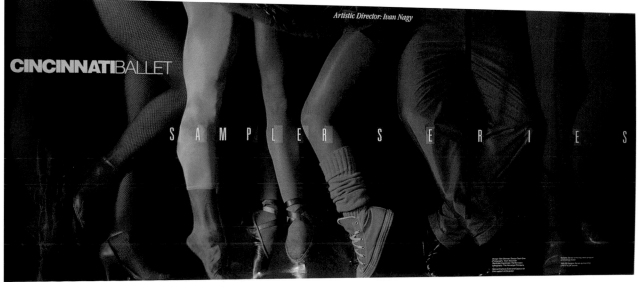

creative firm
   MULLER + CO.
      Kansas City, Missouri
creative director
   JOHN MULLER
art director, designer
   MARK VOSS
client
   KANSAS CITY BLUES & JAZZ FESTIVAL

creative firm
   THE PETERSON GROUP
      New York, New York
design director
   ALEX PENNINGTON
client
   FUJIFILM COMPUTER PRODUCTS

creative firm
FUSION ART INSTITUTE
Shizuoka-ken, Japan
art director
HYOMON FUMIHIKO ENOKIDO
designers
KOSHI OGAWA, HIDEAKI ENOKIDO
photographer
TORU KINOSHITA
client
JAGDA

creative firm
DISNEY DESIGN GROUP
Lake Buena Vista, Florida
creative director
MICHELE KEATING
art director
DAVID WHITAKER
designer, illustrator
ROBERT VANN
client
WALT DISNEY ATTRACTIONS MERCHANDISE

creative firm
  CAHAN & ASSOCIATES
  San Francisco, California
designer
  KEVIN ROBERSON
client
  SAN FRANCISCO CREATIVE ALLIANCE

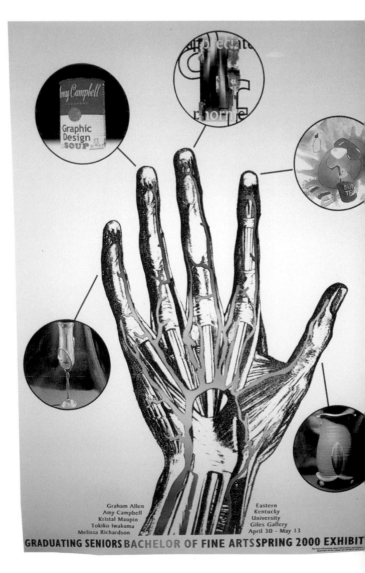

creative firm
  CLEVER LITTLE BOY DESIGNS
  Richmond, Kentucky
designers
  GRAHAM ALLEN, AMY CAMPBELL
client
  GILES GALLERY (EASTERN KENTUCKY UNIVERSITY)

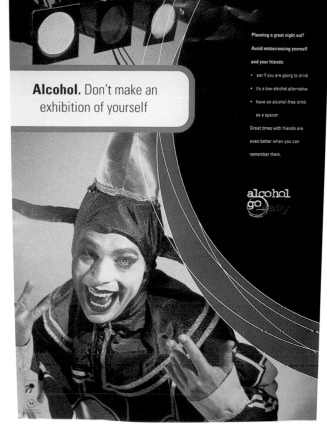

Alcohol. Don't make an exhibition of yourself

Planning a great night out?
Avoid embarrassing yourself
and your friends:

• eat if you are going to drink

• try a low-alcohol alternative

• have an alcohol-free drink
  as a spacer

Great times with friends are
even better when you can
remember them.

alcohol
go easy

creative firm
  BUTLER KEMP DESIGN
  North Adelaide, Australia
art director
  DEREK BUTLER
designers
  HELLEN KIPRIZLOGLOU, JULIE KEMP
photographer
  RICHARD LYONS
client
  DRUG & ALCOHOL SERVICES COUNCIL

creative firm
  THE ARTIME GROUP
  Pasadena, California
creative director
  HENRY ARTIME
art director
  DENVER MINNICH
designer
  LISA SARKISSIAN
client
  AMERICAN CANCER SOCIETY

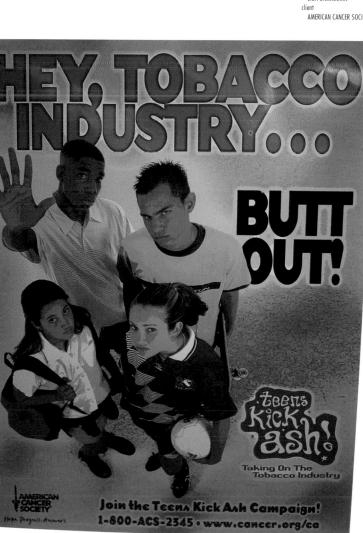

HEY, TOBACCO INDUSTRY...

BUTT OUT!

teens Kick ash!
Taking On The Tobacco Industry

AMERICAN CANCER SOCIETY

Join the Teens Kick Ash Campaign!
1-800-ACS-2345 • www.cancer.org/ca

creative firm
  KOR GROUP
  Boston, Massachusetts
designers
  ANNE CALLAHAN, CHRIS RICHARD
client
  HUNTINGTON THEATRE

creative firm
  MITHOFF ADVERTISING INC.
  El Paso, Texas
designer
  CLIVE COCHRAN
client
  UNIVERSITY OF TEXAS AT EL PASO

creative firm
KOR GROUP
Boston, Massachusetts
designers
ANNE CALLAHAN, JIM GIBSON
client
HUNTINGTON THEATRE

creative firm
FRANK BASEMAN DESIGN
Jenkintown, Pennsylvania
designer
FRANK BASEMAN
client
ZEITGEIST FILMS

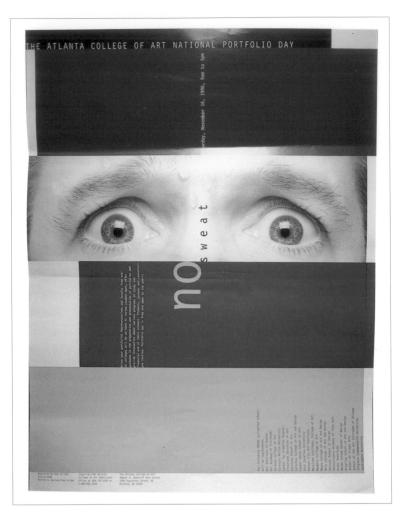

creative firm
ATLANTA COLLEGE OF ART
Atlanta, Georgia
designer
PETER WONG
concept
PETER WONG, MARK ROKFALUSI
client
ATLANTA COLLEGE OF ART

creative firm
ATLANTA COLLEGE OF ART
Atlanta, Georgia
designer
PETER WONG
design assistant
DOUGLAS EVANS
client
AMERICAN CENTER FOR DESIGN

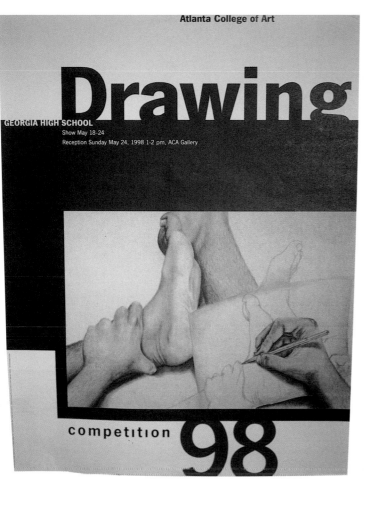

creative firm
  ATLANTA COLLEGE OF ART
  Atlanta, Georgia
art director
  PETER WONG
designer
  JASON LEHRMAN
client
  ATLANTA COLLEGE OF ART

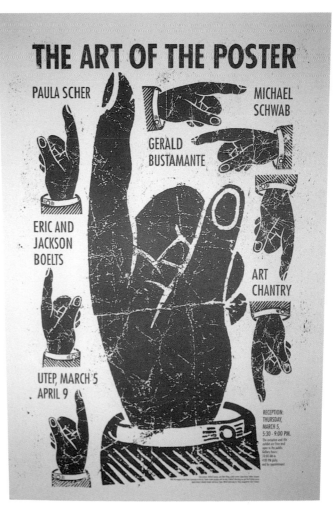

creative firm
  MITHOFF ADVERTISING INC.
  El Paso, Texas
designer
  CLIVE COCHRAN
client
  UNIVERSITY OF TEXAS AT EL PASO

creative firm
GREG WALTERS DESIGN
Seattle, Washington
designer
GREG WALTERS
client
PIONEER SQUARE BUSINESS IMPROVEMENT AREA

creative firm
GREG WALTERS DESIGN
Seattle, Washington
designer, illustrator
GREG WALTERS
client
PIONEER SQUARE BUSINESS IMPROVEMENT AREA

creative firm
DESIGN MACHINE
New York, New York
creative director, art director, designer
ALEXANDER GELMAN
client
GOLDEN BEE BIENNALE

creative firm
   KRISTINE HERRICK DESIGN
   Albany, New York
designer
   KRISTINE HERRICK
client
   TEMPLE UNIVERSITY SOCIOLOGY

creative firm
   NAKATSUKA DAISUKE INC.
   Tokyo, Japan
designers
   DAISUKE NAKATSUKA, TOM NAKATSUKA,
   HIROMI YAMADA, MARIKO ABE
client
   TOKAMACHI REGIONWIDE AREA

creative firm
  KO DESIGN INSTITUTE
  Tachikawa-shi, Japan
art director, designer
  KOSHI OGAWA
calligrapher
  TSUYOSHI RYU
client
  JAGDA, KOSHI OGAWA

creative firm
  KO DESIGN INSTITUTE
  Tachikawa-shi, Japan
art director, designer
  KOSHI OGAWA
calligrapher
  TSUYOSHI RYU
client
  JAGDA, KOSHI OGAWA

creative firm
  KO DESIGN INSTITUTE
  Tachikawa-shi, Japan
art director, designer
  KOSHI OGAWA
calligrapher
  TSUYOSHI RYU
client
  KOSHI OGAWA

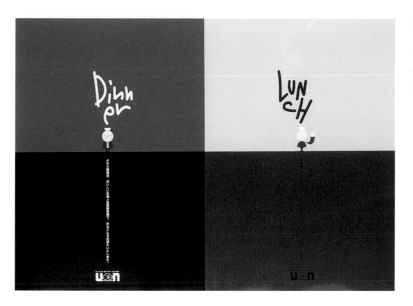

creative firm
  KO DESIGN INSTITUTE
  Tachikawa-shi, Japan
art director, designer
  KOSHI OGAWA
calligraphers
  TSUYOSHI RYU, SHIN OTANI
client
  HAJIME HIROSE

creative firm
  KO DESIGN INSTITUTE
  Tachikawa-shi, Japan
art director, designer
  KOSHI OGAWA
calligrapher
  TSUYOSHI RYU
client
  KOSHI OGAWA

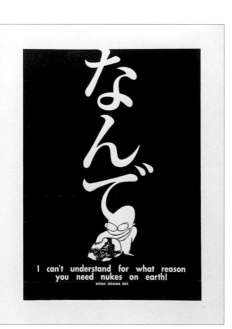

creative firm
  KO DESIGN INSTITUTE
  Tachikawa-shi, Japan
art director, designer
  KOSHI OGAWA
calligrapher
  TSUYOSHI RYU
client
  KOSHI OGAWA

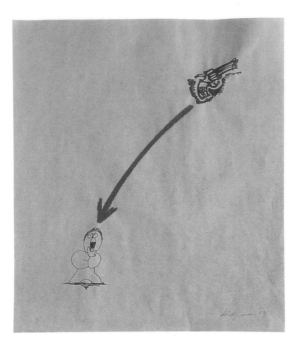

creative firm
KO DESIGN INSTITUTE
Tachikawa-shi, Japan
art director, designer
KOSHI OGAWA
client
KOSHI OGAWA

creative firm
KO DESIGN INSTITUTE
Tachikawa-shi, Japan
art director, designer
KOSHI OGAWA
client
KOSHI OGAWA

creative firm
SQUIRES & COMPANY
Dallas, Texas
designer
BRANDON MURPHY
client
INTERFAITH HOUSING COALITION

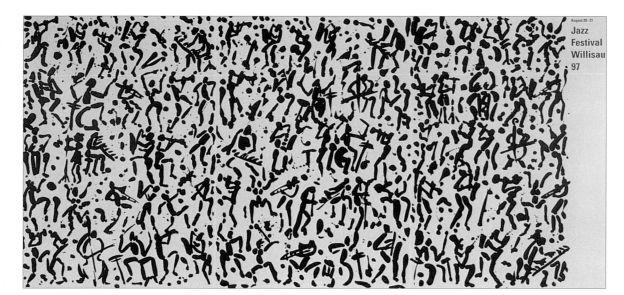

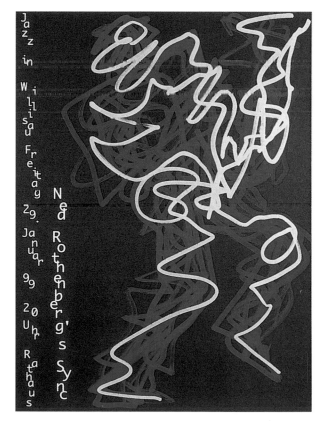

creative firm
  NIKLAUS TROXLER DESIGN
  Willisau, Switzerland
designer, illustrator, typographer
  NIKLAUS TROXLER
client
  INTERNATIONAL LOGO FESTIVAL BEIJING/CHINA

International Logo Festival 98   Beijing
Sept. 13 - 16 1998   Beijing Exhibition Center

The Capital Corporation Image Institution (CCII)

International Trademark Exhibition   International Trademark Festival Design Award   Seminar of "Corporation Image and Brand Image in the 21st Century"

主办 首都企业形象研究会   协办 国际商标中心   北京京华广告公司   鸣谢 北京国际艺苑皇冠假日饭店

35 Years of Graphic Revolution 1964-1999

creative firm
  NIKLAUS TROXLER DESIGN
  Willisau, Switzerland
designer, illustrator, typographer
  NIKLAUS TROXLER
client
  JAZZ IN WILLISAU/SWITZERLAND

creative firm
  MINALE TATTERSFIELD + PARTNERS
  Richmond, Surrey, United Kingdom
creative director
  MARCELLO MINALE
designer
  LEE NEWHAM
client
  MINALE TATTERSFIELD + PARTNERS

25. Jazz Festival
Willisau '99
Aug 26-29

creative firm
  TEAMWORK DESIGN LTD.
  Chai Wan, Hong Kong
design director
  GARY TAM
designers
  JOEL ONG, ALEX CHAN, IVY WONG
client
  NUANCE-WATSON (H.K) LTD.

creative firm
  BOLDRINI & FICCARDI
  Mendoza, Argentina
art director
  LEONARDO FICCARDI
designers
  VICTOR BOLDRINI, PABLO AGAPITO
photographers
  FIGUEWA & STALLARD
client
  INSTITUTO PROVINCIAL DE CULTURA

creative firm
  SAYLES GRAPHIC DESIGN
  Des Moines, Iowa
art director, illustrator
  JOHN SAYLES
client
  ADVERTISING PROFESSIONALS OF DES MOINES

REFINED SCULPTURAL STUNNING

watering can $24.99

tripod frame $12.99

$39.99 toaster

thermometer $19.99

teakettle $34.99

candleholder $16.99

cook's tools $3.99 each

ice bucket $29.99

clock $19.99

MICHAEL GRAVES DESIGN

World-renowned architect and designer Michael Graves has designed a line of products exclusively for Target. Each piece is an inspired balance of form and function, at once sensible and sublime. Michael Graves creates useful objects, which carry their own weight while lifting our spirits high. ⊙ TARGET

creative firm
  DESIGN GUYS
  Minneapolis, Minnesota
art director
  STEVEN SIKORA
designer
  ANNE PETERSON
client
  TARGET STORES

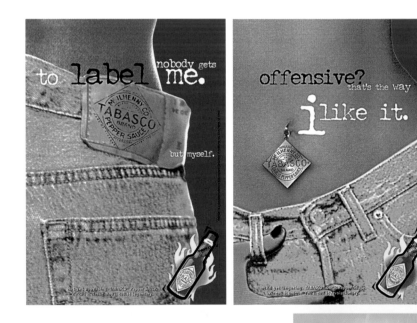

to **label** nobody gets me.

but myself.

offensive? that's the way i **like it.**

creative firm
  UKULELE DESIGN CONSULTANTS PTE LTD
  Singapore
design director
  KIM CHUN-WEI
designer
  LEE SHIN KEE
copywriter
  EVELYN TENG
client
  MCILHENNY COMPANY

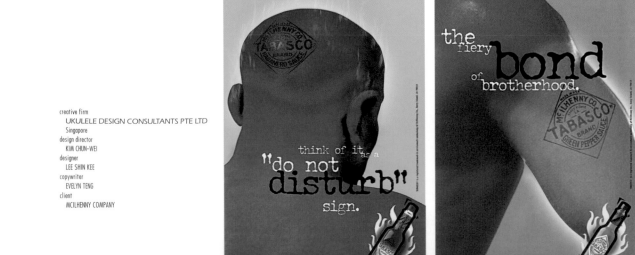

think of it as a "do not **disturb**" sign.

the fiery **bond** of brotherhood.

creative firm
McGAUGHY DESIGN
Falls Church, Virginia
designer
MALCOLM McGAUGHY
client
McGAUGHY DESIGN

creative firm
MITHOFF ADVERTISING INC
El Paso, Texas
designer
PETER FRAIRE
client
ACCUBRAPA CORPORATION

299

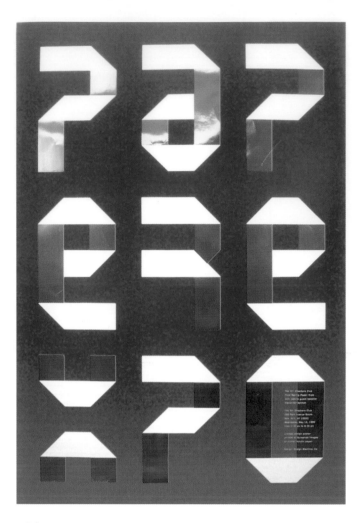

creative firm
  DESIGN MACHINE
  New York, New York
creative director
  ALEXANDER GELMAN
art directors, designers
  ALEXANDER GELMAN, KAOM SATRE
client
  THE ART DIRECTORS CLUB NY

creative firm
  MITHOFF ADVERTISING INC
  El Paso, Texas
designer
  CLIVE COCHRAN
client
  UNIVERSITY OF TEXAS AT EL PASO

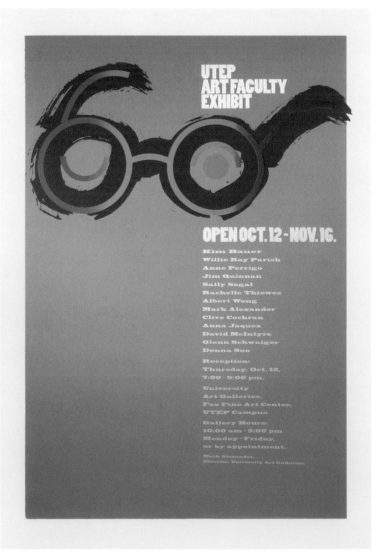

creative firm
   SAYLES GRAPHIC DESIGN
   Des Moines, Iowa
art director, illustrator
   JOHN SAYLES
client
   HOECHST MARION ROUSSEL "2000 EXCELLENCE IN LEADERSHIP"

creative firm
   GREG WALTERS DESIGN
   Seattle, Washington
designer
   GREG WALTERS
illustrator
   ADAM ROGERS
client
   PIONEER SQUARE PUB CLUB

creative firm
SAYLES GRAPHIC DESIGN
Des Moines, Iowa
art director, illustrator
JOHN SAYLES
client
SAYLES GRAPHIC DESIGN

creative firm
SAYLES GRAPHIC DESIGN
Des Moines, Iowa
art director, illustrator
JOHN SAYLES
client
SAYLES GRAPHIC DESIGN

creative firm
 JLN DESIGN
  Eugene, Oregon
art director
 JERRIL NILSON
designers
 JERRIL NILSON, LYNN MARX
photographer
 KENT PETERSON
client
 EUGENE BALLET COMPANY

creative firm
 RGD
  Denver, Colorado
art director
 RICK GRIFFITH
designer
 JUSTIN DOMINGUEZ
client
 MICHAEL D. ROSS, MILLER THEATRE, NY

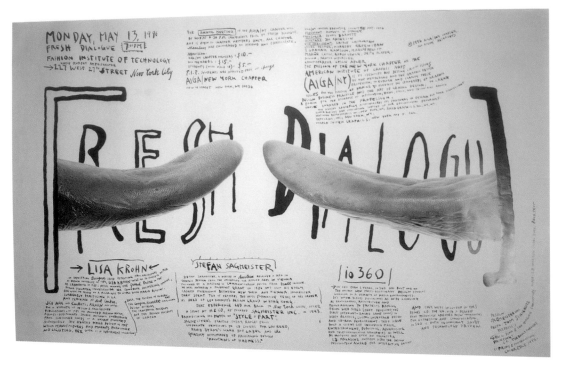

creative firm
SAGMEISTER INC.
New York, New York
designer
STEFAN SAGMEISTER
client
AIGA NEW YORK

creative firm
CLEVER LITTLE BOY DESIGNS
Richmond, Kentucky
creative director, designer
GRAHAM ALLEN
client
GILES GALLERY (EASTERN KENTUCKY UNIVERSITY)

creative firm
  ATLANTA COLLEGE OF ART
  Atlanta, Georgia
designer
  RICHARD MELLOR
client
  ATLANTA COLLEGE OF ART

creative firm
  ARLYN EVE SIMON
  Santa Fe, New Mexico
designer
  ARLYN EVE SIMON
client
  DEPARTMENT OF FILM/VIDEO AT OHIO UNIVERSITY

creative firm
  ROSS ADVERTISING
  Peoria, Illinois
creative directors
  SKIP DAMPIER, BRIAN BRUSH,
  KEVIN CARROLL
designer
  BRIAN BRUSH
production art
  EDEN SCHWINDENHAMMER
copywriter
  KEVIN CARROLL
client
  STRACK & VAN TIL

creative firm
  ROSS ADVERTISING
  Peoria, Illinois
executive creative director
  SKIP DAMPIER
senior art director
  NICK JIBBEN
copywriter
  JOHN RUEBUSH
client
  STRACK & VAN TIL

creative firm
  ROSS ADVERTISING
  Peoria, Illinois
creative directors
  SKIP DAMPIER, BRIAN BRUSH,
  KEVIN CARROLL
designer
  BRIAN BRUSH
production art
  EDEN SCHWINDENHAMMER
copywriter
  KEVIN CARROLL
client
  STRACK & VAN TIL

creative firm
  MIRES DESIGN INC
  San Diego, California
designers
  SCOTT MIRES, MIGUEL PEREZ,
  NEILL ARCHER ROAN, LAURA CONNORS
illustrator
  MARK ULRIKSEN
client
  ARENA STAGE

creative firm
  MIRES DESIGN INC
  San Diego, California
designers
  SCOTT MIRES, MIGUEL PEREZ,
  NEILL ARCHER ROAN, LAURA CONNORS
illustrator
  MARK ULRIKSEN
client
  ARENA STAGE

creative firm
  MIRES DESIGN INC
  San Diego, California
designers
  SCOTT MIRES, MIGUEL PEREZ,
  NEILL ARCHER ROAN, LAURA CONNORS
illustrator
  JODY HEWGILL
client
  ARENA STAGE

creative firm
  ODEN
  Memphis, Tennessee
creative director
  BRET TERWILLEGER
designers
  BRET TERWILLEGER, JEFF BLANKENSHIP
copywriter
  KATIE PRICE
client
  INTERNATIONAL PAPER

creative firm
  A TO Z COMMUNICATIONS, INC.
  Pittsburgh, Pennsylvania
creative director
  ALAN BOARTS
senior graphic designer
  AIMEE LAZER
client
  PNC BANK

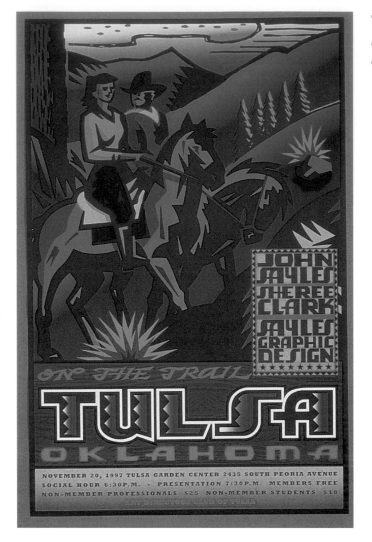

creative firm
SAYLES GRAPHIC DESIGN
Des Moines, Iowa
designer
JOHN SAYLES
client
CRAFTSMEN CLUB OF OMAHA,
ART DIRECTORS CLUB OF DENVER,
ART DIRECTORS ASSOCIATION OF TULSA

creative firm
SAYLES GRAPHIC DESIGN
Des Moines, Iowa
designer
JOHN SAYLES
client
CRAFTSMEN CLUB OF OMAHA,
ART DIRECTORS CLUB OF DENVER,
ART DIRECTORS ASSOCIATION OF TULSA

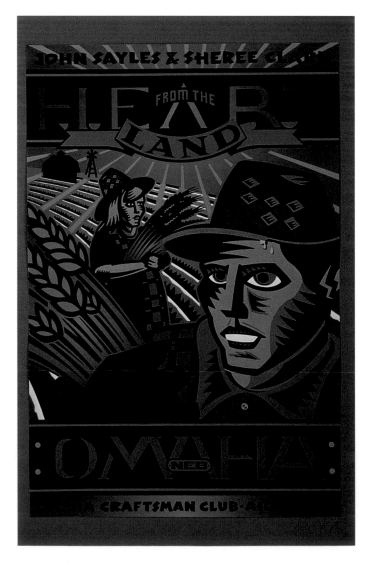

creative firm
  SAYLES GRAPHIC DESIGN
    Des Moines, Iowa
designer
  JOHN SAYLES
client
  CRAFTSMEN CLUB OF OMAHA,
  ART DIRECTORS CLUB OF DENVER,
  ART DIRECTORS ASSOCIATION OF TULSA

creative firm
  BALDWIN FILTERS
    Kearney, Nebraska
art director, designer
  MICHAEL HINTON
illustrator
  ROBERT CASE
client
  BALDWIN FILTERS

creative firm
FOSSIL DESIGN STUDIO
Richardson, Texas
senior art director
BILL MORGAN
product designer
ROBIN BOSWELL
client
FOSSIL

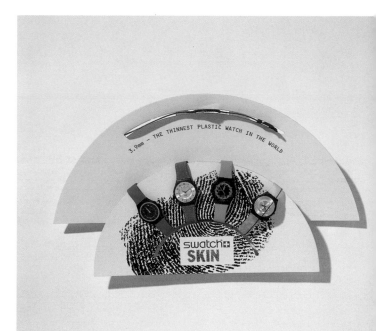

3.9mm — THE THINNEST PLASTIC WATCH IN THE WORLD

swatch+
SKIN

creative firm
RISE AGENCY, INC.
New York, New York
creative director
CAROLINA RODRIGUEZ
art director
ROBERT ZWASCHKA
client
SWATCH

creative firm
FOSSIL DESIGN STUDIO
Richardson, Texas
senior art director
BILL MORGAN
senior product designer
LINDA TSAI
client
FOSSIL

creative firm
DISNEY DESIGN GROUP
Lake Buena Vista, Florida
creative director
MICHELE KEATING
art director, designer
ALEX SANSO
client
WALT DISNEY ATTRACTIONS MERCHANDISE

creative firm
RISE AGENCY, INC.
New York, New York
creative director
CAROLINA RODRIGUEZ
art director
ROBERT ZWASCHKA
client
SWATCH

creative firm
DISNEY DESIGN GROUP
Lake Buena Vista, Florida
creative director
MICHELE KEATING
art director
JIM TRONOSKI
designer
MARK FRANKEL
illustrator
DAVID WILGUS
client
DISNEY CRUISE LINE

creative firm
DISNEY DESIGN GROUP
Lake Buena Vista, Florida
creative director
MICHELE KEATING
art director
DAVID WHITAKER
designer
MICHAEL COLE
client
WALT DISNEY ATTRACTIONS MERCHANDISE

creative firm
FOSSIL DESIGN STUDIO
Richardson, Texas
senior art director
BILL MORGAN
product designers
WILLIAM HO, BROOKE MUDD
client
FOSSIL

She's on the Web.

Fact is, Heartland GlobalNet can promote your business on the Internet quickly and painlessly, making it easier for customers everywhere to get exposed to your company.

creative firm
ROSS ADVERTISING
Peoria, Illinois
senior art director
NICK JIBBEN
copywriter
JOHN RUEBUSH
client
HEARTLAND GLOBAL NET

MAY THE
POWER
BE WITH YOU

www.hp.com.sg/hpvisualize

HP **VISUALIZE** WORKSTATIONS

HEWLETT PACKARD
Expanding Possibilities

creative firm
UKULELE DESIGN CONSULTANTS PTE LTD
Singapore
design director
KIM CHUN-WEI
designer
LYNN LIM
client
HEWLETT-PACKARD SINGAPORE

creative firm
  BBK STUDIO INC.
  Grand Rapids, Michigan
creative director, designer
  YANG KIM
copywriter
  THE GREYSTONE COMPANIES
client
  THE GREYSTONE COMPANIES

creative firm
  OH&CO IN COLLABORATION WITH IDEO
  New York, New York
creative director
  BRENT OPPENHEIMER
strategy director
  ROBIN HAUETER
design director
  MARY ELLEN BUTTNER
designer
  DAVID SHIELDS
client
  AMTRAK

creative firm
  WONG WONG BOYACK, INC.
  San Francisco, California
designers
  BEN WONG, MICHAEL FRANDY
illustrator
  BEN WONG
copywriters
  PENELOPE WONG, JANA BENDER, BEN WONG
client
  CISCO SYSTEMS, INC.

creative firm
    LARSEN DESIGN + INTERACTIVE
    Minneapolis, Minnesota
creative director
    PAUL WHARTON
designer
    TODD MANNES
production
    PAM BORGMAN
copywriter
    PAM POWELL
client
    WAUSAU PAPERS

creative firm
    AIRE DESIGN COMPANY
    Tucson, Arizona
creative director
    CATHARINE M. KIM
art director
    SHARI RYKOWSKI
client
    DESERT WHALE JOJOBA COMPANY

creative firm
    DESIGN GUYS
    Minneapolis, Minnesota
art director
    STEVEN SIKORA
designer
    DAWN SELG
client
    TARGET STORES

creative firm
TOM FOWLER, INC.
Stamford, Connecticut
art director, illustrator
THOMAS G. FOWLER
designers
THOMAS G. FOWLER, KARL S. MARUYAMA
client
CONNECTICUT GRAND OPERA & ORCHESTRA

creative firm
DESIGN MACHINE
New York, New York
creative director
ALEXANDER GELMAN
art directors, designers
ALEXANDER GELMAN, KAORU SATO
client
JANOU PAKTER INC.

creative firm
THE PETERSON GROUP
New York, New York
graphic designer
MAY LOUIE
client
FUJI FILM COMPUTER PRODUCTS

creative firm
MacVICAR DESIGN + COMM.
Arlington, Virginia
art director, designer
CATHY BROADWELL
client
INTER. BOTTLED WATER ASSOC.

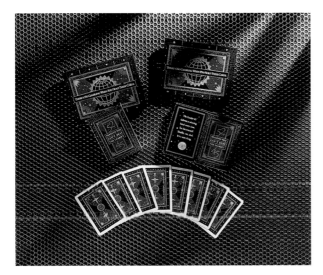

creative firm
GRETEMAN GROUP
Wichita, Kansas
creative director
SONIA GRETEMAN
art directors
SONIA GRETEMAN, JAMES STRANGE
designer
JAMES STRANGE
client
LEARJET

creative firm
SAYLES GRAPHIC DESIGN
Des Moines, Iowa
art director, illustrator
JOHN SAYLES
client
HOECHST MARION ROUSSEL

creative firm
SAYLES GRAPHIC DESIGN
Des Moines, Iowa
art director, illustrator
JOHN SAYLES
client
1998 AMERICAN CANCER SOCIETY

creative firm
SHEILA HART DESIGN, INC.
Strongsville, Ohio
art director
SHEILA HART
client
MERGERSHOP, INC.

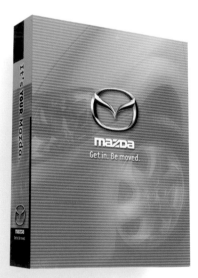

creative firm
THE RIORDON DESIGN GROUP
Oakville, Canada
art director
CLAUDE DUMOULIN
designer
DAN WHEATON
client
CARLSON MARKETING GROUP (MAZDA)

creative firm
  SQUARE ONE DESIGN
  Grand Rapids, Michigan
designers
  MIKE GORMAN, GRANT CARMICHAEL,
  JOHN TOTTEN, MARTIN SCHOENBORN
client
  HAWORTH

creative firm
  GILL FISHMAN ASSOCIATES, INC.
  Cambridge, Massachusetts
creative director
  GILL FISHMAN
designer
  ALICIA OZYJOWSKI
client
  SCHOOL OF THE MUSEUM OF FINE ARTS

creative firm
  A TO Z COMMUNICATIONS, INC.
  Pittsburgh, Pennsylvania
creative director
  ALAN BOARTS
senior graphic designer
  JOE TOMKO
client
  ALCOA

creative firm
  FROST DESIGN LTD
  London, England
creative director
  VINCE FROST
client
  PHOTONICA

creative firm
  GRETEMAN GROUP
  Wichita, Kansas
creative director
  SONIA GRETEMAN
art directors
  SONIA GRETEMAN, JAMES STRANGE
designer
  JAMES STRANGE
client
  COSTA RICA

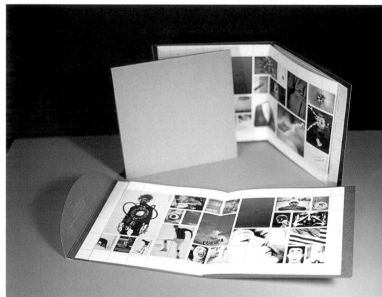

creative firm
  HORNALL ANDERSON DESIGN WORKS
  Seattle, Washington
art director, designer
  JACK ANDERSON
directors
  HEIDI FAVOUR, BRUCE BRANSON-MEYER, MARY HERMES
client
  MAHLUM ARCHITECTS

creative firm
  GRETEMAN GROUP
    Wichita, Kansas
creative director
  SONIA GRETEMAN
art directors, designers
  SONIA GRETEMAN, JAMES STRANGE
client
  HWS HORSE THERAPY

creative firm
  GRETEMAN GROUP
    Wichita, Kansas
creative director
  SONIA GRETEMAN
art directors
  SONIA GRETEMAN, JAMES STRANGE
designer
  JAMES STRANGE
client
  FLEXJET

creative firm
  JA DESIGN SOLUTIONS
    Coppell, Texas
designer
  JEAN ASHENFELTER
copywriter
  LINDA CAPRIOTTI
photography
  JACK WILSON
client
  GTE EVENT MARKETING

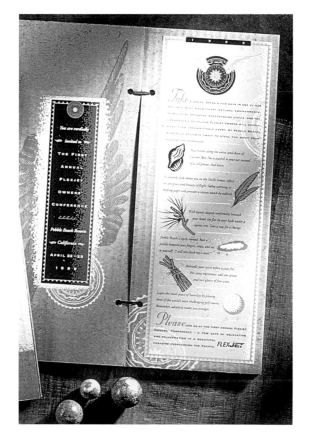

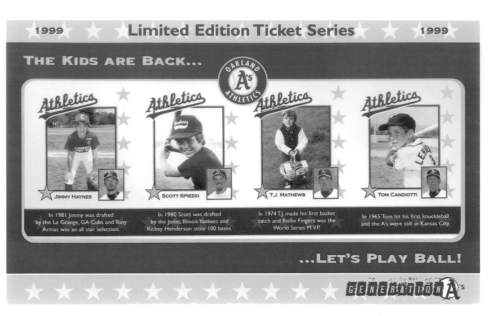

creative firm
STRATFORD DESIGN ASSOCIATES
Brisbane, California
designer
JOHN F. MORGAN
photography
MICHAEL ZAGARIS, MOM'S
client
OAKLAND ATHLETICS

creative firm
MULLER + CO.
Kansas City, Missouri
creative director
JOHN MULLER
art director, designer
MARK VOSS
client
KANSAS CITY BLUES & JAZZ FESTIVAL

creative firm
NBBJ GRAPHIC DESIGN
Seattle, Washington
designer
RODDY GRANT
client
INTERNATIONAL INTERIOR DESIGN ASSOC.

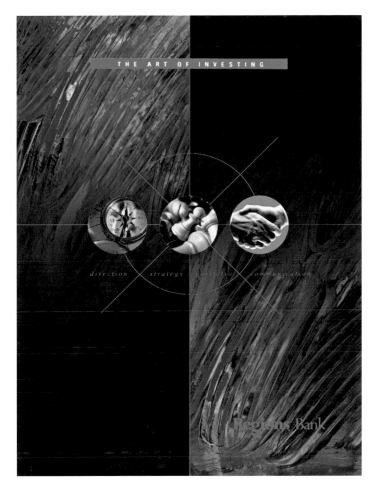

THE ART OF INVESTING

Regions Bank

creative firm
A TO Z COMMUNICATIONS, INC.
Pittsburgh, Pennsylvania
creative director
ALAN BOARTS
senior graphic designer
RICHARD HOOPER
client
FEDERATED INVESTORS REGIONS BANK CAPABILITIES BROCHURE

holiday A day on which custom dictates a halting of general business activity to commemorate or celebrate a particular event.

creative firm
SHOOK DESIGN GROUP, INC.
Charlotte, North Carolina
graphic designer
STEVE FENTON
client
HM WHITE SITE ARCHITECTS

creative firm
GRETEMAN GROUP
Wichita, Kansas
creative director
SONIA GRETEMAN
art director, designer
JAMES STRANGE
client
CANDLEWOOD

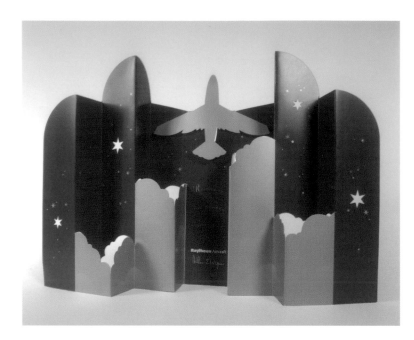

creative firm
GRETEMAN GROUP
Wichita, Kansas
creative director
SONIA GRETEMAN
art director
JAMES STRANGE
designer
CRAIG TOMSON
client
RAYTHEON

We're taking your whiz, we're checking it twice,
we're gonna find out who's naughty or nice.

Happy Holidays!
From the pee-ple at …

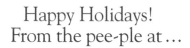

SECON
The Drug Screening Company

In honor of our customers and your contribution to our success, SECON has made a contribution to the Salvation Army.

creative firm
SIDES & ASSOCIATES
Lafayette, Louisiana
creative director
LARRY SIDES
designer
WILL BAILEY
copywriter
DARYL McGRATH
client
SECON

creative firm
ELLEN BRUSS DESIGN
Denver, Colorado
designer
G. CARR
client
UNISOURCE

Washington Mutual

The preferred two-color signature:
yellow square, blue "W" and type

PMS 130C
0c 30m 100y 0k
PMS 116U
0c 30m 100y 0k

PMS 280C
100c 70m 0y 10k
PMS 280U
100c 70m 0y 30k

A bright, clean
color palette
complements
the blue and gold
corporate signature.

Washington Mutual

The preferred reverse two-color
signature: blue background, yellow
square, blue "W", white type

PMS 362C
80c 0m 100y 0k
PMS 369U
60c 0m 90y 0k

PMS 199C
0c 100m 60y 0k
PMS 199U
0c 95m 65y 0k

PMS 021C
0c 69m 100y 0k
PMS 021U
94c 91m 0y 0k

PMS 2665C
94c 94m 0y 0k
Pantone Violet U
94c 91m 0y 0k

PMS 877C/U
metallic silver

PMS 2746C
100c 94m 0y 0k
PMS2746U
100c 87m 0y 0k

8 9

creative firm
HORNALL ANDERSON DESIGN WORKS
Seattle, Washington
art director
JOHN HORNALL
designers
JOHN HORNALL, KATHA DALTON, HOLLY CRAVEN
client
WASHINGTON MUTUAL

creative firm
THE RIORDON DESIGN GROUP INC.
Oakville, Canada
art director
RIC RIORDON
designer
SHARON PECE
client
TMN (THE MOVIE NETWORK)

creative firm
BUTLER KEMP DESIGN
North Adelaide, Australia
art director
DEREK BUTLER
designer
HELLEN KIPRIZLOGLOU
client
EDUCATION ADELAIDE

creative firm
  ODEN
    Memphis, Tennessee
creative director
  BRET TERWILLEGER
designer
  JEFF BLANKENSHIP
copywriters
  KATIE PRICE, SHEPERD SIMMONS
client
  BOYS & GIRLS CLUBS OF GREATER MEMPHIS

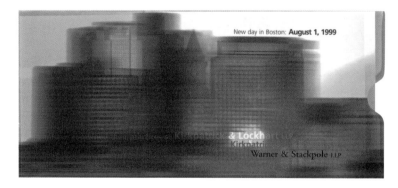

creative firm
  GREENFIELD/BELSER LTD
    Washington, D.C.
art director
  BURKEY BELSER
designer
  JEANETTE NUZUM
copywriter
  GEORGE KELL
client
  KILPATRICK LOCKHART

creative firm
  ID, INCORPORATED
    Portland, Oregon
designer
  KAREN WIPPICH
copywriter
  JON LEE
client
  BRIDGETOWN PRINTING

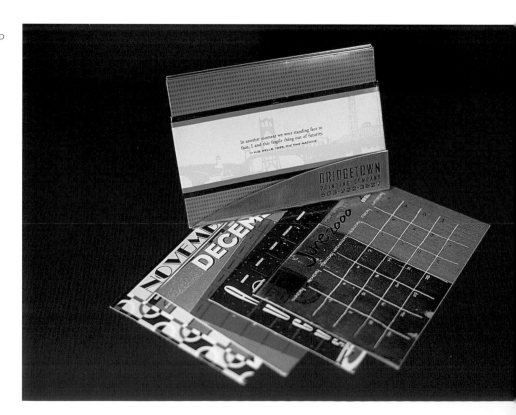

creative firm
 DOMINIC JANNAZZO DESIGN
  Indianapolis, Indiana
designer
 DOMINIC JANNAZO
client
 MELISSA KRISANDA PHOTOGRAPHY

creative firm
 AIRE DESIGN COMPANY
  Tucson, Arizona
creative director
 CATHARINE M. KIM
art director
 SHARI RYKOWSKI
client
 ARIZONA-SONORA DESERT MUSEUM

creative firm
 GARDNER DESIGN
  Wichita, Kansas
art director, designer, illustrator
 BRIAN MILLER
client
 PRINTMASTER

329

creative firm
  MULLER + CO.
  Kansas City, Missouri
creative director
  JOHN MULLER
art director, designer
  JANE HUSKEY
client
  KANSAS CITY BLUES & JAZZ FESTIVAL

creative firm
  TRICKETT & WEBB LTD
  London, England
designers
  LYNN TRICKETT, BRIAN WEBB, HEIDI LIGHTFOOT
paper engineer
  CORINA FLETCHER
client
  ROYAL SOCIETY OF ARTS

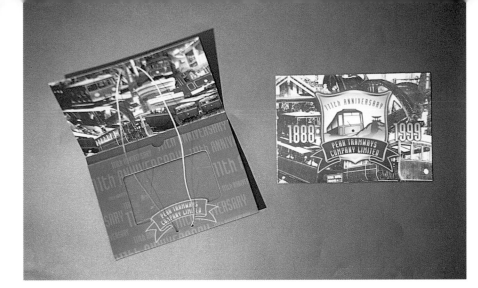

creative firm
UKULELE DESIGN
CONSULTANTS PTE LTD
Singapore
design director
KIM CHUN-WEI
designer
STEPHANIE TAN
client
HEWLETT-PACKARD SINGAPORE

creative firm
TEAMWORK DESIGN LTD.
Hong Kong, China
design director
GARY TAM
designers
JOEL ONG,
ALEX CHANG, IVY WONG
client
PEAK TRAMWAYS CO. LTD.

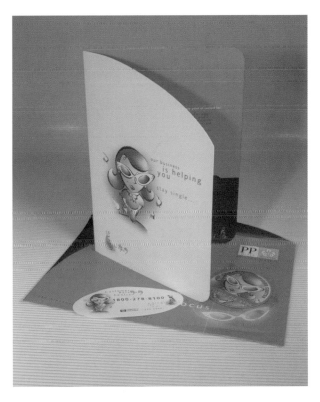

creative firm
SHOOK DESIGN GROUP, INC.
Charlotte, North Carolina
graphic designer
STEVE FENTON
client
THE SUNSET CLUB

creative firm
  ROBERT MEYERS DESIGN
    Fairlawn, Ohio
designer
  ROBERT MEYERS
client
  MARK & MYRNA MASON

creative firm
  JULIA TAM DESIGN
    Palos Verdes, California
client
  HOULIHAN LOKEY HOWARD & ZUKIM

Please join us
for an evening of

cocktails

and

dinner

on Friday, June 12th
at 7:30 p.m.
1129 Beechwood Blvd.

Myrna &
Mark

rsvp weekdays:
Trudy 261-1500

creative firm
  DISNEY DESIGN GROUP
    Lake Buena Vista
creative director
  MICHELE KEATING
designer
  DARREN WILSON
illustrator
  MICHAEL MOJHER
client
  WALT DISNEY WORLD SALES & MARKETING

creative firm
  CYD DESIGN
    Milwaukee, Wisconsin
art director, designer
  CORY DEWALT
photographer
  PORTRAITS ON PILGRIM,
  STENTEN ROWE STUDIOS
client
  YOUR WEDDING

creative firm
  McELVENEY + PALOZZI DESIGN GROUP, INC.
    Rochester, New York
creative director
  WILLIAM McELVENEY
art director
  EMPIRE FORSTER
designer
  GRETCHEN BYE
client
  EMPIRE FORSTER

creative firm
  BARBOUR DESIGN INC.
    New York, New York
art director
  AVA BARBOUR
designer
  MALI COHEN
copywriter
  JOE WOJTOLA
client
  ESPN MAGAZINE

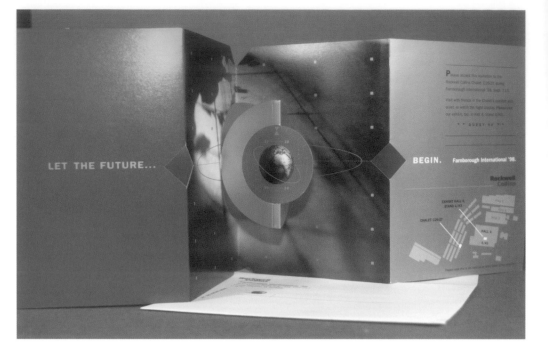

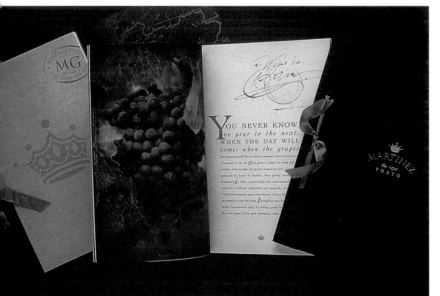

creative firm
GRETEMAN GROUP
Wichita, Kansas
creative director
SONIA GRETEMAN
art directors
SONIA GRETEMAN, JAMES STRANGE
designer
JAMES STRANGE
client
ROCKWELL COLLINS

creative firm
HORNALL ANDERSON DESIGN WORKS
Seattle, Washington
art directors
JACK ANDERSON, LISA CERVENY
designers
JACK ANDERSON, LISA CERVENY, MARY HERMES,
JANA NISHI, JANA WILSON ESSER, VIRGINIA LE
client
MOHAWK PAPER MILLS

creative firm
HORNALL ANDERSON DESIGN WORKS
Seattle, Washington
art directors
JACK ANDERSON, LISA CERVENY
designers
JACK ANDERSON, LISA CERVENY, HEIDI FAVOUR, MARY CHIN HUTCHISON
client
STIMSON LANE

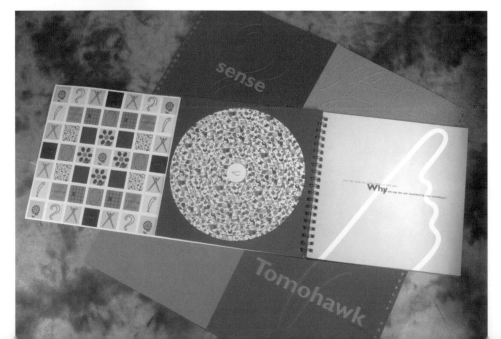

creative firm
GRAPHICULTURE
Minneapolis, Minnesota
designer
BETH MUELLER
client
CLICK MODELS

creative firm
TRICKETT & WEBB LTD
London, England
designers
LYNN TRICKETT, BRIAN WEBB,
KATJA THIELEN
illustrator
JEFF FISHER
client
TOUCHSTONE

creative firm
SACKETT DESIGN ASSOCIATES
San Francisco, California
creative director
MARK SACKETT
designers
JAMES SAKAMOTO, WENDY WOOD, GEORGE WHITE III
photographers
MICHAL VENERA, MARTIN ZEITMAN, CATHERINE BUCHANAN
client
SAN FRANCISCO INTERNATIONAL AIRPORT

creative firm
MEYERS DESIGN, INC.
Chicago, Illinois
designer
KEVIN MEYERS
client
CNA—E+S

creative firm
BELYEA
Seattle, Washington
art director
PATRICIA BELYEA
designer
RON LARS HANSEN
client
CRUISE WEST

creative firm
STRATFORD DESIGN ASSOCIATES
Brisbane, California
art director
TIM GEROULD
designer
SILVIA STEPHENSON
client
PACIFIC FARMS

creative firm
FIVE VISUAL COMMUNICATION & DESIGN
Westchester, Ohio
designers
RONDI TSCHOPP, DENNY FAGAN
client
CONTEMPORARY ARTS CENTER

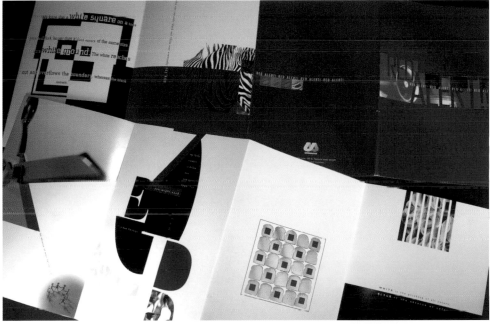

creative firm
5D STUDIO
Malibu, California
art director
JANE KOBAYASHI
designer
ANNE COATES
client
UNISOURCE + NEW OJI PAPERS

creative firm
BBK STUDIO INC.
Grand Rapids, Michigan
creative director
STEVE FRYKHOLM
designer
YANG KIM
typesetter
KIM LAPP
copywriter
CLARK MALCOLM
client
HERMAN MILLER INC.

337

creative firm
D4 CREATIVE GROUP
Philadelphia, Pennsylvania
art director
WICKY W. LEE
client
ANDY & SAMANTHA CHAN

creative firm
SAYLES GRAPHIC DESIGN
Des Moines, Iowa
art director, illustrator
JOHN SAYLES
client
CDW

creative firm
ROSS ADVERTISING
Peoria, Illinois
executive creative director
SKIP DAMPIER
art directors
NICK JIBBEN, BRAD PASCUAL
copywriter
JOHN RUEBUSH
client
GRIDIRON

creative firm
EMERSON, WAJDOWICZ STUDIOS
New York, New York
creative director
JUREK WAJDOWICZ
senior art director
LISA LaROCHELLE
client
DOMTAR, EDDY SPECIALTY PAPERS

creative firm
BBK STUDIO INC.
Grand Rapids, Michigan
creative director, designer, typesetter, copywriter
YANG KIM
illustrator
REBECCA GIBSON
client
THE ETHERIDGE COMPANY

creative firm
MULLER + COMPANY
Kansas City, Missouri
creative director
JOHN MULLER
art director
JEFF MILLER
designers
JEFF MILLER, BROHAN WATKINS
client
THE NELSON ATKINS MUSEUM OF ART

creative firm
  KOR GROUP
  Boston, Massachusetts
art directors
  ANNE CALLAHAN, KAREN DENDY
designers
  ANNE CALLAHAN, KAREN DENDY, JIM GIBSON
client
  FORRESTER RESEARCH

creative firm
  McGAUGHY DESIGN
  Falls Church, Virginia
designer
  MALCOLM McGAUGHY
client
  WRC NBC 4-TV

creative firm
  THE PETERSON GROUP
  New York, New York
design directors
  ALEX PENNINGTON, BOB CRUANAS
client
  FUJI FILM COMPUTER PRODUCTS

creative firm
THE PETERSON GROUP
Now York, Now York
design director
ALEX PENNINGTON
client
FUJI FILM COMPUTER PRODUCTS

creative firm
GRETEMAN GROUP
Wichita, Kansas
creative director
SONIA GRETEMAN
art directors
SONIA GRETEMAN, JAMES STRANGE
designers
JAMES STRANGE, SONIA GRETEMAN, JO QUILLIN
client
DUFFINS

creative firm
THE RIORDON DESIGN GROUP, INC.
Oakville, Canada
art director
RIC RIORDON
designer
SHIRLEY RIORDON
illustrator
DAN WHEATON
client
TMN

creative firm
  ROBERT MEYERS DESIGN
    Fairlawn, Ohio
designer
  ROBERT MEYERS
client
  CLARK & CHAMBERLIN

creative firm
  AERIAL
    San Francisco, California
designer
  TRACY MOON
client
  ALVA RESTAURANT, NY

creative firm
  DESIGN MACHINE
    New York, New York
creative director
  ALEXANDER GELMAN
art directors, designers
  ALEXANDER GELMAN, KAORU SATO
client
  THE ART DIRECTORS CLUB NY

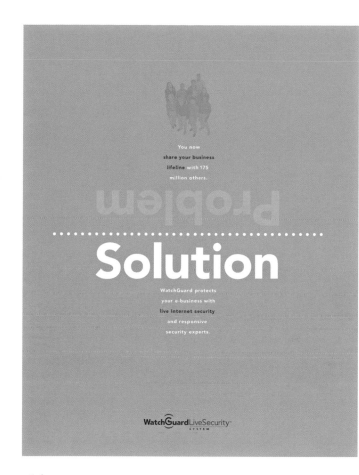

creative firm
GRETEMAN GROUP
Wichita, Kansas
creative director
SONIA GRETEMAN
art director
JAMES STRANGE
designer
CRAIG TOMSON
client
FAIR CHILD DORNIER

creative firm
HORNALL ANDERSON DESIGN WORKS
Seattle, Washington
art directors
JACK ANDERSON, LISA CERVENY
designers
LISA CERVENY, MARY HERMES, KATHY SAITO,
MICHEAL BRUGMAN, HOLLY CRAVEN, BELINDA BOWLING
client
WATCHGUARD

creative firm
CLEVER LITTLE BOY DESIGNS
Richmond, Kentucky
creative director, designer
GRAHAM ALLEN
client
GILES GALLERY
(EASTERN KENTUCKY UNIVERSITY)

creative firm
  HORNALL ANDERSON DESIGN WORKS
  Seattle, Washington
art director
  JOHN HORNALL
designers
  JOHN HORNALL, JULIE LOCK,
  MARY CHIN HUTCHISON, MARY HERMES, DAVID BATES
client
  NEXTRx CORPORATION

creative firm
  SAYLES GRAPHIC DESIGN
  Des Moines, Iowa
art director, illustrator
  JOHN SAYLES
client
  NATIONAL SOCIETY OF FUND RAISING EXECUTIVES

creative firm
  JA DESIGN SOLUTIONS
  Coppell, Texas
editor
  PATRICIA McWILLIAMS-POWELL
designer
  JEAN ASHENFELTER
composition
  JON MOSIER
copywriter
  LINDA CAPRIOTTI
client
  GTE SUPPLY—LYNN HANDLEY

creative firm
STAN GELLMAN GRAPHIC DESIGN, INC.
St. Louis, Missouri
senior designer
MIKE DONOVAN
client
UNIVERSITY OF ILLINOIS FOUNDATION

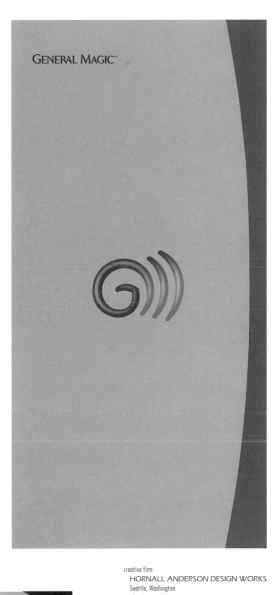

GENERAL MAGIC™

creative firm
AIRE DESIGN COMPANY
Tucson, Arizona
creative director
CATHARINE M. KIM
art director
SHARI RYKOWSKI
client
DESERT WHALE JOJOBA COMPANY

creative firm
HORNALL ANDERSON DESIGN WORKS
Seattle, Washington
art director
JACK ANDERSON
designers
JACK ANDERSON, JANA NISHI, MARY CHIN HUTCHISON
client
GENERAL MAGIC

345

creative firm
MULLER + CO.
Kansas City, Missouri
creative director
JOHN MULLER
designer
BROHAN WATKINS
client
KANSAS CITY ART INSTITUTE

creative firm
GREENFIELD/BELSER LTD
Washington, D.C.
art director
BURKEY BELSER
designers
BURKEY BELSER, ERIKA RITZER
client
LEGAL MARKETING ASSOCIATION

creative firm
5D STUDIO
Malibu, California
art director
JANE KOBAYASHI
designer
GEOFF LEDET
client
VECTA

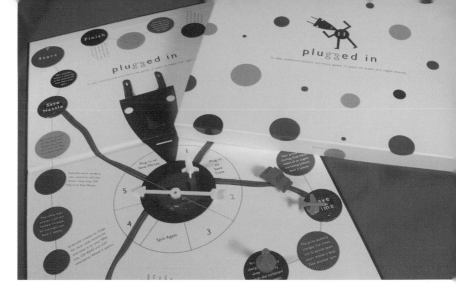

creative firm
**VIVA DOLAN COMMUNICATIONS
AND DESIGN, INC.**
Toronto, Canada
art director, designer, illustrator
FRANK VIVA
copywriter
DOUG DOLAN
client
GRENVILLE MANAGEMENT SERVICES

creative firm
GRETEMEAN GROUP
Wichita, Kansas
creative director
SONIA GRETEMAN
art directors
SONIA GRETEMAN, JAMES STRANGE
designer
JAMES STRANGE
client
ROCKWELL COLLINS

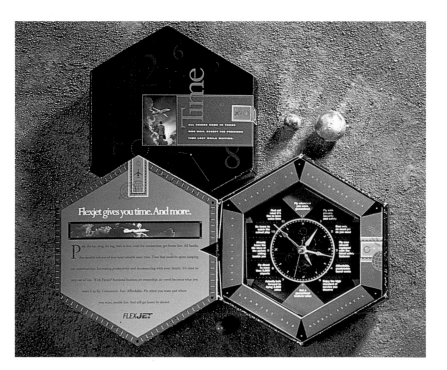

creative firm
GRETEMAN GROUP
Wichita, Kansas
creative director
SONIA GRETEMAN
art directors, designers
SONIA GRETEMAN, JAMES STRANGE
client
FLEXJET

347

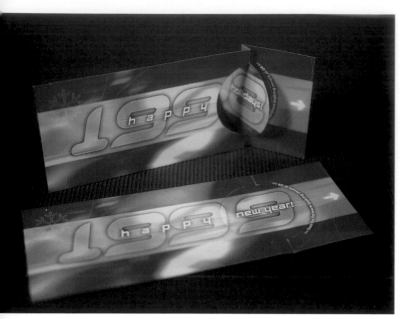

creative firm
D4 CREATIVE GROUP
Philadelphia, Pennsylvania
art director, illustrator
WICKY W. LEE
copywriter
JERRY SELBER
client
D4 CREATIVE GROUP

creative firm
WET PAPER BAG GRAPHIC DESIGN
Fort Worth, Texas
designer, art director, copywriter
LEWIS GLASER
client
WET PAPER BAG GRAPHIC DESIGN

creative firm
ESTUDIO RAY
Phoenix, Arizona
art directors
CHRISTINE RAY & JOE RAY
designers
CHRISTINE RAY, JOE RAY,
LESLIE LINK
illustrators
JOE RAY, FRANK YBARRA
client
ESTUDIO RAY

WHY LIE?
I NEED A HOUSE PAYMENT.

WILL DESIGN FOR CASH, CHECK OR MONEY ORDER.

Wet Paper Bag

CALL 817.257.7697

creative firm
    TOM FOWLER, INC.
    Stamford, Connecticut
art director
    THOMAS G. FOWLER
designer, copywriter
    ELIZABETH P. BALL
client
    TOM FOWLER, INC.

creative firm
    SAYLES GRAPHIC DESIGN
    Des Moines, Iowa
art director, illustrator
    JOHN SAYLES
client
    SAYLES GRAPHIC DESIGN

creative firm
    VIVA DOLAN COMMUNICATIONS
    AND DESIGN INC.
    Toronto, Canada
art director, designer, illustrator
    FRANK VIVA
photographer
    HILL PEPPARD
copywriter
    DOUG DOLAN
client
    VIVA DOLAN COMMUNICATIONS AND DESIGN INC.

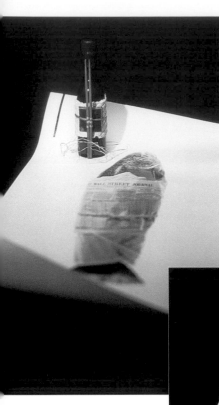

creative firm
  SQUIRES & COMPANY
  Dallas, Texas
designer
  CHRISTIE GROTHEIM
client
  SQUIRES & COMPANY

creative firm
  INDIUM
  New York, New York
director
  DAVID OGANDO
photographer
  JUDY JURACEK
client
  INDIUM

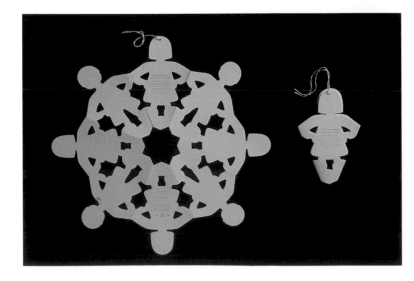

creative firm
  PEARLFISHER
  London, England
creative director
  JONATHAN FORD
designer
  KIM HARDY
client
  PEARLFISHER

creative firm
LIEBER BREWSTER DESIGN, INC.
New York, New York
art director
ANNA LIEBER
designer, photographer
ANTON GINZBERG
client
LIEBER BREWSTER DESIGN, INC.

creative firm
GEORGOPULOS DESIGN
West Chester, Pennsylvania
designer, illustrator, photographer,
programmer, editor, musical composer
JONATHAN GEORGOPULOS
client
GEORGOPULOS DESIGN

creative firm
SHOOK DESIGN GROUP, INC.
Charlotte, North Carolina
graphic designer
STEVE FENTON
client
SHOOK DESIGN GROUP, INC.

creative firm
   THREE FISH DESIGN
   Minneapolis, Minnesota
art director, designer
   CAROLINE VAALER
client
   THREE FISH DESIGN

creative firm
   McELVENEY + PALOZZI DESIGN GROUP, INC.
   Rochester, New York
creative directors
   STEVE PALOZZI, WILLIAM McELVENEY, JON WESTFALL
art directors
   MATT NOWICKI, LISA WILLIAMSON
client
   McELVENEY + PALOZZI DESIGN GROUP, INC.

creative firm
   MIRIELLO GRAFICO INC.
   San Diego, California
designers
   MICHELLE ARANDA, MAXIMO ESCOBEDO,
   CHRIS KEENEY, LISA KAPLAN, LIZ BERNAL,
   MAUREEN WOOD
client
   MIRIELLO GRAFICO INC.

creative firm
KOR GROUP
Boston, Massachusetts
concept, designers, copywriters
ANNE CALLAHAN, KAREN DENDY,
MB SAWYER, JIM GIBSON,
BRIAN ACEVEDO, NICOLE GENDRON
client
KOR GROUP

creative firm
A TO Z COMMUNICATIONS, INC.
Pittsburgh, Pennsylvania
creative directors
ALAN BOARTS, GOLDIE OSTROW
graphic designers
VONNIE HORNBURG, CHERYL RODER-QUILL
copywriter
ANN HORNAK
client
A TO Z COMMUNICATIONS, INC.

creative firm
AERIAL
San Francisco, California
designer
TRACY MOON
photographer
R.J. MUNA
client
AERIAL VISUAL IDENTITY DESIGN

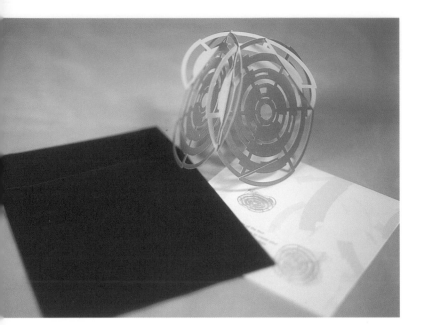

creative firm
O&J DESIGN INC.
New York, New York
art director
ANDRZEJ J. OLEJNICZAK
designer
LIA CAMARA MARISCAL
client
O&J DESIGN INC.

creative firm
30SIXTY DESIGN, INC.
Los Angeles, California
creative director
HENRY VIZCARRA
art director, designer, illustrator
PÄR LARSSON
client
30SIXTY DESIGN, INC.

creative firm
GRETEMAN GROUP
Wichita, Kansas
creative director, art director
SONIA GRETEMAN
designer
JAMES STRANGE
client
GRETEMAN GROUP

creative firm
  MIKE QUON/DESIGNATION
  New York, New York
designer
  MIKE QUON
client
  MIKE QUON/DESIGNATION

creative firm
  GRAHAM ALLEN
  Richmond, Kentucky
designer
  GRAHAM ALLEN
client
  GRAHAM ALLEN

creative firm
  SPENCER ZAHN & ASSOCIATES
  Philadelphia, Pennsylvania
creative director
  SPENCER ZAHN
designers
  JOSEPH McCARTHY, ED McHUGH
client
  SPENCER ZAHN & ASSOCIATES

creative firm
BELYEA
Seattle, Washington
art director, copywriter
PATRICIA BELYEA
designer
RON LARS HANSEN
photographer
JIM LINNA
client
BELYEA

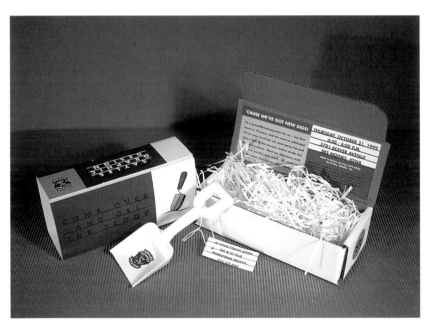

creative firm
SAYLES GRAPHIC DESIGN
Des Moines, Iowa
art director, illustrator
JOHN SAYLES
client
SAYLES GRAPHIC DESIGN

creative firm
D4 CREATIVE GROUP
Philadelphia, Pennsylvania
creative director, copywriter
DAVID LESSER
art director
WICKY W. LEE
client
D4 CREATIVE GROUP

creative firm
  GILL FISHMAN ASSOCIATES, INC.
  Cambridge, Massachusetts
creative director
  GILL FISHMAN
designer
  MICHAEL PERSONS
copywriter
  SUSAN CONWAY
client
  GILL FISHMAN ASSOCIATES, INC.

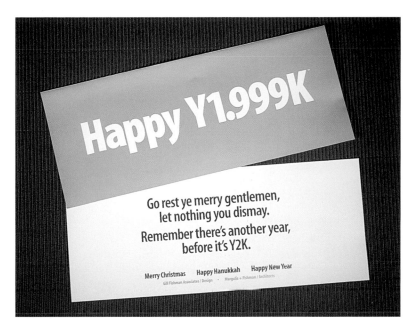

creative firm
  GARDNER DESIGN
  Wichita, Kansas
art director
  BILL GARDNER
designers
  BILL GARDNER, BRIAN MILLER
client
  BILL GARDNER

creative firm
  SWIMMER DESIGN ASSOCIATES
  Prospect Heights, Ilinois
creative director
  KRISTINE MEYER
client
  SWIMMER DESIGN ASSOCIATES

creative firm
 H2D
  Milwaukee, Wisconsin
creative director
 JOSEPH HAUSCH
art director
 ALLAN HAAS
client
 H2D

creative firm
 NBBJ GRAPHIC DESIGN
  Seattle, Washington
designer
 HEATHER HEFLIN
client
 NBBJ GRAPHIC DESIGN

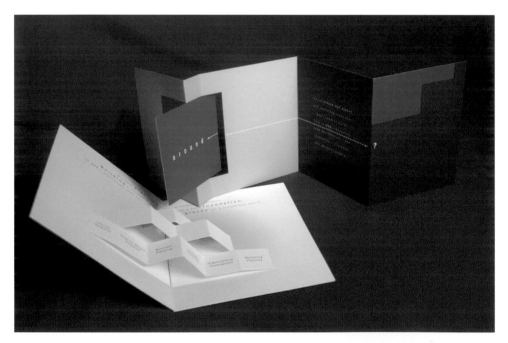

creative firm
 GRAPHICULTURE
  Minneapolis, Minnesota
designer
 CHERYL WATSON
photographer
 JOEL LARSON
client
 JOEL LARSON

creative firm
   GRAPHICULTURE
   Minneapolis, Minnesota
designer
   CHERYL WATSON
photographer
   JOEL LARSON
client
   JOEL LARSON

creative firm
   A TO Z COMMUNICATIONS, INC.
   Pittsburgh, Pennsylvania
creative directors
   ALAN BOARTS, AIMEE LAZER
senior graphic designer
   AIMEE LAZER
copywriters
   ANN HORNAK, DENISE BELIZAR
client
   A TO Z COMMUNICATIONS, INC.

creative firm
   ROSS ADVERTISING
   Peoria, Illinois
creative director
   WENDY BEHRENS
art directors
   JIM JONES, RANDY MARX
illustrator
   LISA LUCAS
copywriter
   JOHN RUEBUSH
client
   ROSS TRAINING AND MOTIVATION

359

creative firm
GRETEMAN GROUP
Wichita, Kansas
creative director, art director, illustrator
SONIA GRETEMAN
designer
JAMES STRANGE
client
GRETEMAN GROUP

creative firm
BBK STUDIO INC.
Grand Rapids, Michigan
creative director, designer
MICHAEL BARILE
illustrators
MICHAEL BARILE, ALLEN McKINNEY
client
BBK STUDIO INC.

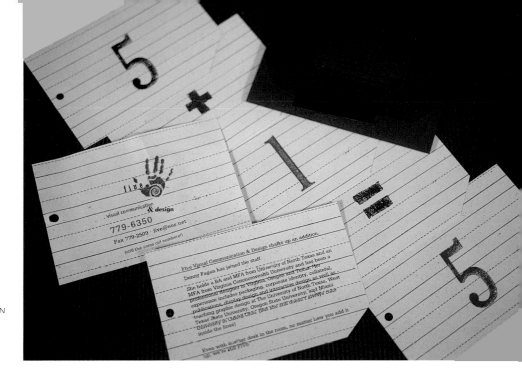

creative firm
  FIVE VISUAL COMMUNICATION & DESIGN
  West Chester, Ohio
designers
  DENNY FAGAN, RONDI TSCHOPP
client
  FIVE VISUAL COMMUNICATION & DESIGN

creative firm
  GRETEMAN GROUP
  Wichita, Kansas
creative director, art director
  SONIA GRETEMAN
designer
  JAMES STRANGE
client
  GRETEMAN GROUP

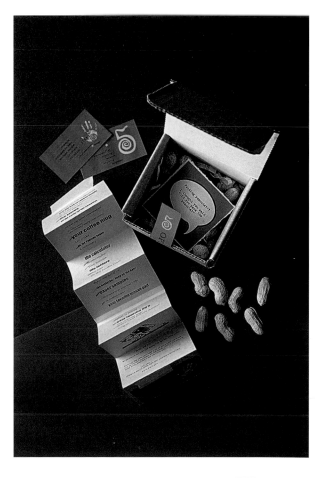

creative firm
  FIVE VISUAL COMMUNICATION & DESIGN
  West Chester, Ohio
designers
  RONDI TSCHOPP, DENNY FAGAN
client
  FIVE VISUAL COMMUNICATION & DESIGN

creative firm
  LAZYWOOD PRESS
  Houston, Texas
concept
  PAULA MURPHY
client
  MY TABLE MAGAZINE

creative firm
  THREE FISH DESIGN
  Minneapolis, Minnesota
art director, designer
  CAROLINE VAALER
production
  ART SERVE
client
  THREE FISH DESIGN

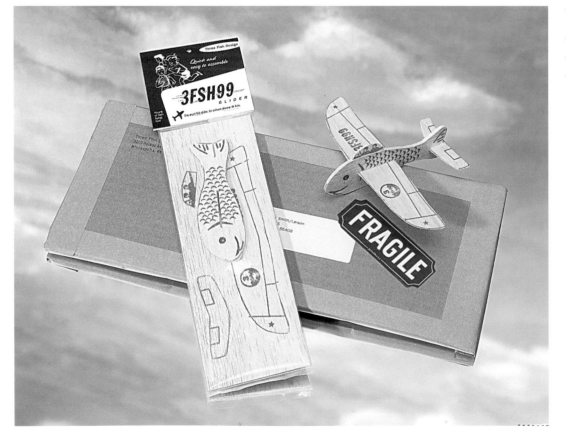

creative firm
NAKATSUKA DAISUKE INC.
Tokyo, Japan
designers
DAISUKE NAKATSUKA, MAYUMI INOUE, SATORU HAMAMURA,
TOMOKO KANOU, RYOKO YAGITA, GORO ARIZONA
client
SHU UEMURA COSMETICS INC.

creative firm
**BRUNAZZI & ASSOCIATI/
IMAGE + COMMUNICATION**
Turin, Italy
art director
GIOVANNI BRUNAZZI
client
BURGO

creative firm
NAKATSUKA DAISUKE INC.
Tokyo, Japan
designers
DAISUKE NAKATSUKA, FUMIYO KITAZUME, MASAKUNI FUJIKAKE
client
SHU UEMURA COSMETICS INC.

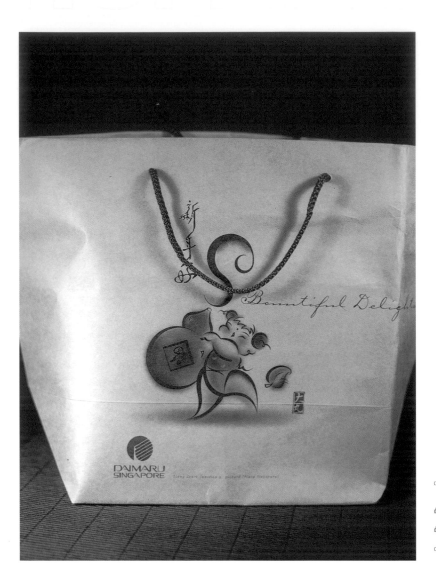

creative firm
UKULELE DESIGN CONSULTANTS PTE LTD
Singapore
design director
KIM CHUN-WEI
designer
LYNN LIM
client
DAIMARU SINGAPORE PTE LTD

creative firm
ADKINS/BALCHUNAS
Providence, Rhode Island
creative director, designer
JERRY BALCHUNAS
senior designer
MICHELLE PHANEUF
client
THE GROCERIA

creative firm
  SAYLES GRAPHIC DESIGN
  Des Moines, Iowa
art director, illustrator
  JOHN SAYLES
client
  GLAZED EXPRESSIONS

creative firm
  RGB DESIGN
  Rio De Janeiro, Brazil
designer
  MARIA LUIZA GONCALVES VEIGA BRITO,
  MARIA ANGELA LUTTERBACH
client
  MARIA FILÓ FASHION STORE

creative firm
  H2D
  Milwaukee, Wisconsin
creative director
  JOSEPH HAUSCH
client
  BRETT FAVRE

creative firm
  MIKE QUON/DESIGNATION
  New York, New York
designer
  MIKE QUON
client
  FIELDCREST—CANNON

creative firm
AERIAL
San Francisco, California
designers
TRACY MOON, STEPHANIE WEST
client
TRIBE PICTURES

creative firm
SQUIRES & COMPANY
Dallas, Texas
designer
CHRISTIE GROTHEIM
client
DEEP ELLUM DASH

367

creative firm
  MIKE QUON/DESIGNATION
  New York, New York
art director
  SCOTT FISHOFF
designer
  MIKE QUON
client
  CLAIROL

creative firm
  MIKE QUON/DESIGNATION
  New York, New York
art director
  SCOTT FISHOFF
designer
  MIKE QUON
client
  CLAIROL

creative firm
  H2D
  Milwaukee, Wisconsin
creative director
  JOSEPH HAUSCH
creative specialist
  TONY TABBERT
client
  RALPH MARLIN

creative firm
  MIKE QUON/DESIGNATION
  New York, New York
designer
  MIKE QUON
client
  CHATTAHOOCHEE COUNTRY CLUB

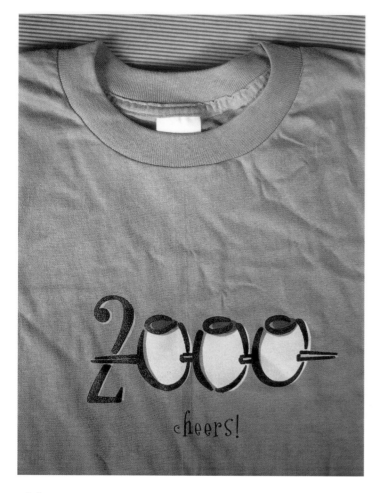

creative firm
AFTER HOURS CREATIVE
Phoenix, Arizona
client
MAX & LUCY

creative firm
MIKE QUON/DESIGNATION
New York, New York
designer
MIKE QUON
client
AMERICAN MUSEUM OF NATURAL HISTORY

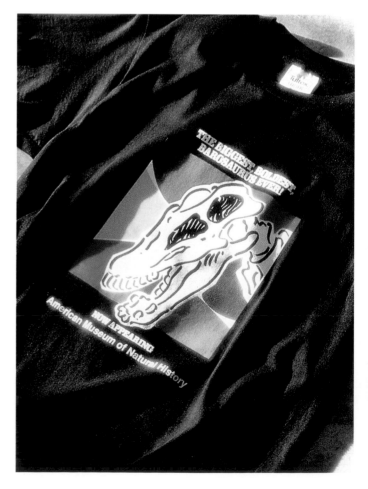

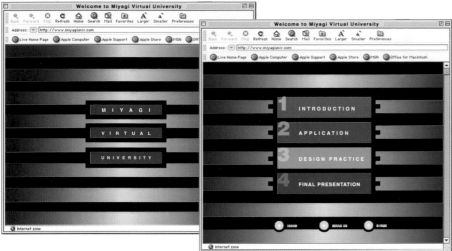

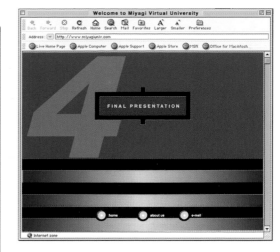

creative firm
SHIMOKOCHI/REEVES
Los Angeles, California
designer
NOBODY LISTED
BUT SOMETHING FOR YOU
TO MARK
client
ROR & MIYAGI

creative firm
WATERSDESIGN.COM
New York, New York
design director
KAYPEE SOH
producer
KIMBERLY LEASS
designer
SOO JIN YUM
content
SHARON TOLPIN
production artists
KIM NIECE, KARRIE FRYBERG
programmer
SETH ZALMAN
client
SOLBRIGHT

creative firm
BBK STUDIO INC.
Grand Rapids, Michigan
art director
KEVIN BUDELMANN
producer
LEAH WESTON
designers
KEVIN BUDELMANN, MIKE CARNEVALE, YANG KIM, ALISON POPP
programmers
MIKE CARNEVALE, LEAH WESTON, VON NEEL, SCOTT KRIEGER
client
HERMAN MILLER FOR THE HEALTHCARE

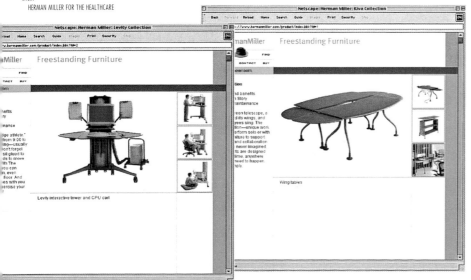

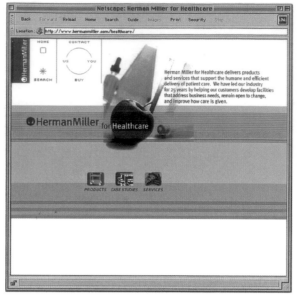

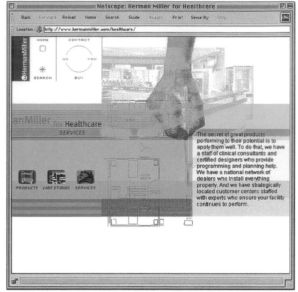

creative firm
BBK STUDIO INC.
Grand Rapids, Michigan
art director
KEVIN BUDELMANN
producer
LEAH WESTON
designers
KEVIN BUDELMANN, MIKE CARNEVALE,
YANG KIM, ALISON POPP
programmers
MIKE CARNEVALE, LEAH WESTON,
VON NEEL, SCOTT KRIEGER
client
HERMAN MILLER FOR THE HEALTHCARE

creative firm
WATERSDESIGN.COM
New York, New York
creative director
JOHN PANOLINI
producer
KIMBERLY LEASS
designer
YOSH OSHIMA
content
DIANA AMSTERDAM
programmer
NICOLE NEOPOLITAN
client
TRIBECA PRODUCTIONS

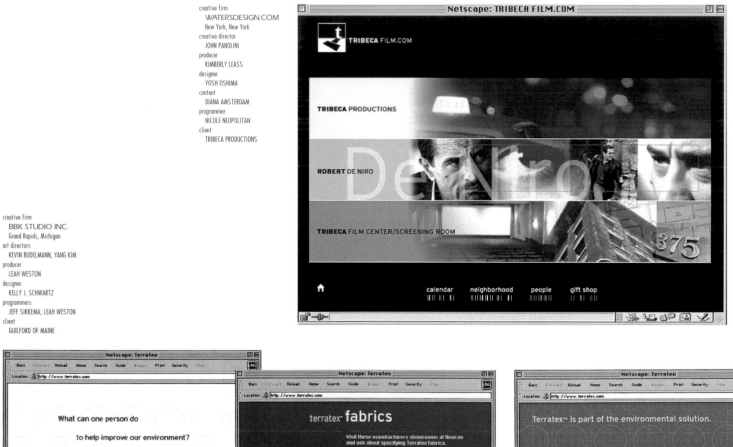

creative firm
BBK STUDIO INC.
Grand Rapids, Michigan
art directors
KEVIN BUDELMANN, YANG KIM
producer
LEAH WESTON
designer
KELLY J. SCHWARTZ
programmers
JEFF SIKKEMA, LEAH WESTON
client
GUILFORD OF MAINE

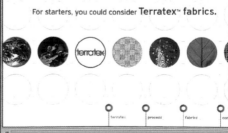

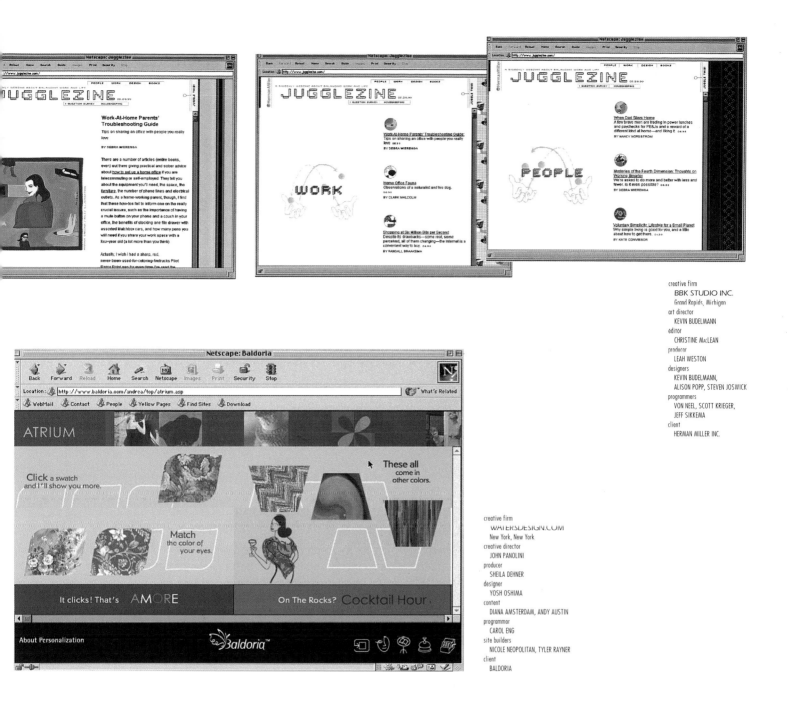

creative firm
  BBK STUDIO INC.
  Grand Rapids, Michigan
art director
  KEVIN BUDELMANN
editor
  CHRISTINE MacLEAN
producer
  LEAH WESTON
designers
  KEVIN BUDELMANN,
  ALISON POPP, STEVEN JOSWICK
programmers
  VON NEEL, SCOTT KRIEGER,
  JEFF SIKKEMA
client
  HERMAN MILLER INC.

creative firm
  WATERSDESIGN.COM
  New York, New York
creative director
  JOHN PANOLINI
producer
  SHEILA DEHNER
designer
  YOSH OSHIMA
content
  DIANA AMSTERDAM, ANDY AUSTIN
programmer
  CAROL ENG
site builders
  NICOLE NEOPOLITAN, TYLER RAYNER
client
  BALDORIA

creative firm
  BBK STUDIO INC.
  Grand Rapids, Michigan
art director
  KEVIN BUDELMANN
editor
  JULIE RIDL
producer
  LEAH WESTON
designers
  KEVIN BUDELMANN, MIKE CARNEVALE,
  YANG KIM, ALISON POPP,
  KELLY SCHWARTZ, MATT RYZENGA
programmers
  LEAH WESTON, JEFF SIKKEMA,
  MIKE CARNEVALE, SCOTT KRIEGER,
  VON NEEL
client
  HERMAN MILLER INC.

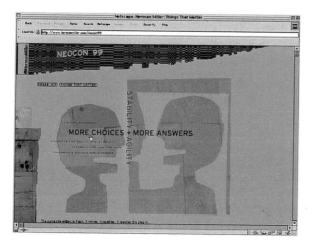

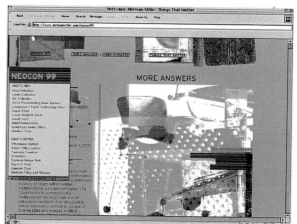

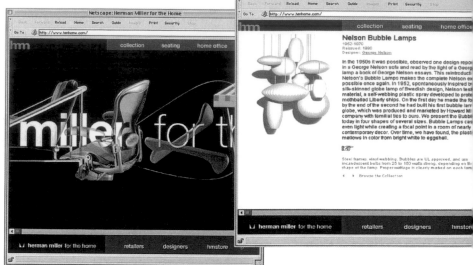

creative firm
  BBK STUDIO INC.
    Grand Rapids, Michigan
creative director
  KEVIN BUDELMANN
producer
  JEFF SIKKEMA
designers
  KEVIN BUDELMANN, ALISON POPP
copywriter
  JULIE RIDL
client
  HERMAN MILLER FOR THE HOME

creative firm
  WATERSDESIGN.COM
    New York, New York
design director
  KAYPEE SOH
producer
  KIMBERLY LEASS
designer
  HENRY KUO
content
  CHRISTOPHER COLLETTE
site builders
  SETH ZALMAN,
  TYLER RAYNER, HENRY KUO
client
  CLICKMAIL

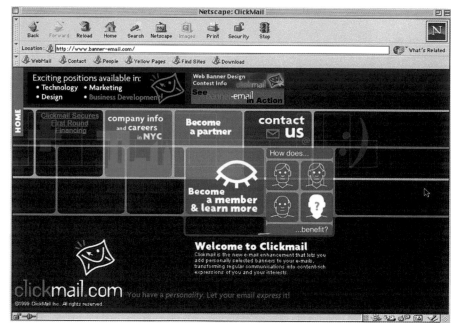

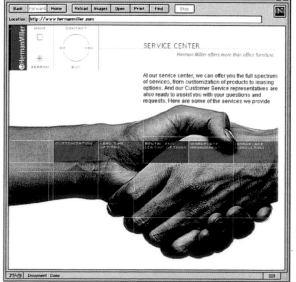

creative firm
  BBK STUDIO INC.
    Grand Rapids, Michigan
art director
  KEVIN BUDELMANN
editor
  JULIE RIDL
producer
  LEAH WESTON
designers
  KEVIN BUEDELMANN, YANG KIM,
  ALISON POPP, MIKE CARNEVALE,
  MATT RYZENGA
programmers
  LEAH WESTON, VON NEEL, JEFF SIKKEMA,
  SCOTT KRIEGER, MIKE CARNEVALE
client
  HERMAN MILLER INC.

creative firm
SAYLES GRAPHIC DESIGN
Des Moines, Iowa
art director, illustrator
JOHN SAYLES
client
MUSCULAR DYSTROPHY ASSOCIATION
"LAST DINNER ON THE TITANIC"

creative firm
GREENFIELD/BELSER LTD
Washington, D.C.
art director
BURKEY BELSER
designer
JEANETTE NUZUM
client
GREENFIELD/BELSER

creative firm
BUTLER KEMP DESIGN
North Adelaide, Australia
art director
DEREK BUTLER
designer
SCOTT CARSLAKE
client
DRUG & ALCOHOL SERVICE COUNCIL
(drink coasters)

All of our buildings
go through an intensive
screening process.

Nothing passes by our quality control screening
process, not even water. Some contractors
skip those boring dry details, so stick with
the experts — we fill in all the cracks.

SAARMAN CONSTRUCTION, LTD
Reconstruction Specialist

683 McAllister Street | San Francisco, CA 94102
Tel: 415.749.2700 | www.saarman.com

When it's raining cats & dogs

It's the leaks you don't see that end up
getting you. Be proactive and stop the leaks.
Work with Saarman, the specialist in multifamily
and commercial defect repair and maintenance.
Now you'll never have to
worry about falling collies again.

SAARMAN CONSTRUCTION, LTD
Reconstruction Specialist

683 McAllister Street | San Francisco, CA 94102
Tel: 415.749.2700 | www.saarman.com

creative firm
BRUCE YELASKA DESIGN
San Francisco, California
art director, designer, copywriter
BRUCE YELASKA
photographer
RICHARD GORDON
client
SAARMAN CONSTRUCTION

creative firm
BRUCE YELASKA DESIGN
San Francisco, California
art director, designer, copywriter
BRUCE YELASKA
client
SAARMAN CONSTRUCTION

creative firm
SAYLES GRAPHIC DESIGN
Des Moines, Iowa
art director, illustrator
JOHN SAYLES
client
SBEMCO INTERNATIONAL

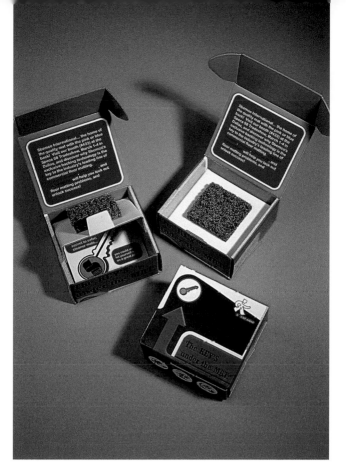

creative firm
  SAYLES GRAPHIC DESIGN
  Des Moines, Iowa
art director, illustrator
  JOHN SAYLES
client
  SBEMCO INTERNATIONAL

creative firm
  BRUCE YELASKA DESIGN
  San Francisco, California
art director, designer, copywriter
  BRUCE YELASKA
photographer
  RICHARD GORDON
client
  SAARMAN CONSTRUCTION

creative firm
  BRUCE YELASKA DESIGN
  San Francisco, California
art director, designer, copywriter
  BRUCE YELASKA
photographer
  RICHARD GORDON
client
  SAARMAN CONSTRUCTION

Just be happy we're not your dentist.

Ouch! Working with your contractor shouldn't hurt. Like a dentist, we'll fill your building's cavities, while making sure that your construction defect repair and maintenance is a painless experience — every last bit of it.

SAARMAN CONSTRUCTION, LTD
Reconstruction Specialist

683 McAllister Street | San Francisco, CA 94102
Tel: 415.749.2700 | www.saarman.com

Stand back, we're professionals.

At the risk of sounding dull, we're the professionals when it comes to multifamily and commercial construction defect repair and maintenance.

SAARMAN CONSTRUCTION, LTD
Reconstruction Specialist

683 McAllister Street | San Francisco, CA 94102
Tel: 415.749.2700 | www.saarman.com

creative firm
  GARDNER DESIGN
  Wichita, Kansas
art directors, designers
  BILL GARDNER, BRIAN MILLER
client
  WILKINSON

creative firm
  UKULELE DESIGN
  CONSULTANTS PTE LTD
  Singapore
design director
  VERNA LIM
designer
  LYNN LIM
client
  THE PAN PACIFIC HOTEL SINGAPORE

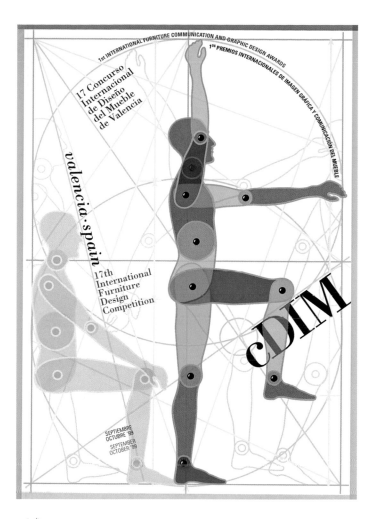

creative firm
PEPE GIMENO—PROYECTO GRÁFICO
Valencia, Spain
designer
JOSE P. GIL
client
FERIA INTERNACIONAL DEL MUEBLE DE VALENCIA

creative firm
SAYLES GRAPHIC DESIGN
Des Moines, Iowa
art director, illustrator
JOHN SAYLES
client
UNITED AIRLINES
"TIME TO OPEN A LITTLE BUBBLY"

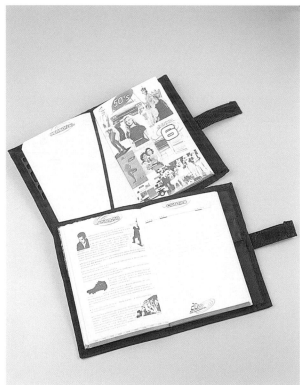

creative firm
RGB GRAPHIC DESIGN
Rio De Janeiro, Brazil
designers
MARIA LUIZA GONÇALVES VEIGA BRITO,
MARIA ANGELA LUTTERBACH
client
COMPANY FASHION STORE

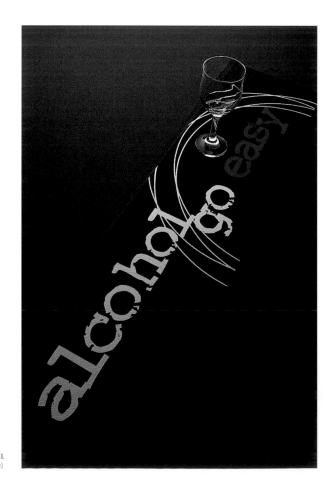

creative firm
BUTLER KEMP DESIGN
North Adelaide, Australia
art director
DEREK BUTLER
designer
JULIE KEMP
client
DRUG & ALCOHOL SERVICES COUNCIL
(alcohol Go Easy logo & bar runner)

CREATIVE FIRMS